THE EPISTOLARY MOMENT

THE EPISTOLARY MOMENT

THE POETICS OF THE EIGHTEENTH-CENTURY VERSE EPISTLE

William C. Dowling

COPYRIGHT © 1991 BY PRINCETON UNIVERSITY PRESS
PUBLISHED BY PRINCETON UNIVERSITY PRESS, 41 WILLIAM STREET,
PRINCETON, NEW JERSEY 08540
IN THE UNITED KINGDOM: PRINCETON UNIVERSITY PRESS, OXFORD
ALL RIGHTS RESERVED

LIBRARY OF CONGRESS CATALOGING-IN-PUBLICATION DATA
DOWLING, WILLIAM C.
THE EPISTOLARY MOMENT : THE POETICS OF THE
EIGHTEENTH-CENTURY VERSE EPISTLE / WILLIAM C. DOWLING.
P.   CM.
INCLUDES BIBLIOGRAPHICAL REFERENCES AND INDEX
ISBN 0-691-06891-7
1. ENGLISH POETRY—18TH CENTURY—HISTORY AND CRITICISM.
2. EPISTOLARY POETRY, ENGLISH—HISTORY AND CRITICISM. I. TITLE.
PR559.E75D69 1991   90-22540   821'.509—DC20   CIP

THIS BOOK HAS BEEN COMPOSED IN ADOBE GALLIARD

PRINCETON UNIVERSITY PRESS BOOKS ARE PRINTED ON ACID-FREE PAPER,
AND MEET THE GUIDELINES FOR PERMANENCE AND DURABILITY OF
THE COMMITTEE ON PRODUCTION GUIDELINES FOR BOOK LONGEVITY OF THE
COUNCIL ON LIBRARY RESOURCES

PRINTED IN THE UNITED STATES OF AMERICA BY
PRINCETON UNIVERSITY PRESS,
PRINCETON, NEW JERSEY

1 3 5 7 9 10 8 6 4 2

For Linda

LUX MEA, QUA VIVA

VIVERE DULCE MIHI EST

CONTENTS

INTRODUCTION
Sociopoetics and the Problem of Audience 3

ONE
Lyric and Epistle 21

TWO
Augustan Audience 53

THREE
Satire and Epistle 83

FOUR
The Commonwealth of Letters 112

FIVE
The Empire of Chaos 144

NOTES 177

POEMS CITED 193

WORKS CITED 201

INDEX 211

THE EPISTOLARY MOMENT

INTRODUCTION

SOCIOPOETICS AND

THE PROBLEM OF AUDIENCE

THIS IS, as its title promises, a study of the verse epistle as the dominant form in eighteenth-century English poetry, my argument being that epistolary verse during that period was an attempt to solve in literary terms the philosophical problem of solipsism as it arose between Locke's *Essay Concerning Human Understanding* and Beattie's attack on Humean skepticism. Yet my interest in the verse epistle originated in a concern with the theory of internal audience in poetry: the listener or listening presence—in epistolary verse, the imaginary reader of the letter—"inside" the poem, created and sustained by its discourse and belonging to its world. Though the following chapters have a great deal to say about internal audience in the verse epistle, they silently assume both the theoretical validity of the concept and its indispensability to poetics, especially in the newer mode, so unremittingly attentive to the claims of culture and history, to which Alain Viala has given the name *sociopoetics*. I should thus like to begin by saying a word about the fortunes of the concept in literary theory.

In modern criticism, the matter of internal audience commanded greatest attention during the formalist ascendancy of the early 1950s, the period when New Criticism was attempting to work out the full implications of what was then called the literary study of literature: interpreting poems and plays and novels as self-contained worlds embodying their own laws and their own logic, and subject to violence and distortion when made to answer to doctrines or epistemologies or ideologies external to themselves. The classic early statement concerning internality of audience is usually taken to be Walker Gibson's well-known *College English* essay on "mock readers,"[1] but the first really influential treatment of the idea was W. K. Wimsatt's compressed but immensely suggestive discussion in *The Verbal Icon*. "The actual reader of a poem," remarked Wimsatt, "is something like a reader over another reader's shoulder; he reads through the dramatic reader, the person to whom the full tone of the poem is addressed in the fictional situation. This is the truth behind that often-quoted statement by J. S. Mill that 'Eloquence is *heard*, poetry is *over*heard'" (xv). This is the essence of the idea as it would then hold sway through the period of New Critical hegemony, to which W. J. Ong's 1975 essay "The Writer's Audience is Always a Fiction" marks a convenient close.[2]

Looking back on the controversies of that period, one immediately sees both why the notion of internal audience was essential to the formalist conception of literary works as worlds-in-themselves and why, nonetheless, it was never much more than an afterthought in the New Critical program. For the great battles on behalf of literary autonomy were fought around the issue of authorial intention—a battle conducted by New Criticism in the name of a speaker or narrator internal to the work. To say that there was a voice speaking from the page in a poem such as *To His Coy Mistress* was, by the lights of that polemical time, to insist that the poem contained a speaker utterly distinct from the deceased author Andrew Marvell, as, in a more obvious but precisely equivalent way, Andrea del Sarto was distinct from his creator Browning or Humbert Humbert from Vladimir Nabokov. No such urgency surrounded the issue of audience, however, which is why it was perhaps merely a nagging sense of neglected symmetry that then prompted such theorists as Wimsatt to point out additionally that the young man speaking inside the poem was addressing a young woman as internal to its world as himself:

> Had we but world enough, and time,
> This coyness, lady, were no crime.

This is a point that retains an obvious importance for literary theory, for to observe that the *lady* of *To His Coy Mistress* is a presence internal to the poem is to declare that she is identifiable with no actual reader of the poem whatsoever: with no actual seventeenth-century ladies, who are all dead in their graves while this lady lives on, perpetually listening to the utterance of her admirer, but also with no modern reader, no deconstructive or phenomenological or subjective reader, nor any subject to the uncertainties posited by affective stylistics. The question that arises thus concerns the relation of this concept of audience to the theory in support of which Wimsatt was arguing twenty-five years ago, that vision of literary autonomy that made New Criticism the last serious defender of the idea of art as a separate reality. This is what Aristotle had in mind when he said that literature portrays not what happened but what always happens, what Sidney meant in saying that poetry gives us a golden world and nature only a brazen one, what Wilde meant in insisting that you and I and our physical surroundings are part of a dissolving reality while *Hamlet* and the *Iliad* will be there to meet other readers in another world two or three hundred years from now.

This idea of literature is today almost universally regarded as a mistake—at best, as an illusion grounded in a false picture of social reality; at worst, as an ideological subterfuge working to perpetuate various modes of illegitimate domination. This immediately raises a complicated issue—the "problem of history" as any project in poetics today inevitably encounters it—but I want nonetheless to begin with a simpler question: why was it that the notion of internal audience seemed ever to make sense in the first place; why did it appear or does it even now appear to do a certain kind of conceptual work at a primary level of literary comprehension? Why, in short, should we want to say that someone who got the relation between speaker and audience in *To His Coy Mistress* wrong—who thought, for instance, that the speaker was addressing his eighty-seven-year-old grandmother, or his two-year-old niece—had misread the poem at a fundamental level? Or, to put the same question in a way that situates it more exactly in relation to contemporary theory: why, if internal audience plays so crucial a role at this level of literary comprehension, has it been so largely ignored by modern theorists—even, after the first dutiful mentions of audience as an internal dramatic coordinate in poetry, by the very New Critical theorists who had given the idea a momentary prominence?

One obvious answer is that any lingering formalist preoccupation with internal audience had by the end of the 1970s been swept away by a wave of what had in the meantime come to be known as reader-response criticism, a movement embracing a great variety of critical approaches but given a rough unity by its focus on the responses of actual readers to literary works. At the furthest extreme, as in the avowed "subjectivism" of David Bleich or the psychoanalytically oriented criticism of Norman Holland, this involved substituting reader response for poems and plays and novels as the object of critical study—the purest example, perhaps, being Holland's *Five Readers Reading*, in which the recorded reactions of five American college students to a Faulkner short story are studied in hopes of uncovering the "identity theme" governing each student's response. More usually, as in the *Rezeptionsästhetik* of Hans Robert Jauss and the Constance group or the separate theoretical projects of Wolfgang Iser and Stanley Fish, the text retained some determinate status in such criticism, with the emphasis nonetheless being on certain forces of indeterminacy giving a role in the creation of meaning to actual or empirical readers.

The reason that reader-response criticism proved to be no more than a passing episode lay, I think, in its inevitable tendency to dissolve the literary work as an object of study,[3] with the one exception—one that seems to me today to suggest a means of moving from a poetics to a sociopoetics of audience—being the semiotic analysis of Roland Barthes. Barthes' work during a certain period of his career is normally grouped with reader-response criticism due to its tendency to dissolve "reader" or "audience" into a system of constituent codes. In a study like *S/Z*, the superficial resemblance between what Barthes is doing and what Fish or Bleich or Holland appear to be doing is very strong. Yet in fact Barthes' analysis in such instances is always controlled by a notion of audience that, at a considerably more abstract level, aligns with the New Critical concept of audience as something created and sustained by discourse itself. In such analysis, as Jonathan Culler well puts it, "the reader becomes the name of the place where the various codes can be located: a virtual site. Semiotics attempts to make explicit the implicit knowledge which enables signs to have meaning, so it needs the reader not as a person but a function: the repository of the codes which account for the intelligibility of the text" (*Pursuit of Signs* 39).

This is what might be called the semiotic horizon of audience theory, implying a mode of analysis barely glimpsed as a possibility by formalists such as Wimsatt, but nonetheless including or subsuming their notion of internal audience in individual literary works. For within the semiotic horizon, what becomes essential is that literary modes or genres—the formal expectations, as we are accustomed to put it, brought into play by terms like "epic" or "lyric"—also presuppose an idea of audience in some sense internal to literature as a total order of meaning. As Fredric Jameson has pointed out, this is what Sartre had in mind in insisting that audience "is implicit in the writer himself, and follows logically from the choices of material and the stylistic formulations which are the acts of his own solitude.... Sartre's analysis takes place on a level which excludes psychology as such, for it merely shows how a certain selection of material, involving a lengthy presentation of certain things and only the most schematic references to others, as though they were already immediately intelligible to his audience, is in itself a selection of the readership" (28).

This is the theory of internal audience in its most generalized form—one that explains, for instance, why what we are accustomed to calling Augustan poetry or Augustan satire always implies a certain *kind* of auditor or reader, someone embodying a determinate system of values and knowledge, and a perception of the world entailed by these, which are carried within the text. Consider, with Sartre's point in mind, several lines from Edward Young's *Letter to Mr. Tickell*, written in 1719 on the occasion of Addison's death. In this poem Young is meditating on the relation between the world of ideas and the world of power, and the conclusion he reaches is that poetry *is* power, that an intelligence such as Addison's, which in one setting plots the destiny of England in foreign policy, composes poetry, for related reasons, in another. Thus it is that those who take poetry to be only "the slight amusement of a leisure hour" resemble Dido dandling the false Ascanius—the god Cupid in the guise of Aeneas's son—on her lap in the banquet scene in the *Aeneid*:

> Poor Dido fondled thus, with idle joy,
> Dread Cupid lurking in the Trojan boy;
> Lightly she toy'd, and trifled with his charms,
> And knew not that a god was in her arms.

This is to make the most serious sort of claim for poetry, for Cupid is no longer the wanton love-god of more innocent fable but the despoiler of empire, the "dread" pagan deity whose shafts set in motion the events that then leave Troy or Carthage a desolation of smoldering ashes. Yet it is not the simile alone that conjures into existence an audience and a world here, but the word *thus*, the insignificant marker of a tremendous semantic expectation. For what is marked by *thus* is an idea of audience thoroughly at home in Virgil's poetry—and at home there, moreover, because of a classical education yet carrying strong overtones of the Renaissance ideal of literary study as a moral enterprise. Implicit in that ideal, in turn, is the entire moral ontology of Renaissance humanism itself, the idea of a permanent or universal human nature, perennially present beneath what Dr. Johnson called the "adventitious and separable disguises" of nation and local culture and historical epoch, that puts the ancient Greek or Roman and the modern Frenchman or Englishman in a nearly identical relation to a timeless realm of moral truth.

At the same time, the audience addressed by Young's poem is not anything so general as "Augustan audience" or "the neoclassical reader," but specifically one Mr. Tickell—the Thomas Tickell who was Young's friend at Oxford, who put in a brief appearance in literary history as Pope's rival in translating Homer, and who then became the editor of Addison's works after his death. If there is a more general audience in view in this situation, it must be, in short, an audience overhearing this address from one friend to another as they converse within the boundaries of their common world about matters familiar to them both. This is where the formalist notion of internal audience begins to take on a specific value missing from the more abstract theorizations of Sartre or Roland Barthes, for should one want to give an account of the verse epistle in eighteenth-century poetry, one would clearly be dealing not with some generalized audience but precisely with a great multitude of addressees like Mr. Tickell, as internal to the poems in which they occur as is the *lady* of *To His Coy Mistress* to hers. An account of Augustan audience would thus necessarily begin, wherever it might end, in an account of resemblances stretching across a large range of particular audiences who belong exclusively to the realm of epistolary discourse.

This, it seems to me, is the great value of internal audience to poetics, one left undeveloped in that moment some years ago when reader-response criticism so decisively shifted the emphasis in literary studies toward the mental processes of actual readers. My own account of the eighteenth-century verse epistle draws very heavily, at any rate, on the principle that some determinate notion of internal audience is invariably involved whenever we speak of the relation between individual texts and the literary mode or genre or form to which they belong, that when we speak of Petrarchan love poetry, for instance, we are normally talking about a dramatic situation in which a young man tries urgently to communicate to a beautiful young woman his desire for her—the *lady* of *To His Coy Mistress* is in this context simply a late representative of the Petrarchan mistress—or that when we speak of the Augustan verse epistle we are normally talking about a situation in which a male speaker, educated in classical values and seeking refuge, in the company of a few kindred souls, from a fallen social reality, addresses a male friend in a way meant to be exemplary for their society as a whole.

The further great value of internal audience to poetics is that it provides a means of mapping the displacements and inversions of this primary ratio through which literary forms, as though fulfilling a set of formal possibilities written into the symbolic relation between speaker and audience at the outset, move toward the implosion or exhaustion of conventions that then creates space for newer forms. Should we take the primary ratio of address for the Petrarchan lyric to be one in which the young lover pleads *with* his lady for her favors, for instance, we are already moving toward an early and important displacement of that ratio in a poem such as Wyatt's *They Flee from Me*, in which a young man speaks bitterly *about* his mistress, now cold-hearted in a quite un-Petrarchan way, to a male companion; already, at such a moment, there comes into view an alternative world of male solidarity based on a shared experience of female betrayal, the world from within whose confines Donne will speak ("Teach me to hear mermaids singing") in the most bitter of his anti-Petrarchan poems. Similarly, the anti-Petrarchanism of a poem such as Shakespeare's Sonnet 130 involves something like an inversion of the ratio originally assumed in Petrarch's sonnets to Laura:

> My mistress' eyes are nothing like the sun;
> Coral is far more red than her lips' red;
> If snow be white, why then her breasts are dun;
> If hairs be wires, black wires grow on her head.
> I have seen roses damasked, red and white,
> But no such roses see I in her cheeks.

Shakespeare's sonnet is anti-Petrarchan, that is to say, not simply in the general sense that it addresses an imaginary audience distinguished by its knowledge of Petrarchan conventions, but also an audience *created by* Petrarchan poetry in the more specific sense that, had no such poetry ever existed, no such audience would be imaginable on just these terms. The dynamic element in this situation emerges when we see that the poem is intended as an act of persuasion, the speaker's aim being to get his audience to recognize the absurdity not only of Petrarchan extravagance but of the whole perspective implied by Petrarchanism, a self-torturing and empty ideality best abandoned—so the argument would run—in favor of a deeper wisdom of the body and its impulses. The "knowledge of Petrarchan conventions" involved here is not just any knowledge—a scholar's knowledge, for instance, would not do at all—but a way of seeing reality, and this is what makes the poem, on the level of the relation between speaker and internal audience, a contest of warring assumptions: there would be no point in addressing the audience this way if it already shared the speaker's views. All this enters into what is meant by the anti-Petrarchanism of the poem.

Any more complete account of audience in the Petrarchan lyric would, clearly, move in the direction of a poetics of audience within an entire body of poetry. This is the project undertaken in the following chapters on the Augustan verse epistle, which in the eighteenth century undergoes a development very like that of Petrarchan poetry in the Renaissance, emerging out of relative literary obscurity to become the dominant poetic mode of its age, giving voice during the period of its formal hegemony to a tremendous range of related moral and imaginative concerns, and then imploding upon itself in a last exhaustion of its dramatic conventions to create space for, in this case, the rise of Romantic lyric. My account of the verse epistle will thus draw constantly on principles I have so far discussed—in particular, the notion of a primary speaker-audience ratio whose inversions and displacements then move a poetic mode toward formal exhaustion—but it will draw as well on a more general principle that in its way subsumes these others. This is the principle that *every poem addresses an internal or imaginary audience created by some prior poem or poems.*

One great value of a poem like Shakespeare's Sonnet 130 is that it exemplifies this principle in a particularly striking way, Shakespeare's anti-Petrarchanism being in some sense unintelligible or incoherent unless we can conceive of a "Petrarchan audience" to whom it is addressed. Yet the same principle is not less importantly but only less visibly at work in a lyric like *To His Coy Mistress*, whose *lady* is a creation of the Petrarchan tradition, and the speaker of Marvell's poem, together with the entire discourse of carpe diem urgency represented in his utterance, will then live on to provide the locus of address in a much later lyric such as Yeats's *The Rose of the World*—"Who dreamed that beauty passes like a dream?"—and even, in a way more radically interiorized, in a more fragmented modern poem such as Eliot's *Love Song of J. Alfred Prufrock*. In the eighteenth-century verse epistle, the same principle is most visible in what might be called fictional situations—the myriad epistles written by an imaginary "Abelard" to the Eloisa created by Pope's poem, for instance—but it is no less importantly at work when such poets as Pope and Gay and Swift write epistles to one another, or when some minor versifier from his personal obscurity addresses an epistle to a Pope he knows only through his poetry.

The Augustan verse epistles addressing Pope as their internal audience are particularly good examples of the process through which poetry itself creates the audience of later poetry, for Pope is in these epistles always the mythologized creation of his own writing, the mighty antagonist of Walpole and modernity and presider over the entire Augustan scene. Thus it is, for instance, that Pope's withdrawal to his country villa is so often taken in Augustan poetry as betokening a silence that must then be filled with other poetic voices, as in Edward Young's *Two Epistles to Mr. Pope*: "Whilst you at Twickenham plan the future wood, / Or turn the volumes of the wise and good, / Our senate meets; at parties, parties bawl, / And pamphlets stun the streets, and load the stall" (334). The symbolic relation between speaker and audience in any such epistle assumes an interior landscape that will then become the setting of Augustan poetry as such: the scene of otium retirement represented by Pope at Twickenham with his few chosen friends, the brawl and bustle of London as symbol of a new speculative or money society, and the peaceful rural countryside where the life of the country house and the values of traditional society yet linger.

In the verse epistle, however, the matter of internal audience is immediately and enormously complicated by what Janet Altman has called epistolarity, which here involves everything a poem may be taken to say about itself in announcing its own status as a letter. For to entitle a poem *Epistle to Mr. Jervas* or *Epistle to Dr. Arbuthnot* is not simply to announce that Jervas or Arbuthnot will be the nominal addressee of the poetic discourse, but also that either will figure only as an imaginary presence in the mind of a letter-writer composing in actual solitude, in a literal absence of any listener or audience. As we shall see in Chapter One, this lonely scene of writing is the chosen ground on which the eighteenth-century verse epistle will move to engage the new terror of a post-Cartesian or post-Lockean solipsism, but it is more immediately the means through which the epistle lays bare a problem of audience always repressed or hidden in the lyric situation. For lyric imitates speech or conversation, and, as Miyoshi Masao has said,

> the conversational forms are by definition interpersonal and social, while writing takes place in isolation. As an individual faces a blank sheet . . . he or she has to imagine a respondent. . . . How does a writer shape his or her respondent? Is there to be a relationship of hostility, intimacy, or equality? How extensive is the respondent's frame of reference, horizon of knowledge, imagined to be? . . . All such questions must be formed, understood, answered, and integrated into the tone, style, and structure of writing. Throughout, as the writer pursues his or her discourse in loneliness, the final audience, too, must be imagined. Is there a specific readership? Which one? And so on. The marvel and terror of writing are in this confrontation with solitude and void, one's encounter with one's own shadow. (32–33)

In general terms, the importance of this lonely scene for Augustan poetry will be that it transposes to the situation of discourse the more abstract terror of solipsism, the haunting fear that one's own consciousness is all there is, and that the world and other people may be no more than figments of the solitary mind. Yet this is just the transposition that will permit the verse epistle, which for this reason becomes normative for Augustan poetry as a whole, to initiate a grand movement out of solitude and back toward community, and moreover to do so precisely by exploiting the purely formal resources of language as a system of signification unimaginable outside some collective or communal form of existence. The Augustan verse epistle will thus stake its moral and epistemological claims on an insight that in philosophy would become current only with the work of the later Wittgenstein—the idea that speech or discourse in and of themselves presume the more primordial existence of both the world and other minds, and that solipsism, although it is not something that could be refuted through argument as such, is nonetheless in a certain way nonsensical, less an error of reasoning than a distemper in one's way of seeing the world.

The notion of community as a reality always silently assumed by discourse gives us the dynamics of audience through which the verse epistle will attempt to bring about a reconstitution of community in a world threatened by fragmentation and alienation. For if the lonely situation of the letter-writer represents the terror of an encounter with one's own shadow, as Masao puts it, a void in which one's audience can only be waveringly or hesitatingly imagined, then the situation of the poet, associated since Homer and Virgil with the voice of the community as a whole, the tale of the tribe listening to its own story, is the opposite of that loneliness. This is what bestows on poetic discourse as such the full traditional weight or value of public utterance in a world in which community is yet a lived reality. By the time Dryden and Pope are writing, that world will have begun to look more and more like a receding memory, but its memory is precisely what they mean to invoke by writing not merely epistles but verse epistles, poems in which the isolation symbolized by epistolary solitude is then opposed and redeemed by verse as an institutionalized mode of public utterance.

As in epic or lyric, in short, the formal features of verse operate in the poetic epistle to signal its status as public object, but only in epistolary verse, which has begun by announcing its own discourse as that of an isolated voice or consciousness, the letter-writer facing the blankness of the page, does this work out to the resolution of a paradox, an attempt to redeem solitude in the name of community. The manner in which the paradox is resolved is of the highest importance for a poetics of audience, for in the verse epistle it is rhyme and meter and all those resources of Augustan prosody that so steadily insist on the status of the discourse as public utterance that then project an audience at one remove—I shall call it *epistolary audience*—as overhearing or listening in on the epistolary exchange between letter-writer and addressee. As we shall see in greater detail in Chapter One, this is the primary means through which the verse epistle will constitute itself as a mode of simultaneous address, a double register within which it is possible to speak to one audience directly while always addressing another by implication.

This double register not only explains our sense that Pope in the *Epistle to Arbuthnot* is speaking through Arbuthnot to a further audience, but permits us as well to understand epistolary audience as a presence internal to the verse epistle, an imaginary reading public created through exactly the same process of formal implication as the *lady* in *To His Coy Mistress*, or Arbuthnot himself as he exists in Pope's poem. (One way of grasping this is to imagine a private letter that had fallen into the hands of a third party: it would have found, contingently, a reader, but it would nonetheless not carry an indirect or secondary audience within itself as does the verse epistle.) Through the double register of epistolary verse, in turn, will be posited a certain charged and dynamic engagement between Augustan poetry and the world, for the verse epistle posits a symbolic situation in which epistolary audience is at once external to the discourse of the speaker and internal to the discourse of the poem, overhearing the exchange between letter-writer and addressee from a middle region in which the ontological claims of poetry and society, otherwise so readily conceived as separate spheres of reality, are suddenly and surprisingly heard to be mutually intelligible.

This gives us a principle lying at the heart of literary Augustanism, the notion of poetry as ideological intervention, poems themselves as symbolic acts with enormous consequences in the domain of the real. The aim of Augustan satire, we have always understood, is to unmask as a hideously false reality the world of Sir Robert Walpole and his Robinocracy and, in so doing, to exert moral pressure on an eighteenth-century public.[4] Yet this is an enterprise that becomes wholly intelligible only when we have seen that the public in question, at once imaginary and real in the sense that readers may be imagined *as* real, is specifically a creation of the Augustan verse epistle. The idea of ideological intervention derives, in short, from an idea of epistolary audience imagined not simply as a presence hovering over the exchange between letter-writer and addressee—*epistoler* and *lector* as I shall be calling them in the chapters to follow—but as one that does so in a state of radical ambivalence, caught between the moral demands of a remembered organic or traditional society on the one hand and, on the other, the glittering mystifications of the new money or market society symbolized by Walpole, an emergent modern order seeming to offer vast possibilities in the way of riches and mobility and individual empowerment.

To see epistolary audience this way is to glimpse the process through which, over the course of hundreds of eighteenth-century verse epistles, it will emerge as an autonomous presence within Augustan poetry, always displaying a tendency to detach itself from this or that individual epistle and assume the status of a more generalized Augustan reading public. This tendency may be explained as an immediate consequence of that epistolary double register that projects an audience already partly outside the poem, existing in a problematic middle region belonging wholly neither to poetry nor to history, but it must also be taken as a consequence of the principle that every poem addresses an imaginary audience created by prior poems. For the presence that will by the time of Pope and Swift be felt as a generalized Augustan audience makes its first hesitant appearance in the verse epistles addressed to each other by such writers as Congreve and Dryden in the late seventeenth century, begins in the early eighteenth century to assume a stable identity as a public addressed by a multitude of previous poems, and only then emerges as the morally vigilant readership in which Augustan satire will invest its last hope for the regeneration of English society.

This is the point at which a poetics of audience encounters the problem of history. For epistolary audience, precisely as it is imagined as mind or consciousness dwelling uneasily in a middle region between poetry and the world, here becomes the specific means through which Augustan poetry will propose to intervene in a historical reality separate from its own discourse, to enunciate in symbolic terms a moral regeneration that will then actually occur in society. The name of this regeneration in Augustan writing is always the *ricorso* of Machiavellian political theory, that dismantling of the Walpole order and return to organic or traditional society that would inevitably take place if enough readers of Pope identified their own best selves with the imaginary audience of the *Epistle to Arbuthnot* or the Horatian epistles, internalizing a moral perspective and system of values that had begun as poetry but were now taking on force in the domain of the real. The problem for poetics occurs not because Augustan poetry imagines its relation to its own society in this way, but because that relation is, after all, imaginary: everything—readers, the Walpole-society they inhabit, the very possibility of change—is a projection of the poetry itself.

This is a symbolic situation with which recent theories of subjectivity or consciousness, taking Althusser's theory of interpellation as their starting point, have tried to come to terms by speaking of the reader not, as Teresa de Lauretis puts it, as "an undivided identity, a stable unity of 'consciousness,' but the term of a shifting series of ideological positions" (14). The importance of Althusser to such theories lies in their stress on the manner in which, as de Lauretis also says, men and women are as social beings "constructed through effects of language and representation" (14). For interpellation in Althusser's theory is the means through which a cultural system determines not simply the contents of consciousness, mere attitudes or beliefs or opinions, but consciousness itself, the primordial "I" as it feels itself to be itself in relation to the world. This is the basis of Althusser's more general theory of ideology as, in the now-familiar formulation, the way human beings live an imaginary relation to the real, the means through which they are constructed as "autonomous" or "responsible" agents within a social system that then perpetuates itself through their thoughts and actions.

Yet the newer theories of subjectivity that honor this premise—particularly those associated with Stephen Heath and Paul Willeman and other writers for the journal *Screen*,[5] are not simply extensions of Althusserian theory but critiques of it, especially of the notion of interpellation-by-a-text that, suggested originally by Althusser's famous essay on ideological state apparatuses, has enjoyed a certain vogue in literary and film studies. For the innocent or malleable subject sometimes posited in such studies could not, one sees, exist: to take the idea of interpellation seriously on its own terms is to see that the consciousness of a reader who picks up a book or that of a viewer who walks into a cinema has already been constructed in a complex way through an unending process of previous interpellations by what Willeman calls a plurality of discourses. We are to speak in this situation not of anything so simple as imaginary readers or actual readers, either of which an adequate theory must regard as unreal abstractions, but of "the relation of forces of competing discourses intersecting in the place of the subject-in-history, the individual's location in ideology at a particular moment and place" (Willeman 63).

One great virtue of Willeman's account, as of the similar account of reader or audience given by Pêcheux (see Morley 189–93), is that it gives us precisely the terms on which the eighteenth-century verse epistle will project as its ultimate audience an Augustan public imagined to have power to alter the course of history. For where Althusserian theory was prone to speak of interpellation, such newer theories wish us to speak of a virtual war of interpellations. This is the point at which we once again encounter Barthes' abstract reader—now conceived, however, not as a mere repository of codes but rather as the site of what Laclau has called the struggle in ideology. This will be, as we shall see, precisely the role of epistolary audience in the perpetual Augustan warfare against Walpole and modernity. Yet an even greater virtue of such theories is the solution they propose to the problem of history. For the engagement of Augustan poetry with a world of its own imagining is not a genuine problem, on an account like Willeman's, to just the degree that Augustan poetry must be envisioned simply as one among a plurality of discourses: the entities that we call society or history are simply the sum total of such projections or imaginings. To think otherwise—the cardinal error of so many current materialisms—is to make the common mistake of imagining reality, in the very moment one is calling it into being through discourse, as something nonetheless wholly independent of language or representation.[6]

The manner in which the Augustan verse epistle imagines eighteenth-century society as its own arena of ideological warfare, by the same token, will depend on an idea of epistolary audience as a preconstructed subject: the consciousness of reader or audience as, in Althusserian terminology, bearing the sedimented traces of past interpellations. In specific terms, this gives us the grounds on which Augustan poetry will be able to use an idea of organic or traditional society assumed to be lingering in cultural memory as a point of moral leverage against the new society of stockjobbers and speculators symbolized by Walpole. This in turn gives us Augustanism as what Raymond Williams has called retrospective radicalism: a critique of emergent capitalism that, recognizing in urgent terms the grim tendency of a money or market society to dissolve human community into a mere aggregation of isolated individuals, attempts to expose the danger by summoning an image of traditional society as the moral measure of what is being lost.

Williams arrives at this understanding of Augustanism from a Marxist perspective, as had Isaac Kramnick before him in *Bolingbroke and His Circle*, the seminal study that put to rest so many earlier conceptions of Augustan writing as "conservative" in the nineteenth- or twentieth-century sense. One important implication of such a view, perhaps, is that such writers as Pope and Swift and Gay demand to be seen in this light because they were carrying out a proto-Marxian critique of early capitalism, alert as Marx would subsequently be to the terrible consequences of an economic system working blindly to transform human beings into mere interchangeable integers or market units. Yet there is a contrary perspective, no less important to an understanding of these writers, in which such an account may be seen to work to precisely the degree that Marx's own writings preserve an "Augustan" sense of organic or traditional society as a measure of genuine human community, as in, famously, *The Communist Manifesto*:

> The bourgeoisie, wherever it has got the upper hand, has put an end to all feudal, patriarchal, idyllic relations. It has pitilessly torn asunder the motley feudal ties that bound man to his "natural superiors," and has left remaining no other nexus between man and man than naked self-interest, than callous "cash payment." . . . It has resolved personal worth into exchange value and, in place of the numberless indefeasible chartered freedoms, has set up that single, unconscionable freedom—free trade. In one word, for exploitation, veiled by religious and political illusions, it has substituted naked, shameless, direct, brutal exploitation. (9–10)

The ground common to Marx and the Augustan writers is a sense of social crisis as deriving from certain violent subterranean movements at the level of material or property relations, which explains why a classic Marxist study such as C. B. Macpherson's *The Political Theory of Possessive Individualism*, even as its merits as a general analysis of eighteenth-century thought have increasingly come into question, remains so valuable a guide to the way such writers as Pope and Swift perceived the new world of the Bank of England and the South Sea Bubble and the Royal Exchange. For what Macpherson calls possessive individualism, the new epistemology brought about by a market system allowing human beings value only as owners of their own labor, their labor as just another commodity in an impersonal world of exchange value, is what the Augustan verse epistle will encounter as the dilemma of solipsism, a process of alienation or estrangement threatening to dissolve society into an assemblage of free-floating egos or monadic selves. The skepticism that impels Hume to expose personal identity as a groundless fiction in the *Treatise of Human Nature* will appear from this perspective as merely the symptom of an underlying crisis, the abstract or philosophical formulation of a dilemma elsewhere being lived out in existential terms.

The great reason that such writers as Macpherson and Kramnick and Raymond Williams have been able so clearly to see this underlying crisis at work in eighteenth-century thought, no doubt, is that a Marxist perspective instructed them in advance what to look for, the invariable relation between base and superstructure that, in a world of shifting or illusory social appearances, had always been held within classical Marxism to contain the secret of human social development.[7] Yet it is precisely when we have begun to grasp the essential truth of the Marxist analysis, the manner in which it brings into view an English society actually posited by Augustan poetry as its own arena of ideological conflict, that we begin to glimpse as well certain important truths made unavailable to Marxism by its theoretical assumptions, a situation enormously more complex than can be accounted for in terms of either the base-superstructure relationship or the ascendancy, as destined and inexorable as History itself, of an emergent bourgeoisie. This is the point at which my own argument will so frequently be drawing on the work of various non-Marxist historians—Dickinson, Brewer, Appleby, Pocock, Stone, and others—who have been attentive to the singularities and anomalies created by the submerged crisis of which Marxism gives such an otherwise compelling account.

The major figure is Pocock, whose monumental analysis of classical republicanism in *The Machiavellian Moment* has permitted us to glimpse an unbroken intellectual continuity stretching from the Rome of Horace and Virgil to the England of Dryden and Pope, to grasp civic humanism as the shared paradigm of literary Augustanism and Country ideology, and to understand the eighteenth century, in a way for which no Marxist analysis allows, as a time as much of ideological collapse as of ideological struggle. In particular, my argument will be drawing on one important implication of Pocock's analysis, which is the notion of Augustan England as an ideological interregnum during which an aristocracy and gentry increasingly rendered powerless in economic terms nonetheless retains its control over civic mythology while the emergent bourgeoisie celebrated in such works as Defoe's *Complete English Tradesman* remains ideologically naked, unable to generate a sustaining ideology or myth. My own claim will be that this ideological nakedness is something directly brought about by Augustan satire, that it is the single most visible consequence of Augustan poetry as ideological intervention.

The point on which Pocock and such Marxist historians as Kramnick fundamentally agree, however, suggesting the perspective from which a New Historicism is today emerging in eighteenth-century literary studies, is that there is a great deal more at stake in this situation than a mere ideological warfare between tradition and modernity. For Augustanism speaks not simply as the troubled consciousness of an organic or traditional society threatened by modernity, but as that consciousness encountering, as John Ellis puts it in a more general discussion of ideological crisis, an external process that it has not yet succeeded in symbolizing.[8] The external process that thus resists symbolization is emergent capitalism felt as something at once implacable and mysterious, the forces of a new credit or commercial society as Pope has them in mind in railing against "paper credit," or Defoe in his wondering meditation on the operations of credit in early eighteenth-century society: "Like the soul in the body it acts as all substance, yet it is itself immaterial; it gives motion, yet it cannot be said to exist; it creates forms, yet has it self no form.... If I should say it is the essential shadow of something that is not, should I not puzzle the thing rather than explain it, and leave you and myself more in the dark than we were before?" (qtd. in Kramnick 40).

The specter that Defoe is glimpsing here is capitalism as Marx would describe it in impassioned terms more than a century later, a blind or impersonal system endowed with tremendous powers of social transformation and yet obeying no human laws or logic, the runaway engine of a historical process that would only much later be grasped as, in Lukács's phrase, a system "setting its own goals and being its own master" (238). In the eighteenth century, as Pocock has shown, the great effort was to grasp this same process of transformation within the categories of classical republicanism, especially that of Luxury, the too-great indulgence of material prosperity leading inevitably to corruption and decline. The disintegrative energies of emergent capitalism as they escape or exceed these categories, on the other hand, the new money or market society as something utterly unimaginable in the Greece of Pericles or the Rome of Horace and Virgil, will then always be felt within Augustanism as something monstrous or demonic. Thus Walpole eventually becomes for Augustan poetry an actual monster, the ravening beast or demon-figure of a capitalism graspable in no other terms.

This is the situation in which eighteenth-century social and political history comes to exist for Augustan writing as an already-constituted field of symbolic meaning, a domain of the real in which everything takes on symbolic significance in terms of an underlying crisis in social relations. Thus it is that Augustan satire, swarming with particulars, all those names and allusions and local references that can make the poetry seem so opaque to modern readers, sees every such particular surrounded by a halo of cosmic implication precisely because of the abstract struggle going on in the immediate background: a vanishing traditional society that may yet, through a gigantic effort of the collective will, be brought back to life and civic vitality (the Machiavellian ricorso) versus an emergent market society in which all merely human bonds or ties must be corrosively eaten away and ultimately dissolved by, as we have heard Marx say, exchange value and the cash nexus. It is the notion of contemporary social reality as already charged with symbolic meaning that explains not simply the relentless topicality or particularity of Augustan poetry but, as David Morris splendidly puts it, "the bold claim of immortality for verse so choked with the debris of time and history" (257):

> Is this too little? would you more than live?
> Alas! 'tis more than Turner finds they give.
> Alas! 'tis more than (all his visions past)
> Unhappy Wharton, waking, found at last!
> What can they give? to dying Hopkins heirs;
> To Chartres, vigor; Japhet, nose and ears?
>
> (*Epistle to Bathurst* 83–88)

The notion of emergent modernity as involving these dark or mysterious energies gives us, by the same token, a context in which a great deal of older literary and historical scholarship becomes immediately relevant to our newer understanding of Augustanism as ideological warfare, and in which my own argument will be drawing constantly and with gratitude on the work of such earlier scholars as Loftis and McKillop and Havens, as well as on that of such contemporary exponents of the "old historicism" as Bertrand Goldgar and Isabel Rivers and Howard Erskine-Hill. For the great charge leveled against the old historicism was that it was blind to the universal or cosmic dimension of works such as *Gulliver's Travels* or *The Dunciad*, reducing them to the status of mere documents in eighteenth-century social and political history, the wranglings and local disputes of party politics during the long ministerial reign of Robert Walpole. To see history as existing for Augustan poetry as a cosmic or universal drama in its own right, however, is at once to possess a translator mechanism through which the endlessly patient researches of the old historicism may today be permitted to speak at a more universal level of literary or symbolic implication.

In the following chapters, then, my argument will be based on the assumption that eighteenth-century society, "history" as a warring field of significations, exists in intelligible relation to the verse epistle most importantly as what Michael Riffaterre has called a semantic precondition.[9] This is the ground on which a poetics of audience inevitably becomes, to apply Viala's term to my own researches, sociopoetics: not a generalized New Historicism (at least as that term is today sometimes understood) nor yet the cultural poetics associated with Stephen Greenblatt and *Representations*, which so often achieves brilliant results through a simultaneous symbolic reading of text and society, but a reading of eighteenth-century society and culture as they exist *for* the verse epistle as its arena of ideological warfare, the course of history as it is meant to be altered or transformed by poetry as symbolic action. For in the verse epistle, it seems to me, where the projection of epistolary audience so unmistakably insists on an engagement between poetry and the world, and where the world is always nonetheless so undeniably a reality of its own imagining, this is a perspective urgently demanded by the poetry itself.

· · · · ·

The primary research for this book was begun when I was a Fellow of the Institute for Advanced Studies in the Humanities at Edinburgh University, and I should like to thank Professor Peter Jones and his staff for their many kindnesses during my residence there. In subsequent years, support for research and the actual writing of the book was provided by the John Simon Guggenheim Memorial Foundation and the George A. and Eliza Gardner Howard Foundation; I am grateful to both for having made available to me the time to think and write.

For many kindnesses, too, I should like to thank the staffs of the National Library of Scotland, the British Library, the Bodleian Library, the Newberry Library, the Special Collections Department of the University of Edinburgh Library, the Houghton Library at Harvard, the Beinecke Rare Book and Manuscript Library at Yale, and the Rare Book and Manuscript Collection of the Firestone Library at Princeton. In addition, I owe special thanks to Georgiana Bradford and the reference staff at the Cincinnati Public Library for having arranged the special loan of noncirculating materials at a crucial period in my work.

Conversations with a number of friends and colleagues—Cleanth Brooks, Thomas Edwards, David Falk, John Gordon, Paul Ricoeur—have helped me at various points over the years to get straight my thoughts about theory of audience and epistolarity, and I thank them. Some particular debts demand special mention. Carol Lanham was my guide to epistolary humanism and the *ars dictaminis* tradition; without her early and timely help, I would still be trying to make sense of neo-Latin epistolography. James Moore permitted me, at a time when my understanding of Pocock's work was fragmentary and confused, to begin to see what it all meant systematically; important parts of the argument as it now stands took shape in our conversations in Edinburgh. Leo Damrosch and David Morris, both of whom have written books about Pope to which I owe a great deal of my understanding of Augustan poetry, each made painstaking and illuminating criticisms of the manuscript. The book as it now appears owes much, finally, to the patience and generosity of spirit displayed by Robert E. Brown of Princeton University Press from its early stages to the end of what must have seemed an interminable process of rewriting.

ONE

LYRIC AND EPISTLE

EVEN TO GLANCE through the standard literary histories of England is to gain some sense of the eighteenth century as a literary moment dominated by epistolarity, for even the simplest of inductive surveys is compelled to look past *Pamela* and *Clarissa* and *Humphry Clinker* to the hundreds of minor epistolary novels produced during the period, past Locke's *Letters Concerning Toleration* or Hurd's *Letters on Chivalry and Romance* or Chesterfield's *Letters to his Son* to the hundreds of works of philosophy, theology, aesthetics, political theory, controversy, conduct, and travel whose titles give no hint that they, too, are written in the form of letters or epistles. Indeed, it is the way in which the epistolarity of so many works lies hidden beneath their titles that sometimes leads us to overlook its enormous literary importance in the eighteenth century. Bolingbroke's *Letters on the Study and Use of History* come to mind readily enough, but it takes an effort to recall that *The Idea of a Patriot King* is also epistolary in form. Everyone remembers that Goldsmith's *Citizen of the World* is written in the mode of Montesquieu's *Lettres Persanes*, but not everyone recalls that Goldsmith also composed a *History of England* as a series of letters from a nobleman to his son. And whole studies have been written of a work as major as the *Reflections on the Revolution in France* that give no hint that it is in the form of an extended letter from Burke to a young Frenchman.

Viewed against this background, the emergence of the verse epistle as the dominant form in eighteenth-century poetry might be seen as inevitable. Yet no merely inductive survey is able to explain the movement through which the verse epistle gravitates steadily during the later seventeenth century from its marginal position in the work of such poets as Wyatt and Donne and Jonson toward the literary center previously occupied by lyric, until at the moment of high Augustanism marked by Pope's Horatian poems it has become the major form in English poetry. To explain this, one must begin to think of epistolarity in terms more dynamic than any mere inventory of works or titles can suggest, to conceive of epistolarity in poetry, as have such critics as Janet Altman and Christina Gillis so well in writing about the eighteenth-century novel, as any "use of the letter's formal properties to create meaning" (Altman 4). For it is only an awareness of such meaning that then allows one to understand the eighteenth-century verse epistle as a response to an underlying epistemological dilemma, and ultimately, I want to argue, as an attempt to solve in literary terms the philosophical problem of solipsism.

The manner in which solipsism arose as an unintended consequence of Lockean empiricism belongs not to literary history but to the story of eighteenth-century philosophy, where it is already wholly implied in Hume's declaration that "it is impossible for us so much as to conceive or form an idea specifically different from ideas and impressions": "Let us chase our imaginations to the heavens, or to the utmost limits of the universe; we never can really advance a step beyond ourselves" (67). Yet even the most neutral assertions of the empirical argument, even those of Hume himself in those moments when his usual mood of robust skepticism deserts him—that other Hume who once describes himself as "affrighted and confounded with that forlorn solitude in which I am placed in my philosophy" (264)—seem haunted by a sense of barely repressed anxiety or dread, and at such moments certain literary problems leap into a new focus. For the deepest relations between literature and philosophy in the eighteenth century derive from their uneasy awareness of the epistemological dilemma that arose together with Locke's philosophy—"the troubling possibility," in John Richetti's phrase, "of a complete rupture between language and a shadowy order of things" (15), which then subsequently emerges as the specter of a solipsism threatening to transform the world and other people into mere delusive figments of the solitary mind.

Whenever the purely logical arguments for solipsism seem unwittingly to have summoned up this particular anxiety, we find ourselves in a region common at once to philosophy and literature. It is the specter of utter meaninglessness, of human beings shivering out their lives in a cold and oblivious universe, that will move Pater in the nineteenth century to revive Hume's argument in a more grimly existential register:

> And if we continue to dwell in thought on this world, not of objects, . . . but of impressions, unstable, flickering, inconsistent, which burn and are extinguished with our consciousness of them, . . . the whole scope of observation is dwarfed into the narrow chamber of the individual mind. . . . Every one of those impressions is the impression of the individual in his isolation, each mind keeping as a solitary prisoner its own dream of the world. (187-88)

In the same way, F. H. Bradley will develop, as the nineteenth century gives way to the twentieth, an argument intended simply as a contribution in philosophy—"My external sensations are no less private to myself than are my thoughts or my feelings. . . . In brief, regarded as an existence which appears in a soul, the whole world for each is peculiar and private to that soul" (qtd. in Spacks 94)—which then nonetheless goes on to gain wide currency among students of literature because it is incorporated into the notes to *The Wasteland*, taken by Eliot as a bleak epigraph to his own modern landscape of meaninglessness and despair.

The grim specter of solipsism that haunts Eliot's modern wasteland, Patricia Spacks has persuasively argued, is the same as that haunting Pope's Augustan landscape, with the crucial difference that the "solipsism which is assumed by such later poets as Eliot to be a necessary condition of life seems to Pope a symbol of ultimate evil" (94). Indeed, the very landscape of eighteenth-century poetry as a whole comes into a certain comprehensible focus as soon as we think of Augustanism as the enterprise of resisting the evil of solipsism through the powers of literary expression, and of non-Augustan poetry as what occurs when those powers of resistance have failed. It is some such perspective, at any rate, that allows us to gaze through the religious despair of Cowper's *The Castaway* to a despair even more bottomless—

> No voice divine the storm allayed,
> No light propitious shone,
>   When, snatched from all effectual aid,
> We perished, each alone;
> But I, beneath a rougher sea,
>   And whelmed in deeper gulfs than he.

—or that gives us the speaker of a poem such as Gray's Eton ode as Stephen Cox describes him, as the very image of "the isolated self, reflecting bitterly on its inability to accomplish anything of significance in either thought or action" (91). This, the specter of solipsism not simply as isolation but as spiritual paralysis, is the ultimate evil against which the verse epistle enters into symbolic combat.

The same perspective accounts, too, for the dynamics through which the verse epistle takes over the center earlier occupied by lyric, which, though itself always harboring a certain threat of solipsism, had so far been able to banish that threat through its promise of consummation in the world of the body. For lyric by the later seventeenth century is no longer able to deny the reality of desire as something that reaches out to other minds in the same way, as Lacan has taught us to see, that language reaches out to a world outside itself. "It is quite simply . . . as desire of the Other," says Lacan, "that man's desire finds form" (311); "what I seek in speech is the response of the other. What constitutes me as a subject is my question" (86). And Anike Lemaire's remark that such Lacanian pronouncements always turn on the notion of absence or lack may be taken incidentally—or not so incidentally, given that Renaissance lyric is nothing other than the convergent moment of language and desire—as a revelation of the hidden drama always playing itself out behind the lyric speaker's protestations of personal misery: "lack is the void, the zero, that which lies before the instinct. . . . Lack implies the idea of the lived drama of an irreversible incompleteness rather than that of some erotic appeal" (162). The triumph of the lyric from Petrarch to the late Renaissance would thus have been to contain this drama within the limits of a conventional vocabulary of sexual frustration.

This is why Marvell's *To His Coy Mistress* stands in relation to the verse epistles of the later seventeenth century as the last lyric, a great valedictory attempt to posit sexual consummation not simply as a reenactment on the physical level of spiritual communion but also as a guarantee that the lady and the world exist separate from the mind of the speaker. For the lady that one convinces through speech or argument may be a figment of one's discourse, but the woman one then touches is indubitably real. We have always known that lyric promises a consummation in which are dissolved all distinctions between mind and body, the spiritual and the physical; what matters now is to see the sense in which that consummation is simultaneously a triumph over the void or absence at the heart of human consciousness. Yet lyric, doomed to remain an endless gesture in the direction of this triumph, remains forever unable to describe it, which is doubtless why such description occurs only when the lyric moment is past, in the passionate remembrance of Pope's Eloisa:

> Oh happy state! when souls each other draw,
> When love is liberty, and nature, law:
> All then is full, possessing, and possest,
> No craving void left aching in the breast:
> Ev'n thought meets thought ere from the lips it part,
> And each warm wish springs mutual from the heart.

This is the context in which Lockean epistemology, with its dissolution of the physical world into private or mental impressions, dissolves the premise of lyric as well. For the Renaissance lyric had always known that even in sexual consummation one is embracing only one's *idea* of the other person—this is, after all, the moment in Shakespearean romance when the husband sleeps with his own wife thinking she is another woman—but only after Locke does this appear as the possibility of what might be called Berkelian intercourse, in which the lady of a poem such as *To His Coy Mistress* dissolves into a mere assemblage of tactile sensations. This is why, no doubt, the eighteenth-century verse epistle will so often dwell on sexual consummation as union with a figment of the mind, as in those epistles from Ratisbon in which Etherege imagines English ladies while having sex with German women—"True to my country-woman's charms; / While kissed or pressed in foreign arms" (*A Second Letter*)—or the Ovidian epistle by Lady Mary Wortley Montagu in which young sparks rush urgently to a brothel after paying a call on a married lady—"There pleas'd with fancy'd quality and charms, / Enjoy your beauties in a strumpet's arms" (*Arthur Grey*)—or the remarkable epistle in which Earl Nugent instructs a married woman to imagine at the moment of sexual climax that her lumpish husband is Nugent himself: "Ah! be those joys for me design'd, / And let me rush upon thy mind! . . . / For me unlock the nectar'd store, / Then sigh, and dream the transport o'er!" (*To Clarissa*).

The implosion of traditional lyric occurs when the notion of human existence as an irreversible drama of incompleteness, the mind reaching ceaselessly out to the Other and finding nothing there, begins in a new climate of Cartesian doubt and Lockean empiricism to appear in the guise of a naked solipsism. For lyric in such a climate will appear at best as the strategem of an exploded metaphysics, and at worst, as in a mid-eighteenth-century jeu d'esprit like Robert Lloyd's *Familiar Letter of Rhymes* to a lady, as a sort of literary joke:

> The poet can, with little pain,
> Create a mistress in his brain,
> Heap each attraction, every grace
> That should adorn the mind or face,
> On Delia, Phyllis, with a score
> Of Phyllises and Delias more.

Yet the lyric moment is long past when such lines as these come to be written. Already, in Ambrose Philips's demurring epistle to a friend who had demanded a poem on the death of King William—"To blooming Phyllis I a song compose, / And, for a rhyme, compare her to the rose"— we see lyric being demoted to the sort of consciously "minor" poetry that will then survive in the diminished poetic world of Lloyd and his circle. And even after the rebirth of lyric as a Romantic mode, a memory of its eighteenth-century eclipse will linger in something like Paul Valéry's description of poetry as (in René Girard's paraphrase) "a purely solipsistic activity practiced by the more able solely out of love for art, while the less able persist in the belief that they are actually communicating with someone" (6–7).

In the later seventeenth century, then, with lyric fading into insubstantiality, the verse epistle grows steadily more visible as though in a sort of metaphysical counterpoint. Nor is it imprecise to speak of metaphysics or visibility here, for in this new epistemological context it is precisely the materiality or autonomy of written language, the verse epistle's formal insistence on its own status as written discourse, that explains its rise to literary dominance. For the curious and important fact is that the same relentlessly empirical impulse that moved Locke to dissolve the world of tables and chairs and trees and mountains into mere mental impressions brought him simultaneously to a compensatory sense of written discourse as something possessing autonomous powers. I write, says Locke wonderingly, "nor when those characters are once made on the paper, can I choose afterwards but see them as they are. . . . Whence it is manifest, that they are not barely the sport and play of my own imagination, when I find that the characters that were made at the pleasure of my own thoughts, do not obey them" (*Essay* 634).

The reason why language assumes for Locke an enormous importance as a surety against the solipsistic implications of his own empiricism has been well explored by Rosalie Colie[1] and, more recently, John Richetti. The point here is that, as an emphasis on writing as language in its permanent or autonomous aspect, the same notion becomes a commonplace of eighteenth-century poetics. "Alone," says Richardson the painter, explaining why he writes poems as well as paints, "I think, . . . and what I think I write": "The naked thought, an unsubstantial shade, / Embody'd thus, a living creature's made (qtd. in Guilhamet 158). And this, in turn, raises to visibility something always implicit in epistolarity: the sense in which a letter, sent forth into the world, becomes a voice independent of its author. Thus epistolary poetry must always involve, as Barbara Ewell puts it, "the transformation of self into artifact," as when in *Englands Heroicall Epistles* a letter written by one of Drayton's Ovidian lovers assumes its own defiant voice:

> This cannot blush, although you do refuse it,
> Nor will reply, however you shall use it;
> All's one to this, though you should bid despair,
> This still entreats you, this still speaks you fair.
>
> (Ewell 237)

"I make account that this writing of letters," said Donne, thinking of the same phenomenon, ". . . is a kind of extasie, and a departure and secession and suspension of the soul, which doth then communicate itself to two bodies" (10).

The epistle as written discourse thus has a power, in the phrase of Richardson the novelist, to make "distance, presence; and . . . makes even presence but body, while absence becomes the soul,"[2] and in this begins its direct confrontation with a specter of solipsism lying at the heart of the epistolary situation, the letter-writer's isolation in time and space. A friendly letter, said Dr. Johnson in the "Life of Pope," is a performance "in the cool of leisure, in the stillness of solitude": a letter is read in a world different from the one in which it was written, and at a time different from that in which it was composed. This is no doubt why the eighteenth-century verse epistle dwells so often on an epistolary space separating writer from addressee, as in William Julius Mickle's *Almada Hill*, an epistle from Lisbon to a friend at home in England—

> While you, my friend, from low'ring wintry plains,
> Now pale with snows, now black with drizzling rains,

> From leafless woodlands, and dishonour'd bowers
> Mantled by gloomy mists...
> ....
> Pleas'd from the threat'ning tempest to retire,
> And join the circle round the social fire;
> In other climes through sun-bask'd scenes I stray.

—with an obvious implication: distance, separation, and absence are figures of the mind's aloneness in the world, and an epistolarity that so unperplexedly overcomes them already represents an evident resource for meeting and vanquishing solipsism on its own ground.

Yet epistolary solitude poses its own threat to any such gesture toward community, for in a scene of writing where nothing exists but the writer and the blankness of the page the possibility always lurks that audience or community are themselves mere figments of discourse. The ghost of lyric solipsism lingers here, as Claudio Guillén has pointed out, in the very notion of epistolarity as "absent speech," for "letter-writing . . . can always prompt a process of alienation, objectify a man's image of himself, present his 'I' as an 'other'" (249). The verse epistle will ultimately respond to this threat, as we shall see, through a complex dialectics of audience that conjures out of blankness a world beyond the epistolary exchange, but in the later seventeenth century it does so initially through a split or division within the sphere of epistolary verse in which the Ovidian verse epistle, having been made into the lonely embodiment of lyric solipsism, is repressed in favor of a public or Horatian mode of epistolary wisdom.

The Ovidian epistle had always been taken to represent the lyric impulse within epistolary poetry, the women of Ovid's *Heroides*, abandoned by their lovers, the possibility of tragic isolation. The Ovidian epistle, Joseph Warton would observe in his *Essay on Pope*, is not really a letter: "it is indeed no other than a passionate soliloquy in which the mind gives vent to the distresses and emotions under which it labors" (1.286). And as such, as Gillian Beer has said in a brilliant discussion of the Ovidian tradition, its central question is how "the self which has lost mutuality" may "ever discover its own limits or escape its own confines" (383). Yet in the contemporaneity of the *Heroides* and Horace's *Epistulae* in Roman poetry we see a balance or positive tension between Ovidian solipsism and the social or communal perspective of Horatian ethical verse, and in English poetry a similar equipoise, no doubt now between a fading Petrarchanism and an emergent Augustanism, is evident as late as the moment when Drayton is writing *Englands Heroicall Epistles* even as Jonson is reinventing Horatianism in an English voice. Yet by the time of Pope's *Eloisa to Abelard*, the single great Ovidian epistle of the eighteenth century, the triumph of the Horatian perspective is nearly complete.

In this context, *Eloisa to Abelard* may be taken not as a last exploration of the Ovidian dilemma of romantic abandonment, in which an unexpressed solipsism hovers darkly around the edges of the heroine's isolation, but as a diagnosis of Ovidian solipsism itself. For Pope's poem seizes immediately and dramatically on the one element in the medieval story that puts it outside Ovidian conventions: Abelard, caught with Eloisa in their guilty enjoyment, has been castrated by the males in her family ("what sudden horrors rise! / A naked lover bound and bleeding lies!"), and Eloisa, even as she dreams of a renewal of their sexual passion, is wholly aware that it is physically impossible. This, the situation of a heroine not doomed unwillingly to solipsistic reverie but embracing it, gave the poem in the eighteenth century both its terror and a certain gloomy fascination. It is the fascination that will make *Eloisa to Abelard* the great source poem for the Wartons and the midcentury revival of "pure poetry," the terror that throughout the century will prompt replies from imaginary Abelards that, as in James Cawthorn's, attempt at once to restore Eloisa to her role as holy abbess and God to his heaven:

> Th' Eternal Spirit o'er thy cell shall move
> In the soft image of the mystic dove:
> The longest gleams of heavenly comfort bring,
> Peace in his smile, and healing on his wing;
> At once remove affliction from thy breast,
> Melt o'er thy soul, and hush her pangs to rest.

Yet *Eloisa to Abelard* retains at a fundamental level the premise that will allow the eighteenth century, and Pope himself in his later poetry, to dwell consciously within a world of public or Horatian ethical concern. This is the conviction that isolation and powerlessness represent not an anxiety universal to human consciousness, but merely and contingently the cultural predicament of women. It was the powerlessness of women in Roman society, no doubt, that led Ovid originally to make the female voices speaking from the *Heroides* a general metaphor of human isolation, but no degree of Ovidian pathos could prevent the hardening of metaphor into ideology that would then lead the Renaissance to read them simply as poems about women.[3] Thus we encounter, for instance, the wrenching words of Daniel's Octavia as Gillian Beer invokes them, in which Pater's prison of the solitary mind can still appear in the light of a merely female dilemma: "We, in the prison of ourselves confin'd, / Must here shut up with our own passions live, / Turn'd in upon us, and denied to find / The vent of outward means" (qtd. in Beer 392).

The gesture of ideological dismissal that will portray isolation and inner paralysis as accidents of female circumstance, in turn, clears the space of ethical concern that will become the domain of the Horatian epistle. What this space looks like, Beer points out, the Ovidian epistle had always known. It is the public space from which Julia laments her own exclusion when, in *Don Juan*, she declares that love is "woman's whole existence": "man may range / The court, camp, church, the vessel and the mart, / Sword, gown, gain, glory . . . to fill up his heart" (qtd. in Beer 391). We are to view the eighteenth-century emergence of epistolarity as a masculine mode, then, against the busy background of a male-dominated scene of camp and forum—"The writing of letters has so much to do in all the occurrences of human life," Locke had observed, "that no gentleman can avoid showing himself in this kind of writing" (*Works* 9.180)—and then also, within it, the specific emergence of the Horatian epistle as the poetry of a world of active purpose. "He labors," said Dryden about Horace, incorporating a remark of Dacier's into the *Discourse Concerning Satire*, "to render us happy in relation to ourselves; agreeable and faithful to our friends; and discreet, serviceable, and well bred in relation to those with whom we are obliged to live, and to converse" (595).[4]

In the Horatian ethical perspective begins the great countermovement through which the verse epistle will deploy the *Nosce teipsum* of Western philosophy since Socrates against the new terror of epistemological solipsism. It is not wrong to think of the seventeenth century, as we now generally do, as the emergent moment of a radical Cartesian skepticism or doubt, so long as we recall that the inward gaze could still be for Descartes's own age a wholly positive gesture, a source of permanent wisdom about the world inhabited by men. "Seek we then ourselves in ourselves," writes Donne to Rowland Woodward. "I study myself more than any other subject," says Montaigne. "It is my supernatural metaphysic, it is my natural philosophy" (3.33). "The world that I regard is my self," declares Sir Thomas Browne. "Nature tells me that I am the image of God, as well as Scripture; he that understands not this much . . . is yet to begin the alphabet of man" (1.104–5).

The engagement of the verse epistle with solipsism thus begins in a scene where solitude or isolation, far from holding any terrors, may yet be viewed as a wholesome sanctuary from the world. Nor is there terror in the blankness of the epistolary page, that literal absence of audience that might otherwise so obviously be taken as the very image of the mind's isolation in the world. In the ethical security of this situation begins the dialectic of audience that consists in a complex interplay, beginning as the first words are written on the page, between the letter-writer and an imagined presence that assumes a more and more specific identity until, long before the epistle has come to a conclusion, it has taken on the reality of another mind or person looking outward from the page; "you are just here upon this little paper," writes Swift to Stella, "and therefore I see and talk with you every evening constantly and sometimes in the morning" (1.232). This dialectic is not peculiar to epistolary writing, of course—a lyric, quite as much as a verse epistle, no doubt gets written this way—but only in epistolary writing is it formally a feature of the way the discourse means, transforming the very process of its own composition into an ongoing epistemological drama.

The notion of inward contemplation as moral sanctuary, that refuge from the world for which Montaigne's withdrawal to his tower may be taken as the outward symbol, thus becomes a refuge from the precariousness or vulnerability of the epistolary enterprise. Outside the sanctuary provided by philosophical tradition, this would give us the eighteenth-century verse epistle as Paul Fry describes the ode—a poetic form whose very point is "the creation of an auditor," the "projecting from the self a precedent other who will then be able to take the self seriously" (99). Permitted that sanctuary, on the other hand, the verse epistle is able to draw steadily on a certain nonchalance about the literal absence of audience that had always been part of epistolary tradition. "Reader," says Nicholas Breton in *A Post with a Packet of Mad Letters*, one of the earliest English formularies, "I know not what you are, and therefore I cannot well tell what to say: only this at adventure: if you be wise, you will not play the fool in scoffing at that which perhaps may deserve a better countenance" (30).[5]

Within the tradition of the eighteenth-century verse epistle itself, this nonchalance is preserved mainly in the strain of mock-heroic address running from Mason's *Heroic Epistle* to Sir William Chambers to the jocular irreverence of Wolcot's Peter Pindar, where the imaginary status of audience becomes as often as not part of the satiric joke. Thus, for instance, T. J. Mathias, pausing halfway through an epistle to the Reverend Richard Watson for a jocular footnote: "Hitherto I have addressed the Doctor under the distant title of Thou, but as I have now made a more intimate acquaintance with him, and as it is the property of familiarity to lessen awful respect, I shall venture to use the word *You* from hence to the end of the epistle." In the more serious context of the Horatian epistle, all such nonchalance is dispelled, even in moments of jocularity, by the dialectic through which audience assumes an actual presence, as with the friend who suddenly speaks out in Fenton's epistle to Lombard:

> "Wither," you cry, "tends all this dry discourse?
> To prove, like Hudibras, a man's no horse...."
>   Faith, sir, I see you nod, but can't forbear;
> When a friend reads, in honor you must hear.

The same dialectic gives us the voice of the adversarius in the epistles of Horace and Pope, which has sometimes been mistakenly viewed—in

Pope's case, no doubt partly due to the textual meddlings of Warburton—as a sort of dramatic impurity in the epistolary situation.

To imagine that epistolary decorum is somehow violated when audience comes alive on the page, however—very often so that the solitary letter-writer seems to hear a voice in the room—is to miss not simply the way in which the verse epistle is presenting its own discourse as a drama, but then the whole point of that drama as the power of discourse to posit and populate a world. To take the epistolary dialectic on its own terms, on the other hand, is to be prepared for that ensuing moment in which the epistle will shift its gaze to an audience lying beyond the circumference of its immediate address. As Gillis has pointed out, Benveniste's reflections on the ontology of the pronoun, originally suggested by certain terms used by the Arab grammarians, provide the essential perspective here: "For them, the first person is *al-mutakallimu* 'the one who speaks'; the second, *al-muhatabu* 'the one who is addressed'; but the third is *al-ya'ibu* 'the one who is absent'" (197). The move through which the epistle reveals its awareness of an unaddressed audience—one thinks of Jean-Louis Guez de Balzac's comment on his own epistolary conduct: "When I treat with you, (my Lord) I suppose myself to be before a full assembly" (316)—thus draws on something already written into the abstract or formal nature of discursive systems.

The normal register of the verse epistle, that is, must be viewed as one of double address—a discourse that, as Jean Starobinski says in a related context about Augustine's *Confessions*, "takes form by creating, almost simultaneously, two addresses, one summoned directly, the other assumed obliquely as a witness" (77). Yet the audience listening in on the epistolary exchange is also one that may at any moment leap into visibility through a simple shift in address, as often happens, for instance, in the commendatory epistle. Thus Dryden, ostensibly speaking to a young poet whose work he admires ("Thou hast inspired me with thy soul"), suddenly and abruptly shifts to a new audience—"Reader, I've done, nor longer will withhold / Thy greedy eyes" (*To John Hoddesdon*)—and thus Walter Harte, from addressing the young lady to whom he has sent a copy of Fenton's poems, is able to raise his eyes to a wider public:

> Attend, ye Britons, in so just a cause,
> 'Tis sure a scandal to withhold applause;
> Nor let posterity reviling say,
> Thus unregarded Fenton pass'd away.

The essential point about this wider audience is that it is, quite as much as the addressee of the letter, internal to the epistolary situation, a presence summoned up by the conventions of discourse and having no real existence outside them. We are dealing, in short, with a phenomenon very similar to the one that allows Starobinski to derive the double audience of Augustine's *Confessions* from a purely formal contradiction within the autobiographical narrative: Augustine addresses his confessions to God, but on his own account God is an omniscient being who does not need to be told his innermost thoughts. Thus we encounter an immediate paradox, and a choice: either Augustine, on all other accounts intelligent enough, has embarked here on a discourse nonsensical in its own terms, or the ultimate audience of the *Confessions* is not God but a humankind listening in on Augustine's fervent address to his Creator. And so, of course, it is: "My soul, tell this to the souls that you love. Let them weep in this valley of tears, and so take them with you to God" (83).

The eighteenth-century verse epistle exploits most of those resources of internal paradox that signal double audience in discourse, as when, for instance, John Byrom writes within the conventions that allow us to recognize that a modern letter to the editor is only incidentally to the editor, or Charles Churchill writes within the conventions that, in a modern trial transcript, would tell us that the cross-examination of a key witness is for the benefit of an unaddressed judge and jury:

> HOGARTH stand forth—I dare thee to be tried
> In that great Court, where Conscience must preside;
> At that most solemn bar hold up thy hand;
> Think before whom on what account you stand—
> Speak, but consider well—from first to last
> Review thy life, weigh every action past.

And then, invisibly sustaining all such local exploitations of the conventions of oblique address, there is the simultaneous role of rhyme and meter in summoning up an audience external to the epistolary exchange.

The high degree of formal complexity associated with Augustan verse—that is to say, all those resources through which Dryden or Pope manages an endlessly witty elaboration of sense within the tight constraints of the heroic couplet—has to do beyond its local effects with the paradox of meaning as borne by a materiality itself meaningless. On the face of it, this is only the familiar paradox of language itself as meaning somehow arising from brute matter. I trace a message in the sand: the stick does not mean, the sand does not mean, and it is not clear how it helps to say that these tracings mean, since those tracings over there (made by a starfish) do not. And yet you read my message. In speech, we are accustomed to saying, the same paradox is present but overlooked: I know that your words to me are made out of the same brute material as a car's backfire or the sound of a dish smashing against the wall, but what I hear is your "pure meaning."

Only poetry, or what was called poetry in the centuries before free verse, insists that we remain aware of the paradox as we listen.

The way in which poetry insists on the paradox is doubtless what Wordsworth had in mind when he spoke of "the tendency of meter to divest language, in a certain degree, of its reality" (1.147). For what "reality" can only mean in such a context is the sort of speech-act situation we are most used to, in which we are so unconscious of language as brute sound or material medium that, hearing "pure meaning," we quite simply forget that it exists as such. It is the way that poetry from Homer onward calls us back to remembrance that Sir Joshua Reynolds has in mind when, writing only a few years before Wordsworth but in much closer cultural proximity to the formal complexities of Augustan verse, he describes poetry as being composed "in a language in the highest degree artificial, a construction of measured words, such as never is, nor ever was used by man. Let this measure be what it may, whether hexameter or any other meter used in Latin or Greek—or rhyme, or blank verse . . .—they are all equally removed from nature, and equally a violation of common speech" (2.67).

Nor are we mistakenly projecting onto Reynolds some post-Saussurean linguistic awareness when we note that the ways poetry dwells on the materiality of language—all those features, including things like alliteration and assonance as well as rhyme and meter, that Reynolds has in mind when he speaks of poetic language as "in the highest degree artificial"—always involve an emphasis on linguistic arbitrariness. For the eighteenth century was wholly aware of this as well. Long before Johnson speaks routinely in *The Idler* of words as "signs accidental and arbitrary" (106), the *Guardian* has reflected that the first affixing of signs to sounds must have been "as arbitrary as possible, there being no more connection between the letters and the sounds they are expressive of, than there is between those sounds and the ideas of the mind they immediately stand for" (2.491), and even before that the *Athenian Oracle* had some time since pointed out to its readers that "in every letter we are to consider the power, and the character distinct from each other," for "the power, force, or sound, which is the same, or little differing in all nations or languages: the character or figure whereby those powers are expressed, which almost infinitely disagree, seem perfectly arbitrary, alterable, and still altering at pleasure" (1.335).

To offer the sort of account of rhyme and meter given in contemporary theory—"By putting his words into the hands of a preexisting material scheme, an external, nonsemantic organizing force which no syllable can escape, the poet . . . exchanges the expressive potential of the individual utterance for that of the literary institution within which the poem takes its place" (Attridge 245)—is thus only to translate into modern terms something already perfectly understood by the Augustan poets, and to bring to light as well the paradox through which the verse epistle reaches out to an audience beyond the epistolary exchange: the ostensible purpose of language is to mean or communicate, and a continuous stress on the nonsemantic dimension of language, those arbitrary or accidental elements insisting on an underlying reality of meaningless sound, must have some other point, the most obvious being to turn attention back on the poem as an object of public contemplation. Yet it is only in epistolary writing, letters being an exemplary instance of language as it is available to serve the purposes of bare communication, that rhyme and meter point insistently not to some vaguely imagined "public" but to an audience specifically overhearing or listening in on the ostensibly private address of epistoler to lector.

At the same time, the stylistic decorum of Augustan verse includes, beyond a demand for rhyme and meter as they direct attention to the poem as public object, the further demand that they never direct attention to themselves—meter as a mere metronomic regularity, rhyme as those "two catchwords in the rear," as Robert Lloyd once puts it, "which stand like watchmen at the close, / To keep the verse from being prose." The genesis of Augustan poetry as such, we have always recognized, was in an ideal of "correctness" that the Augustans themselves saw as having originated with Waller and Denham, what William Walsh had in mind when he told the young Alexander Pope that England had had great poets but never a correct one. This is the ideal for which Lloyd's verse, for all its attempts to pass its own clumsiness off as part of the joke, is seriously nostalgic. Poetry may have no choice, now that Pope is dead, but to return to a mode of Hudibrastic inconsequentiality, but the Augustan memory lingers:

> When genius steers by judgement's laws
> When proper cadence, varied pause
> Show Nature's strength combin'd with art . . .
> Then numbers come, and all before
> Is bab, dab, scab—mere rhymes—no more.
>
> (*On Rhymes*)

The ideal of Augustan decorum or correctness, that is to say, becomes fully comprehensible only when translated into terms of internal audience, and in particular of the mode of double or simultaneous address associated with the verse epistle. For the requirement that rhyme and meter make the poem available as a public object is one shared with other poetry, but the demand that they work so invisibly that the audience thus summoned is allowed to gaze as through a window into an otherwise private world of civilized discourse and high ethical concern—and is, as we shall see, compelled to choose between entering that world or rejecting it—is peculiar to the epistolary situation. The centrality of this internal or dramatic situation to the Augustan mode no doubt explains why so many poems sounding like spontaneous utterance proclaim themselves nonetheless to be epistolary—one thinks of the opening lines of the *Epistle to Arbuthnot*, or Pope's address to Bolingbroke throughout the *Essay on Man*—but it explains prior to that why a clumsy use of rhyme or meter, the "bab, dab, scab" of Lloyd's bad poet, threatens the Augustan enterprise itself: what is shattered is not some rule of stylistic regularity but an entire drama of ethical choice.

When the illusion is sustained, we are given that epistolary situation in which an audience hovers invisibly over the scene of writing and, supposing itself to be unnoticed because it is unaddressed, gives its entire attention to what is going on in the world of the epistoler and his acquaintance. And what is occurring, though the essential theme has a thousand variations in epistolary literature, is a conjuration of community out of distance or absence or flux, the gesture through which written language, as in Mickle's address to his friend at home in England, assumes the power to annihilate time and space. This is the possibility that makes Steele's reflections on writing in *Guardian* 172, for instance, a meditation on the ontology of discourse itself, and on a relation of written language to community that lies at the heart of Augustan values: "by it the English trader may hold commerce with the inhabitants of the East or West Indies, without the trouble of a journey. . . . This silent art of speaking by letters, remedies the inconvenience arising from distance of time, as well as place. . . . This preserves the works of the immortal part of men. . . . To this we are beholden for the works of Demosthenes and Cicero, of Seneca and Plato" (2.492–93).

The importance of the epistle in the eighteenth century, however, has less to do with its mere ability to remedy the inconveniencies of distance, as Steele puts it, than with its power as written discourse to resurrect an intimacy otherwise lost, to restore to momentary wholeness a world of sundered personal relations. The eighteenth-century focus, in short, is always on epistolary discourse as Horace had described it, as absent speech or conversation taking place at a distance: "*epistulis ad absentes loquimur, sermone cum praesentibus*" (see Haight). A similar notion had been present in England from the beginnings of its own epistolary tradition—a letter, Angel Day had said in *The English Secretary*, is "the familiar and mutual talk of one absent friend to another" (8)—but by the eighteenth century it has gained the status of an axiom. "Epistolary writing," says Hugh Blair shortly after midcentury, is "conversation carried on upon paper, between two friends at a distance" (370). "What are letters," asks Vicesimus Knox at century's end, "but written conversation?" (1.64).

The impulse in such remarks is to dwell on the intimacy wondrously restored through the epistolary exchange, and to pass lightly over its origins in separation or distance or loss. Before the invention of writing, acknowledges Lady Winchelsea in verses to a friend, "absence separated like the grave," but through the long ages since there has always been correspondence to, as she puts it, "baffle absence and secure delight." Yet while the focus of commentators and individual letter-writers is usually on the delights of intimacy thus restored, epistolary tradition as a whole speaks eloquently enough of the absence that separates like the grave, and of epistolarity itself as a gesture toward community in a world where some preexisting order is threatened with decline or disintegration. The sense of epistolary tradition invoked by the eighteenth-century verse epistle is one that remains perpetually mindful of the moment of loss or absence in which the letter originates, the movement toward dispersal or fragmentation that makes necessary an attempt to reconstitute community in alternative terms. This is the context in which epistolarity then becomes so often associated with a sense of imperiled community against a background of cultural decline.

In poetry, this gives us the verse epistle in its normal association with literary movements, the assertion of a community of literary or ethical sensibility in the context of a perceived decline. The epistles of Ronsard may thus be taken as the outward expression of the impulse toward community that gave birth to the Pléiade, the epistles of Ben Jonson as the token not simply of a revived classicism but of the similar sense of community giving birth to the Sons of Ben. Against this same background, even a literary phenomenon as apparently isolated as the superb neo-Latin verse epistles of Sarbiewski in the seventeenth century demands to be seen as a last expression of the Renaissance humanism that perceived itself as a community sustained by a shared sense of classical values and permitted through the newly eloquent medium of a restored Latinity to speak to each other across the narrow boundaries of nation or local vernacular. Sarbiewski's verse epistles may be viewed in this context as the culmination of a movement that had begun with the epistles of Petrarch, for whom his own *Epistulae Metricae* were the natural complement of his prose letters.

In the very impulse of Renaissance humanism to constitute itself as a community of learned souls suspended above the divisions of nation or locality,[6] in turn, lies the explanation of humanism as an epistolary phenomenon, an intellectual movement taking the *De Conscribendis Epistulis* of Erasmus as its handbook and the actual letters of a Petrarch or Erasmus as a central literary achievement. The humanists wrote their letters, observes Huizinga in his biography of Erasmus, "with a view to publication, for a wider circle, or at any rate, with the certainty that the recipient would show the letter to others" (97), and in fact such showing-about of letters is a constant motif in Erasmus's surviving correspondence. This is the context in which humanism itself may be viewed as developing out of the survival in the *ars dictaminis* tradition of what R. W. Southern has called medieval humanism, and a controversy such as that surrounding the *Epistulae Obscurorum Virorum* as the emergent moment of a community that would then, against a background of growing national and religious antagonisms, sustain an improbable existence for nearly two hundred years.[7]

In the ancient world, though letters dealing with practical or commercial matters are as old as the cuneiform writing of the Sumerians, the letter as a mode of personal or philosophical expression once again arises as an attempt to assert the possibility of ethical community in a context of cultural decline. The great exemplum here is the correspondence of Cicero, representing a retreat into private relationships after the disintegration of the Republic, and this no doubt explains Cicero's role as a literary model for the Renaissance humanists and the specific excitement generated by Petrarch's discovery of the lost manuscript of the *Ad Atticum*, which may be taken as the major event in the rise of epistolary humanism. As we shall see in a subsequent chapter, the verse epistles of Horace may be regarded as the poetry of the same moment that produced Cicero's disillusionment, an attempt to regenerate the Republic as a private ethical ideal within a fallen social or political reality. And as we shall also see, Seneca's epistles to Lucilius and the *Epistulae* of Pliny the Younger simply continue the same enterprise against a darker and more foreboding background of Roman decline. To grasp this is to grasp the sense in which such poets as Dryden and Pope, who recognized in the cultural situation surrounding Horace's *Epistulae* a mirror of their own cultural dilemma, saw themselves as Augustan.

At the same time, the letter-writer whose own situation lies behind that of Cicero or Horace or Seneca as an ultimate source of moral authority wrote epistles that have come down to us only in scattered fragments, so that we are left to speculate about the shape and tonality of the entire correspondence. This is Epicurus, retreating after the disintegration of the Greek polis into his Garden and a private society based on ethical friendship, attempting in an age when power now emanated from distant centers and civic participation was lost to the citizen to create an inward community in which philosophy as Plato and Aristotle had understood it, not as abstruse speculation but as a total form of life, would once again become possible for individuals.[8] As has been pointed out by Benjamin Farrington, whose account of Epicureanism viewed in this aspect remains unrivaled, the lost correspondence of Epicurus must be seen less as an attempt to impart philosophical doctrine than to create philosophical community, to carry the ethical message of the Garden outward into a disordered and declining world.

This is the context in which, for instance, Farrington speculates that the Epicurean epistles may have provided a model for St. Paul and the early

Christian community. Whether or not the earliest Christians were aware of the Epicurean model, the truth Farrington is seeing here is a structural truth, one having less to do with actual historical influence than with the role of the letter as it is able to summon into existence an alternative community in periods when an older order is thought to be in a state of disintegration. For Epicurus, as philosopher of the Garden, this involves a recognition that the Greek polis is irrecoverable not simply as a political entity but as a sphere of ethical expression; for Horace and Virgil it involves an awareness that the Republic whose virtues they celebrate is lost except as a literary or imaginative ideal. For Paul, however, writing his epistles against the same general background of disorder and decline as Seneca and Pliny, sending to the scattered Christian communities of his time the word that a new and timeless community is arising out of the slow disintegration of the Roman order, the same notion has somewhat different implications. These, too, enter into epistolary tradition as it will lead ultimately to the eighteenth-century verse epistle.

In the letters of Paul in the New Testament, the materiality of written discourse once again permits, paradoxically, a demonstration that the material world is unreal. For if we think of Paul's letters as mere documents, they are only tokens of an irrecoverable past, linguistic mementos of a community that no longer exists, sender and receivers both having gone into the abyss of time. Yet as soon as we recall that the community Paul addresses had a perilous existence and was still in the making, we recover a sense Farrington has in mind when he posits Epicurus as a model, of letters not simply as a medium of exchange within a community but, in their public aspect as written discourse, as invitations to join that community, to make a conscious decision to include oneself in the audience to which they are ostensibly addressed. And, taken out of historical time, that is of course still the purpose of Paul's epistles—a purpose that is simply given formal recognition in their being included in the New Testament as revealed Christian doctrine. The truth thus affirmed is only incidentally doctrinal; it is a truth about epistolarity, through which a timeless Christian community is summoned into being by these letters to the early Christian communities of the Mediterranean world.

The major contribution made by Paul to subsequent epistolary tradition thus has to do not with any formal innovation but with the postulation of audience as a universal community existing outside of time and, beyond that, with a redramatization of the epistolary situation in the terms in which Augustine would later portray the two worlds symbolized by the city of man and the City of God. For in Paul, the local background of cultural decline we find in the secular epistle, the lost world of the Greek polis for Epicurus or the vanished Republic for Cicero or Horace or Pliny becomes, as it will be for Augustine, the entire disorder of the world as men inhabit it—a world of sin and death from which no actual city or society is exempt. And the private ethical community toward which the epistle traditionally gestures, the world of the Garden for Epicurus or of friendship with a Maecenas or Bolingbroke for Horace or Pope, assumes in Paul's letters just the form it will have in Augustine, of that scattering of souls who already, here and there among the corruptions of every human dispensation, dwell in the City of God.

In specific terms, the manner in which this sense of timeless or universal community lies in the immediate background of the Augustan verse epistle has to do with the Pauline or Christian transformation of the *Nosce teipsum* of classical philosophy—the "Know thyself" of Socrates and the Delphic oracle—into the mode of what I shall call Augustinian introspection. For it is in Augustine, himself powerfully influenced by the general intuition of Greek philosophy that to look into one's own mind is somehow to have access to humanity as a whole, that the world of one's own thoughts becomes a point of entrance to the world of humanity in its universal aspect, a turning away from an outward world of sin and delusion and inward toward the City of God itself. This is the context in which, as Peter Brown has wonderfully said, Augustine's *Confessions* are "a manifesto of the inner world": "Above all, it is man's tragedy that he should be driven to flee 'outwards', to lose touch with himself, to 'wander far' from his 'own heart'. . . . This emphasis on the fall of the soul as a turning outwards, as a loss of identity, as becoming 'a partial thing, isolated, full of cares, intent upon the fragment, severed from the whole,' is a clear echo of the thought of Plotinus" (168).

We have long since learned to say, in light of arguments made by Paul Fussell and others, that literary Augustanism is grounded in an Augustinian moral perspective, a sense of human existence as a gloomy and disordered state of alienation from the divine: "My soul . . ." cries Augustine, "do not let the din of your folly deafen the ears of your heart. For the Word himself calls you to return. . . . In the land of death you try to find a happy life: it is not there" (81–82). The introspective movement in which the soul seeks its true identity not in this world but in a universal human community that moves and has its being in God is an immediate consequence of the same perspective, which may then be seen to lie as well behind the tradition of philosophical self-scrutiny from within which the verse epistle in the later seventeenth century moves toward its eventual confrontation with solipsism. For when the isolation or solitude of the epistolary situation may still appear in the positive light of the seclusion from the world that produced Montaigne's *Essays*, we are in the near vicinity of Augustine's timeless community of souls. This is, once again, Montaigne's "I study myself more than any other subject" ("It is my supernatural metaphysics, it is my natural philosophy"), but now in a context in which one may hear its insistent theological or Augustinian overtones. "We are to be found truly," says Walter Mountague in terms echoing both Augustine and Montaigne, "nowhere but in ourselves, everywhere else we meet but with our fantasm or our shadow" (qtd. in Røstvig 1.234).

The reason that Augustinian introspection assumes such importance in the very moment of Cartesian doubt is that the battle between literary Augustanism and solipsism in its philosophical guise will turn precisely on the issue of introspection as a means to knowledge about human nature. Within philosophy, this involves a story at which we have already glanced, one leading from Descartes's meditations by his fireside to the dwindling dominion of man in what Locke will call "the little world of his own understanding" (*Essay* 120) to Hume's mid-eighteenth-century gloom to, finally, Pater's haunted image of the mind keeping as a solitary prisoner its dream of the world. Yet the origins of the story, far removed from any such scene of spiritual isolation, lie paradoxically just where the spirit of the new empiricism is seen at its most confident and optimistic, in the conviction that Locke's great achievement had been to extend to the investigation of human nature the principles of Baconian science. "As the science of man is the only solid foundation for the other sciences," we find Hume averring in accents of undiminished optimism a half-century after Locke's *Essay*, "so the only solid foundation we can give to this science itself must be laid on experience and observation. 'Tis no astonishing reflection to consider, that the application of experimental philosophy to moral subjects should come after that to natural at the distance of a whole century" (xvi).

The usual account of Lockean empiricism as a movement within the new experimental philosophy, the epistemology of the same intellectual climate that produced the founding of the Royal Society and Hobbes's denunciations of the schoolmen, has always been so persuasive as to gloss over certain anomalies that, already present at the moment Locke was writing the *Essay*, would later surface as an irresolvable dilemma. The most troublesome of these concerns the matter of method: though the Baconian program provided empiricism with a powerful slogan, and though Locke himself would then make a revolutionary move in positing sense impressions as the mental equivalent of the experimental data demanded by Baconian induction in the natural sciences, it was never clear what was to count as the equivalent in epistemology of laboratory tests and careful measurement in chemistry or physics. Yet for Locke the problem was not a problem. One was to experiment, in effect, by closing one's eyes: "Let anyone examine his own thoughts, and thoroughly search into his understanding, and then let him tell me, whether all the original ideas he has there, are any other than of the objects of his senses; or of the operations of his mind, considered as objects of his reflection" (*Essay* 106).

Nor, strictly speaking, was the problem recognized as such by Hume, who is still talking in the mid-eighteenth century about the absolute necessity in philosophy of mind for "careful and exact experiments, and the observations of those particular effects, which result from its different circumstances and situations," and who, since his own method is identical to Locke's, obviously supposes that simple introspection answers those requirements: "When I shut my eyes and think of my chamber, the ideas I form are exact representations of the impressions I felt. . . . Ideas and impressions appear always to correspond to each other" (3). The same notion, always present as an unexamined premise, is nearly indistinguishable from the history of empiricism as a doctrine. "Whosover looketh into himself . . . ," Hobbes had said at the beginning of it all, "he shall thereby read and know, what are the thoughts, and passions of all other men" (xix). "To what purpose is to dilate on that which may be demonstrated with the utmost evidence in a line or two, to anyone that is capable of the least reflection?" asks Berkeley some years later. "It is but looking into your own thoughts" (1.166). "Our idea of an orange really *consists* of the simple ideas of a certain color, a certain form, a certain taste and smell, etc.," J. S. Mill will still be saying over a century later, "because we can, by interrogating our consciousness, perceive all these elements in the idea" (2.433).

By the time we get to Mill's *System of Logic,* introspection has enjoyed so long a favor as the empiricist method in philosophy that Mill or his contemporaries would have thought it pointless to trace its origins back further than Locke's *Essay Concerning Human Understanding.* Yet when we actually go back to Locke's *Essay,* it becomes clear that introspection is not, as a philosophical method, anything that arises from within empiricism; it is the *Nosce teipsum* of Socrates and the Greeks as then transmuted into Augustinian introspection in theology and only then, in a moment of methodological necessity, pressed into service by Locke in the name of what Hume calls "the application of experimental philosophy to moral subjects." If Locke felt no deep contradictions at work here, it is because he is still very close to the older theological tradition in which introspection operates as a wholly intelligible means of construing reality. This is why the inward gaze may still be taken by Locke, as by Descartes, as an immediate demonstration of God's existence: "from the consideration of ourselves, and what we infallibly find in our own constitutions, our reason leads us to the knowledge of this certain and evident truth,—*that there is an eternal, most powerful, and most knowing being*" (*Essay* 621).

There is obviously a deep and lingering problem here for empiricism as a doctrine, however—one that goes well beyond that of Locke's unconscious indebtedness to the very metaphysical tradition from which the *Essay* is an attempt to break free. For the effect of his unconscious borrowing is to introduce a logical incoherence into the heart of the empiricist program. This is something that Prior, in a moment of extraordinary intuition, had seen almost immediately; "if no man's ideas be perfectly the same," he wrote in 1721, "Locke's Human Understanding may be fit only for the meditation of Locke himself" (1.639)—that is, if empiricism is to work as a mode of philosophical inquiry, then what one sees when one examines one's own mind must not be something contingently or idiosyncratically true about one's own mental experience, but something universally true about human consciousness. Here, once again, is Hume: "When I shut my eyes and think of my chamber, the ideas I form are exact representations of the impressions I felt; nor is there any circumstance of the one, which is not to be found in the other. In running over my other perceptions, I find still the same resemblance and representation."

At any such moment, it is clear that Hume supposes the results he gets by shutting his eyes to be those that any other human being would get by doing the same, nor is there any sign that he sees that the premise needed to sustain such a conviction—a metaphysics giving Hume's own consciousness a share in some universal human consciousness—is altogether missing from his philosophy. Yet it is always clear as well that the whole thrust of Hume's enterprise, that relentless skepticism that so effortlessly dismantles such ideas as causality and human identity, would in an instant, if given the opportunity, triumphantly dissolve any notion of universal or transcendent human consciousness as well. The reason that this moment never arrives is that Hume's mind functions as a skeptical intelligence only by repressing its grounding in an unacknowledged metaphysics, which is why the contradiction returns instead, famously, as an unanalyzed source of personal anxiety:

> The *intense* view of these manifold contradictions and imperfections in human reason has so wrought upon me, and heated my brain, that I am ready to reject all belief and reasoning, and can look upon no opinion as even more probable or likely than another. Where am I, or what? From what causes do I derive my existence, and to what condition shall I return? Whose favour shall I court, and whose anger must I dread? What beings surround me? and on whom have I any influence, or who have any influence on me? I am confounded by these questions, and begin to fancy myself in the most deplorable condition imaginable, environed with the deepest darkness, and utterly deprived of the use of every member and faculty. (268–69)

To explain Hume's despondency as the psychological penalty of denying or repressing an unacknowledged metaphysics,[9] however, is to miss the meaning it would have had for Dryden or Swift or Pope, to whom it would have appeared as the wholly natural consequence of his having cut himself off from the transcendent ground of his conscious being—in Augustinian terms, not simply of dwelling in the "land of death" that is this world but then of mistaking it for one's home. As we shall see, it is the way William Law revives this Augustinian notion in the moment of Swift and Pope that makes him, in effect, the theologian of literary Augustanism, insisting in urgent tones that as human beings we dwell simultaneously in two worlds, the divine and the temporal, and that the truth of Divine Scripture thus concerns not some long-vanished historical reality but a story being played out around and within us even now: "We do not want Moses to assure us that there was a First Man; that he had something from Heaven, and something from Earth in him. . . . For every man in himself is the infallible proof of this" (*Divine Knowledge* 39–40).

As it plays a major role in the development of Law's later theology, this view has complex and far-reaching consequences, but its more immediate intent was to turn the gaze of eighteenth-century readers away from the outward world of sham and delusion and toward, as John Sitter well puts it, "the timeless and archetypal world revealed by introspection" (78). This is precisely the ground of moral intent that Law shares with Augustanism, which will stage its own counterattack against eighteenth-century skepticism by insisting not simply on that same timeless world as an ultimate reality, but on introspection as the privileged means of discovering its truths. To look within the human mind is, on this account, not, except trivially and incidentally, to discover the realm of decaying sense impressions and arbitary mental operations proclaimed by Hume or Condillac;[10] it is to discover the same universal humanity-in-God once imperfectly glimpsed by Plato and Plotinus and then wholly revealed to Paul and Augustine, the inward community through which human ethics are grounded in a transcendent morality and human beings are made intelligible to one another as moral subjects.

In purely doctrinal terms, this yields the *Nosce teipsum* of Greek philosophy and Augustinian Christianity in the specific form of what W. K. Wimsatt called the Augustan universal, the belief in a universal human nature obscured by accidents of language and culture and historical period. Thus Samuel Johnson in *Rambler* 60: "there is such a uniformity in the state of man, considered apart from adventitious and separable decorations and disguises, that there is scarce any possibility of good or ill, but is common to human kind. . . . We are all prompted by the same motives, all deceived by the same fallacies, all animated by hope, obstructed by danger, entangled by desire, and seduced by pleasure" (3.320). Yet the existence of a universal human nature might be, quite as much as the existence of God or an absolute ground of morality, a matter of mere assertion, which is why the peculiar genius of Augustanism lies in having engaged philosophical empiricism not on doctrinal grounds but on those of procedure or method, presenting its own claims to truth in terms that directly contest the introspective claims of Hobbes or Locke or Hume. "Every man may," says Imlac in *Rasselas*, "by examining his own mind, guess what passes in the mind of others" (100).

The move through which Augustanism thus engages philosophical empiricism on its home ground, in effect laying a public wager that introspection will always reveal a moral reality rather than a mere jumble of sense impressions, is so far inconclusive, however, for the result might well be nothing more than a war of competing introspective claims. The implicit threat of such an impasse gives us the situation in which Augustanism then makes the more momentous move of positing art as a mode of moral explanation, thus at once defining its own mission as a literary movement and appealing to the judgment of an audience outside the limited confines of theological or philosophical controversy. This is a move through which a universal human nature becomes, as Pope had said almost in the dawning moment of high Augustanism, at once the source, and end, and test of art, and in which the moral reality revealed by the introspective gaze is made available within the social or public realm as literature. "He needed not the spectacles of books to read nature," says Johnson about Shakespeare; "he looked inwards and found her there" (7.112).

The notion of literature as moral explanation should not be discounted as unphilosophical simply because literature is not philosophy. For it is this that will allow Augustanism to focus relentlessly through much of the eighteenth century on the logical weakness at the heart of the empiricist program: even if it is true that Locke and Hume see nothing but sense impressions when they look within their minds, their own empiricism provides no grounds for supposing that this is what Pope sees, or Swift, or you and I. If, on the other hand, when I look within my own mind I have an overwhelming intuitive conviction that I can by this means tell what is going on in yours, I have discovered for myself the ground on which Augustan literature stands in explaining the world as a sphere of moral choice, and in then invoking the notion of a timeless or universal human nature as the only intelligible context of such choice. Augustanism does not summon Socrates and Augustine and Shakespeare as its witnesses out of some nostalgia for a time before skepticism, but because it has staked its own position on the strong ground of moral intelligibility.

The verse epistle thus emerges as the dominant form in Augustan poetry against the background of an intellectual conflict in which the public that responds to literary works has power to decide between the opposing doctrines. Yet this power is neither plenary nor absolute: since the actual or temporal world is a scene of sin and folly, there will always be skeptics like Hume who through pride or blindness deny the transcendent basis of human existence, readers who through guilt or perversity are brought to subscribe to such views, and a vast populace of others so caught up in a round of vanity and greed and sensuality that they have never thought about the matter at all. The name of the judgment that Augustan poetry passes on this teeming world is satire, which thus becomes the means of compelling an invisible audience to choose between the crowded outward scene and an inward world of ethical consciousness. This is the situation in which the epistoler and lector of the verse epistle come to symbolize a private ethical community besieged by the outside world, its implied audience those souls who, projected as overhearing the epistolary exchange while yet in a state of moral suspense, have yet to choose one or the other world as their own.

At the same time, the epistolary audience that thus becomes a symbolic presence in the Augustan drama of ethical choice is still only a figment of discourse, and the verse epistle does not pretend otherwise. To the contrary, the Augustan belief in the power of an inward moral order to transform the outward world of social relations, and specifically of a moral community summoned into existence by Augustan literature to regenerate the declining world of eighteenth-century England, derives from the conviction that an abstract audience projected by discourse may take on body within the world of social beings. The manner in which this is projected as occurring is logically the last act in the ethical drama, the moment of ultimate moral choice in which actual readers, having been privileged to listen in on the private world of Pope and Swift and Bolingbroke and Arbuthnot, then take the abstract audience projected by the verse epistle as being identical with their own best selves. In such a moment epistolary audience would cease to be merely epistolary, solipsism would have been overcome, and there would be an alteration in the actual order of things.

This is epistolary audience as the site of what Laclau has called the struggle in ideology. The struggle as waged by the verse epistle begins in the close relationship between Augustan satire and the classical ideal of otium, or virtuous retirement from the world. This gives us, to take an entirely typical example, the friend in Yorkshire to whom Francis Fawkes addresses an epistle at midcentury, living as a "stranger to faction, in his calm retreat, / Far from the noise of cities, and the great," or the man living in a state of rural retirement as Wycherley had pictured him a half-century earlier:

> Here may he sit, and on the rocky shore
> See distant storms, and hear the billows roar,
> And count the wrecks on the tossed ocean spread,
> Safe from each surge that curls its ridgy head.
> Here may he laugh, in privacy and ease,
> At guilty grandeur, and its fopperies.

The movement through which Augustan poetry will generate satire out of solitude, with the verse epistle becoming the means of carrying the values of the otium scene outward into a corrupt world, begins in a sense of personal isolation as a state of deprivation. In the epistolary situation, as we have seen, this gives us the letter as Angel Day describes it, as "the familiar and mutual talk of one absent friend to another." In the otium scene, on the other hand, it gives us in even more immediate terms an ideal of ethical friendship. An identical sense of solitude as deprivation no doubt explains why Epicurus, the great theorist of otium in the ancient world, was also the most famous exponent of the theory of ethical friendship earlier developed by Aristotle: "We think, and we are conscious that we think," says Farrington, summarizing this doctrine. "This is the source of the good man's pleasure in himself. . . . But his friend is to him another self, and to share with a friend the awareness each has of the other's goodness is the specific pleasure of friendship" (30). This gives us the specific context in which ethical friendship becomes a companionship that does not detract from solitude—it is not, says Roscommon in his *Ode Upon Solitude*, "for my solitude unfit, / For I am with my friend alone, / As if we were but one"—and in which Epicurus and the Garden become the great archetype standing behind the eighteenth-century or Augustan ideal of otium.

The community surrounding Epicurus in the original Garden in Athens may be taken to demonstrate the way that the otium ideal, ostensibly involving only a withdrawal from the corrupt world, almost inevitably ends with its private circle of virtue having become a moral alternative to it. In the Garden, the ideal sustaining the enclosed community was one of moral self-sufficiency: like the gods of Epicurean doctrine, completely absorbed in the contemplation of their own divine nature, the company of the Garden demanded no more from life than a steady consciousness of its own virtue. This is a notion that may be seen to survive virtually unchanged, for instance, in an eighteenth-century poem like *The Friend*, Richard Savage's epistle to Aaron Hill, in which friendship leads to knowledge and knowledge to "bliss," "for wisdom virtue finds, / And brightens mortal to immortal minds." More normally, however, the otium ideal in eighteenth-century poetry leads to a countermovement back outward toward the world; "th'immortal blessings that attend / The just and good, the patriot and the friend," says Earl Nugent, speaking within the context of a Christian theology unknown to Epicurus, are not some "distant prospect" of eternal reward: "they taste heav'n's joys anticipated here" (*Of Human Enjoyments*).

The countermovement occurs because Christian theology, while in one aspect wholly congenial to the classical ideal of otium—the little community of Augustine at Hippo may in this context be taken as the Christian counterpart of the Garden, and the same sense of otium remains strong in such humanists as Erasmus and More—implies in another a powerful critique of ethical retirement. The manner in which this comes to bear may be traced in the way a certain perspective of Lucretian detachment gives way in Augustan poetry to satiric engagement. For the great passage in *De Rerum Naturae* in which Lucretius likens withdrawal from the world to safety in a storm—"When the winds are troubling the waters on a mighty sea it is sweet to view from the land the struggles of another man"—had always been taken as the highest poetic expression of Epicurean doctrine, and it never quite loses its spell over eighteenth-century otium poetry. "What is that world which makes the heart its slave?" asks John Langhorne in an epistle to a friend. "'Tis no more / Than the vext ocean while we walk the shore. / Loud roar the winds and swell the wild waves high" (*Epistle to Mr. _____*).

The celebrated detachment of the original passage in Lucretius corresponds to the Augustan sense that the moral decline of eighteenth-century England was due in part to impersonal forces of history, the implacable working-out of cycles in human civilization from which no society is exempt. Yet even Lucretius had suggested that the souls drowning in the ocean of the world sometimes do so by choice or through moral blindness; "from those tranquil places which have been strongly fortified aloft by the teaching of wise men," he says, one "can look down upon other men and see them wandering purposelessly" (*De Rerum Naturae* 2.1–35, trans. A. A. Long). Whenever otium poetry ascends toward this other Lucretian perspective, from the level seashore to a moral elevation or height, the corresponding emphasis on ethical choice moves toward something very like satiric judgment; as here, for instance, in George Granville's verses to Elizabeth Higgons:

> Farewell then cities, courts, and camps, farewell,
> Welcome, ye groves, here let me ever dwell. . . .
> From hence, as from a hill, I view below
> The crowded world, a mighty wood in show,
> Where several wanderers travel day and night,
> By different paths, and none are in the right.

The otium scene begins to generate satire when its own private circle of virtue enforces in new terms this moral contrast with the outside world. This is, once again, Epicurus in the Garden, Augustine at Hippo, Pope among his friends at Twickenham, and in every such instance the distinction between the otium community and what Granville calls the "crowded world" is felt as a collapse of ethical symmetry: within the otium scene, a private circle of friends exists in perfect sympathy because they have chosen both to renounce the world and to live in the company of one another. In the outside world, on the other hand, men are caught up in a ceaseless round of vice and folly not because they have made wrong choices but because they do not understand that moral consciousness begins, before any actual choice, in seeing the need to choose. This gives us the context in which vice and folly as they most often appear in Augustan satire are really forms of moral solipsism, as, for instance, in Epistle I of Langhorne's *Enlargement of the Mind*:

> Behold, ye vain disturbers of an hour!
> Ye dupes of faction! and ye tools of power!
> Poor rioters on life's contracted stage!
> Behold, and lose your littleness of rage!
> Throw envy, folly, prejudice behind!
> And yield to truth the empire of the mind.

This gives us the inward scene of the Augustan verse epistle, in which the epistoler—as with Pope in his Horatian poems—is a symbolic figure because he speaks for the entire philosophical tradition of otium retreat in a corrupt or disordered world, a lonely voice of beleaguered virtue preserving as a memory older and better days when good men were active in public affairs. This is the context in which the lectors of the verse epistle, the Bolingbrokes and Bathursts and Arbuthnots, become symbolic figures because, as members of the otium community similarly driven into retreat by a degenerate world, they collectively come to represent virtue in exile, an inward sphere of ethical consciousness that might yet, could the outside world be brought to pause in its noisy round, transform the outward order of things. There is an almost unbearable pressure in the direction of ethical choice in this situation, and yet—the otium community having chosen, the outside world oblivious—there is no one in sight to choose. This is the moment when epistolary audience, hovering above and outside the otium scene, feeling still an uneasy kinship with the outside world, becomes felt as a symbolic presence.

This is also the moment at which otium begins through an internal critique to call into question its own value as withdrawal or retreat, something that had already begun to occur when an otium community inadvertently emerged as a model to the corrupt world, but that is now more insistently heard as a demand to save those souls who are able to be saved; in this context, epistolary audience will come to represent the possibility of a society morally regenerated by the values of the otium world. In theological terms, this imperative gives us Augustine rising from the circle of friends around his table to preach to the crowds in church; in the secular terms of eighteenth-century England, where politics has increasingly become the only surviving vocabulary for ethical expression in the world, the same imperative gives us Pope and a great host of lesser writers as they are drawn into literary opposition to Walpole and the Robinocracy. In every case, the name of the voice exposing otium withdrawal as an abdication of moral responsibility is Stoicism, which from Hellenistic times onward had counterposed its own ideal of the *vita activa* to the Epicurean ideal of otium retirement from the world.

A Stoic strain had always been present in English ethical poetry—"You do not duties of societies," remonstrates one of Donne's speakers—but in the eighteenth century it runs as a steady counterpoint to the Augustan version of the otium ideal. The Greek philosophers, observes Thomas Gray, did not "run away from society for fear of its temptations: they passed their days in the midst of it" (1.263). The Stoics, says one Mr. Harris, quoted by Joseph Warton to correct a common error about Stoic "apathy," "considered it as a duty, arising from our very nature, not to neglect the welfare of public society" (2.147). "Not him I praise," says Lyttelton in a verse epistle to a friend, "who, from the world retir'd, / By no enlivening generous passion fir'd, / . . . fears bright Glory's awful face to see" (*To Mr. Poyntz*). To dare this, on the other hand, as Thomas Tickell had reminded his countrymen some years earlier in a mood of Roman elevation, is to die at peace: "Our own strict judges our past life we scan, / And ask if glory hath enlarg'd the span; / If bright the prospect, we the grave defy, / Trust future ages, and contented die."

The Stoic ideal comes to exert this force in the Augustan moment because, as Warton's Mr. Harris points out, it derives its principle of the vita activa from the moral nature of man, and in terms, moreover, that were then to enter directly into Christian theology; "the faculty in man which enables him to think, to plan, and to speak," says A. A. Long in *Hellenistic Philosophy*, "—which the Stoics called *logos*—is literally embodied in the universe at large. The individual human being at the essence of his nature shares a property which belongs to Nature in the cosmic sense" (108). In Christian terms, the world of the logos is precisely that inward world of a universal humanity discovered through contemplation—"the Word himself," we have heard Augustine cry, "calls you to return"—and this in turn is what the private circle of friends dwelling in the otium world have discovered among each other. In this situation, the Stoic injunction to civic duty, the obligation of those endowed with a rational nature to play a rational role in human affairs, takes on strong theological overtones, and the otium ideal dwindles away to mere selfishness or sloth, the choice of him who, as Lyttelton puts it, "on flowery couches slumbers life away, / And gently bids his active powers decay" (*To Mr. Poyntz*).

At the same time, an obvious paradox lurks here, for to send members of the otium community out to enter into public affairs would be to dissolve the community as a sanctuary of moral virtue. In Christian tradition, of course, a sense of the world as inescapably corrupt lay behind the great monastic movement of the early Middle Ages, but a nearly identical strain is visible before that in Roman syncretic philosophy; "contact with the crowd is deleterious," writes Seneca in one of his moral epistles; "inevitably vice will be made attractive or imprinted on us or smeared upon us without our being aware of it" (172). This gives us the situation in which the Epicurean injunction to live in unpolluted retirement and the opposing Stoic injunction to play an honorable part in civic affairs is felt in the

Augustan milieu as a strong dialectical tension, dialectical in precisely the Hegelian sense that it proceeds to unify the opposing imperatives at the level of a higher synthesis. One is to remain steadfastly within the otium scene, in short, and to send one's written works, making available the wisdom gained through virtuous retirement, outward into an unregenerate world. This is the moral solution for which Lyttelton praises the Reverend Dr. Ayscough of Oxford in an epistle written from Paris in 1728:

> Happy who thus his leisure can employ!
> He knows the purest hours of tranquil joy;
> Nor vex'd with pangs that busier bosoms tear,
> Nor lost to social virtue's pleasing care;
> Safe in the port, yet lab'ring to sustain
> Those who still float on the tempestuous main.

The same solution had of course been anticipated by the ancients. The Garden sent its letters out into the world, and Horace had reinvented the verse epistle as a major poetic form under the pressure of a similar dilemma. The eighteenth-century response, however, has the specific effect of moving to the center of Augustan literature the symbolic situation that Maynard Mack memorably called "the pursuit of politics from the vantage point of retirement" (116) and then, in turn, of moving to the center of that situation the verse epistle, with its singular promise of regenerating society from within the sphere of private life. This is a situation in which epistolary audience, as a symbolic presence mediating between the otium scene and the larger world, initiates the moral regeneration of society not through any active gesture but simply by allowing itself to be drawn toward the private circle of virtue to which epistoler and lector belong. The result is always the prospect of a steadily expanding moral community, the ideal vision that prompts such addresses as that of William Somerville to Pope in the shining moment when poetry could still seem to promise the regeneration of English society: "Thy kind reforming Muse shall lead the way / To the bright regions of eternal day" (*To the Author of the Essay on Man*).

When verse epistles are also satires, as in Pope's later poetry, the urge to expand the circle of virtue and the urge to annihilate vice and folly are simultaneous impulses within the same poem, and the ideal outcome of the Augustan enterprise may be glimpsed as one in which the teeming world of knaves and fools attacked by satire gradually dwindles away to nothing while the otium community of the verse epistle expands to become the world. Within this scheme of things, the poetry that regenerates society would have become an embodiment of the logos in both its Stoic and Christian versions, and a great moral poet such as Pope would stand revealed as the voice of the universal humanity that has its inward home in the divine. The genius of a Pope, says Walter Harte, viewing the poet of the Horatian imitations in just this light, must be seen as guided by "Some fairer image of perfection, giv'n / T'inspire mankind, itself deriv'd from Heav'n" (*To Mr. Pope*). "Fantastic wit," echoes John Brown in his *Essay on Satire*, "shoots momentary fires, / And like a meteor, while we gaze, expires":

> But Genius, fir'd by Truth's eternal ray,
> Burns clear and constant, like the source of day:
> Like this, its beam prolific and refin'd
> Feeds, warms, inspirits, and exalts the mind; . . .
> This praise, immortal POPE to thee be given:
> Thy genius was indeed a gift from heav'n.

This is the moment of high Augustanism caught even as it is passing into memory, an image of poetry in the radiant instant when its address to its audience seemed an actual power to create moral community. The collapse, when it comes, will occur through a sudden exposure of epistolary audience as, after all, nothing more than a figment of discourse, an invisible presence that, having once seemed able to take on body in the actual world of people and events, is now revealed as having been no more than a shadow summoned in vain against the specter of solipsism. In satire, as we shall see, this gives us the Juvenalian moment in which the satirist abandons all hope of regenerating his society and simply rails at it—"Why loves not HIPPIA rank obscenity?," asks Joseph Warton in *Fashion: A Satire*. "Why would she not with twenty porters lie? / Why not in crowded malls quite naked walk?; / Not aw'd by virtue—but 'The world would talk'"—and the beginning of the countermovement, so energetically exploited by writers on the Walpole side, in which satire may be turned against satirists: "Satire herself, a public grievance grown, / Nor spares the altar, nor reveres the throne" (*Candour*). This is the countermovement that will come to an end, along with the eighteenth century itself, in William Gifford's last bitter epistle to Peter Pindar.

The implosion of satire has momentous consequences for the Augustan verse epistle because satire had always been the medium through which it had been able to engage solipsism on the social level, as a process of alienation or estrangement at work everywhere in Hanoverian England. When this possibility vanishes, there remains only a last encounter with an underlying epistemological solipsism, which in the first instance produces the brief and astonishing career of Charles Churchill and what I shall call satiric solipsism—"If to thyself thou canst thyself acquit, / Rather stand up assur'd with conscious pride / Alone, than err with millions on thy side" (*Night*)—and then in the diminished poetic world of his friend Robert Lloyd, taking as its patron saint the poet who, "prancing in his easy mode, / Down this epistolary road," as Lloyd once puts it, "First taught the Muse to play the fool" (*On Rhyme*). Lloyd's diminished world is, as we shall see, also the world of Christopher Anstey, William Mason, T. J. Mathias, John Wolcot's Peter Pindar, and a multitude of other poets writing verse epistles after the death of Pope.

At the same time, a new poetic world is also visible amid the disintegration of Augustanism, one in which solipsism, as the aloneness of the mind in an infinite universe, will begin to appear as an imaginative resource. This is the world of the eighteenth-century sublime, of the Wartons as they turned away from Pope's Horatian poems to the gloom and solitude of *Eloisa to Abelard* and Milton's *Il Penseroso*, of the midcentury revival of medievalism and "pure poetry." Its landscape is the twilight scene of lonely woods and solitary groves that we glimpse suddenly and unexpectedly at the end of Joseph Warton's *Fashion: A Satire*, as the dying Juvenalian echoes of the speaker's voice give way to a quieter tone:

> O, teach me friend, to know wise NATURE's rules,
> And laugh, like you, at FASHION's hoodwink'd fools;
> You, who to woods remov'd from modish sin,
> Despise the distant world's hoarse, busy din:
> As shepherds from high rocks hear far below,
> Hear unconcern'd loud torrents fiercely flow.

Yet the distant world on which the speaker turns his back, the hoarse, busy din of mankind from which he seeks refuge in the woods and groves, is a world earlier conjured into being by Augustan poetry and its literary traditions. It is only from the collapse of otium and the subsequent demise of the verse epistle, as we shall see, that this gesture toward an alternative world of the solitary imagination assumes its meaning.

TWO

AUGUSTAN AUDIENCE

RAYMOND WILLIAMS'S *The Country and the City* has nowhere more conclusively demonstrated its influence, perhaps, than in having restored to sudden respectability an idea of literary Augustanism otherwise long disregarded in eighteenth-century studies. This is the notion of Augustan England as gazing continuously backward across the abyss of the interregnum to a traditional English society presumed to have lingered on intact until the civil war. In the literary histories written thirty or forty years ago this was a gaze thought to involve little more than simple nostalgia, and yet its object was the same society brought into view in Williams's story of change and cultural crisis—an England still visible in the country-house poems of poets like Jonson and Carew, in which life yet moved to the slower rhythms of the agricultural year, and lord and peasant were bound to each other within a system of mutual responsibilities taken by the community as a whole to be inviolable. This was a community assumed to have been shattered not simply by military conflict and political upheaval but by the powerful alternative Puritan vision of England as, in Milton's sounding phrase, "a great and warlike nation instructed and inured to the fervent and continual practice of truth and righteousness" (3.78).

To the scholars who spoke a generation ago so unperplexedly about an English Augustanism, the meaning of the analogy between Restoration England and the Rome of Virgil and Horace and Livy lay in the shared experience of a return to sanity after civil war. The analogy was undeniably foremost in the minds of Dryden and a multitude of other poets at the Restoration ("Oh happy age! Oh times like those alone / By fate reserved for great Augustus' throne!"), but then it could be invoked to explain a great deal more. The Dryden who undertakes in his old age to translate the *Aeneid*, William Frost could persuasively argue thirty years ago, is the same Dryden who so bitterly looks back on civil war ("seams of wounds, dishonest to the sight") in *Absalom and Achitophel*, and what draws him to the project is Virgil's own haunted memory, present everywhere in his poetry, of the civil wars of Rome. Augustan England was on this account a nation to whom the return of Charles II represented less a political occurrence than a divine intervention in human history, as in Cowley's famous ode:

> Already was the shaken nation
> Into a wild and deform'd chaos brought.

> And it was hasting on (we thought)
> Ev'n to the last of ills, annihilation.
>
> Lo, the blest Spirit mov'd, and there was light. . . .
>   We by it saw, though yet in mists it shone,
> The beauteous work of order moving on.[1]

The England seen to be restored to itself at such a moment was less a political entity than a community sustained by natural law, which for a generation of scholars such as Frost and Reuben Brower was also assumed to give meaning to the Roman analogy. For the great strength of the older view, as we have come to see in light of arguments advanced by Williams and Pocock and others, is that it recognized in literary Augustanism a response to the dissolution of organic or transcendently grounded community under the pressure of impersonal historical forces. To understand these forces as they are understood in *The Country and the City* or *The Machiavellian Moment* is, to be sure, to perceive the crisis of Augustan England as one in which society is decomposing into an assemblage of isolated souls before any new ideology of self-interest has emerged to sustain them in their isolation. Yet the older view retains its persuasiveness precisely because the Augustan writers themselves, knowing nothing of any future ideologies of individual autonomy, experienced not an ideological but a moral crisis. This was why such poets as Dryden and Pope were able to discover in the situation of Virgil and Horace a mirror of their own dilemma.

The importance of the Roman analogy to a poetics of the verse epistle is that it assigns to poetry a specific moral agency within a fallen social reality, providing the model on which Augustan poetry, aiming to project an abstract audience created by discourse outward into the actual world of stockjobbers and corrupt politicians, will attempt the moral regeneration of English society. This vision of a poetic audience transmuted into actual moral community is what I shall mean by "Augustan audience." It begins, as had the Roman poetry from which it drew its inspiration, in the reimagining of an unfallen social reality called the Republic, a time of simple virtue and lived community from which the world has ever since been in decline. This is the Republic as remembered throughout the eighteenth century in poems such as Dyer's *The Ruins of Rome*:

>   From the plough
> Rose her dictators; fought, o'ercame, returned,
> Yes, to the plough returned, and hailed their peers;
> For then no private pomp, no household state,
> The public only swelled the generous breast. . . .

> They, content,
> Feasted at nature's hand, indelicate,
> Blithe, in their easy taste; and only sought
> To know their duties.

The great significance of the Roman analogy for Augustan poetry, however, is implied less by this gaze back toward a vanished Republic than by the theory of moral regeneration from which it derives. For the important thing now will be that, as Gary Miles has recently reminded readers of Virgil's *Georgics*, Roman society at the time of Augustus had no notion of social progress in the modern sense. Rome was a traditional or archaic society looking back to an ideal past, the era of Rome's founding and early rise to power: "However much the Romans may have changed their ways in fact, they continued to justify their own actions and judge those of others by the example of the past" (5). *Moribus antiquis res stat Romana virisque*, Ennius had written early in the second century B.C.—"the Roman state is what she is because of her ancient customs and her men"—and Cicero's constant appeal in his public speeches nearly two centuries later is to the *mos maiorum* "the way of our ancestors." This is a perspective, at once moral and political, from which the workings of historical change seem at best unsettling and at worst blindly destructive of traditional values: "*Res novae* ('new things')," Miles recalls, always referred for the Romans "to seditious attacks on established ways and institutions" (4).

The backward gaze to an ideal Republic involves not simply a notion of the past as a source of moral regeneration but one of the future, of what will occur unless the blind processes of historical change can somehow be arrested through an exertion of collective will, as inherently dangerous and threatening. For Dryden and Pope and Swift, the moment at which English society was exposed to the perils of uncontrollable historical change is conventionally said to have been 1688, with the arrival in England of William and his foreign advisors and a new system of financial arrangements—Pope's "blest paper credit"—previously associated with Dutch trade and commerce. Yet an "Augustan" sense of emergent capitalism as a demonic force is already evident well before this in a poem such as Marvell's *Last Instructions to a Painter*—"She stalks all day in streets conceal'd from sight," says Marvell about Excise, uncannily anticipating not only the Excise Crisis of 1733 but the language of *The Craftsman* and *The Dunciad*, "And flies like bats with leathern wings by night"—and with it a sense of England as being carried by imponderable social and economic forces into a dark and inscrutable future.

Yet a tendency merely to dwell on the virtuous past, either of the vanished Republic or a traditional English society thought to have remained inviolate until the civil war, might be nothing more than a weak and demoralized response to a sense of inevitable historical decline. This is the context in which the poets of Augustan Rome, whose work could be read as a splendid refusal to surrender to the forces of such decline, were to be claimed as the symbolic forebears of the poets of Augustan England. The Virgil and Horace whose voices echo throughout the English poetry of the late seventeenth and early eighteenth centuries are not mere utterers of a prolonged lament for the past—

> Soon, these royal palaces will be empty
> Acres for the plough . . .
> . . . Romulus never meant it
> So, nor long-haired Cato, nor any of
> Our simple fathers.
>
> They owned almost nothing, but Rome
> Was rich beyond measure.
>
> (Ode 2.15)

—but the makers of an imaginative reality existing as an alternative to the corruptions of the present. The poetry of Augustan Rome thus becomes the custodian of the moral ideals identified earlier with the Republic itself, and as such the great example to which Dryden and Pope and their literary generation are able to turn in their own moment of cultural crisis.

The martyr of the vanished Republic is always taken to be Cato, but there is a sense in which the exemplary figure for Augustanism is Cicero, whose own eyes saw the extinction of the Republic and the emergence of the new order in which Virgil and Horace would write their poetry. This is Cicero as resurrected by Conyers Middleton, trying amid the propaganda wars under Walpole to provide an ideological counterweight to the powerful symbolism that Opposition writers had developed out of Cato's suicide.[2] It is Cicero, first, as he almost succeeds in restoring the Republic through the naked power of his public eloquence: "how amazing, how almost incredible was the success of it!" exclaimed Colley Cibber in his remarks on Middleton's volume. "That this vast turbulent city . . . should at last by this animating, this coercive eloquence of Cicero, so strongly recover into its native power, as . . . to drive Antony . . . from the gates of Rome" (255). And then it was the Cicero whose bloody hands and severed head were set on stakes in the forum in a macabre mockery of his former eloquence, making him a martyr of the Republic in a sense that Cato never was, a tragic symbol of the days in which Roman energies flowed unimpeded into civic speech and action. "What drew tears from every eye," writes Middleton, was "to see those mangled members, which used to exert themselves so gloriously from that place, in defence of the lives, the fortunes, and the liberties of the Roman people, so lamentably exposed to the scorn of sycophants and traitors.... It was a triumph over the Republic itself" (3.281).

The deeper significance of Cicero's death, however, lies less in this mournful scene than in the writing he managed to do before he died. For Cicero's attempt to do what no one had done before—make the wisdom of the Greeks systematically available to educated Romans—exposes an important truth about the Republic, which had remained so far largely innocent of poetry and philosophy precisely because it was its own work of art, the *res publica* or public object to the molding of which its best citizens had devoted the whole of their creative energies. Cicero in involuntary retirement from public life, writing ethical treatises and letters to his friends, provides the general image of the writer in the Augustan situation, and the first exemplary moment of Augustan writing occurs in the passage of *De Officiis* in which he laments that the occasion of his sitting down to compose in solitude is the demise of the Republic:

> As long as our country was still governed by men it had voluntarily elected as its rulers, I was delighted to dedicate all my efforts and thoughts to national affairs. But when the entire government lay under the domination of a single individual, no one else but he any longer had the slightest opportunity to exert statesmanlike influence in any way whatever.... If things had gone better I should never have been devoting my attention to writing, as I am now. No, I would have been delivering public addresses, as I used to in the days when we still had a government: and if I wrote anything it would have been those speeches. (121)

The Republic had been for its citizens, in short, the polis of the Greeks reborn in Roman actuality, and poetry and philosophy begin only in the moment of its vanishing.

For Virgil and Horace, writing after Augustus has assumed the role of *princeps*, and Roman civic life has been reduced to an empty ceremony, poetry becomes a moral enterprise precisely because their society now exists in a middle state between virtue and corruption, freedom and tyranny. To say this is not to project back onto the *Georgics* or Horace's satires some unlikely premonition of Visigoth horses tramping in the forum, but only to say that the Roman poets existed inside a civic mythology telling them that things could be far worse than Rome under Augustus: outright tyranny or despotism—the expulsion of the kings was a crucial symbolic moment in Rome's founding myth—or the bloody anarchy of civil war as both had lived through it, either one representing a state of affairs in which poetry is powerless as a moral agency in society. Under Augustus, on the other hand, where the memory of the vanished Republic is still close enough to provide a moral resource for poetic expression, the poet is someone with a power to bring it to alternative life within the sphere of language.

Roman poetry, remarked Shaftesbury, giving early expression to what would become an eighteenth-century commonplace, went into decline along with Roman liberty, which explains why Virgil and Horace, the two great poets "who came last, and closed the scene, were . . . such as had seen the days of liberty and felt the sad effects of its departure" (1.143). The Augustan situation is one in which poetry has come to embody the Republic in exile, an ideal or imaginary commonwealth both serving as a moral sanctuary and offering the possibility of moral choice in a time of historical dissolution. The middle state of the Augustan poet, moreover, is one in which language or discourse has assumed a certain nobility of expressive purpose precisely because the actual Republic has vanished from the historical scene, which is the context in which Atterbury's famous remark—"I question whether in Charles the Second's reign, English did not come to its full perfection; and whether it has not had its Augustan Age, as well as the Latin" (qtd. in Erskine-Hill, *The Augustan Idea* 236)—should be taken not as an estimate of Restoration literature but as a perceptive comment on the situation in which literature found itself at the Restoration.

The same notion of poetry as the Republic in exile explained for the eighteenth century why Augustus played so relatively minor a role in the literature of his own age, appearing mainly as an offstage figure presiding conscientiously over the political realm while poetry, now the real embodiment of Roman values, gets written. "Contemplation and action have their different seasons," said Thomas Rymer in *A Short View of Tragedy*. "It was after the defeat of Antony, and the business of the world pretty well over, when Virgil and Horace came to be so distinguished at court" (8). And it is, in turn, precisely because Roman poetry can so often and so unconstrainedly sing the glories of an age before Augustus that his rule appears not as tyranny but as a sad inevitability, the outcome of the same inexorable forces that had earlier dissolved Rome into civil anarchy. "Such was the people whose exploits I sung," says the shade of Virgil at the end of a verse epistle to Pope written from Rome by the young Lord Lyttelton, a Virgil reimagined now as the tutulary spirit of English Augustanism: "Brave, yet refin'd, for arms and arts renown'd . . . / Dauntless opposers of tyrannic sway, / But pleas'd a mild Augustus to obey."[3]

The mild Augustus of Lyttelton's epistle becomes a symbolic presence in eighteenth-century English poetry precisely because he brought about the circumstances in which the vanished Republic could assume an alternative life as a literary or imaginative reality. This is, first of all, the Augustus who appears in Virgil and Horace as the restorer of peace after a hateful and vicious time of civil anarchy:

> The ox tramps safely in our fields,
> Ceres and Faustita nourish our corn. . . .
>
> Families stay chaste, undefiled,
> Law and morality prevail over sin,
> Women's children resemble their fathers,
> Punishment chases after guilt. . . .
>
> Every Roman walks his own hills,
> Marrying vines to the widowed elms,
> Then feasts at his own table, rejoicing,
> Pouring a libation to Caesar as if
> To a god.
>
> (Ode 4.5)

And then it is the Augustus of St. Évremond, familiar to every English reader of Rollin, who honors the Republic in his own way: "he made no other use of his power, than to take away the confusion which universally prevailed. He restored the people to their rights. . . . He restored the senate to their ancient splendor, after he had first banished corruption from it. For he contented himself with a moderate power, which did not leave him the liberty of doing ill" (Rollin 4.159).

The spirit of Virgil is speaking in Lyttelton's epistle as well for one of the enabling premises of eighteenth-century Augustanism—the idea that the imaginary Republic living on now in the *Georgics* and the *Aeneid* and the odes of Horace represents the same moral resource for English poetry that the actual Republic had for the poets of Augustan Rome. This is the context, for instance, in which Addison's *Letter from Italy* represents, for all Addison's own subsequent Whig sympathies, one of the inaugural moments in English Augustanism, for Addison in Italy is a poet living inside poetry: "Gay gilded scenes and shining prospects rise, / Poetic fields encompass me around, / And still I seem to tread on classic ground." From the same premise derives the hope that Augustan poetry may rescue from the ravages of history a similarly ideal England—"Oh Granville!" cries Elijah Fenton, urging his noble friend to preserve in verse the golden interlude of England under Anne, ". . . make her memory rever'd by all, / When triumphs are forgot, and mouldering arches fall" (*Epistle to Southerne*)—and, consequently, a sense of poetry as the voice of genuine civilization. "By secret influence of indulgent skies," Roscommon had said some years earlier, "Empire and Poesy together rise. / True poets are the guardians of the state" (*Essay on Translated Verse*).

At the same time, the notion of poets as guardians of the state amounts in some sense to an admission that, the Republic having vanished from the scene of history, the state now has an authentic existence only within the realm of poetry. This is why Horace's repeated insistence on the immortality bestowed by poetry is really a disguised declaration of poetic autonomy, or, as Pope's paraphrase of Horace's Ode 4.9 so clearly brings out—

> Vain was the chief's and sage's pride
> They had no poet and they died!
> In vain they schem'd, in vain they bled
> They had no poet and are dead.

—a demotion of the warrior and the statesman in favor of the poet who now presides over an alternative commonwealth. The idea of the poet as unacknowledged legislator, found in its neoplatonic form in Sidney or Shelley, is in its Augustan form always a response to the dissolution of authority and community in the realm of the actual. "He which can feign a commonwealth (which is the poet)," Ben Jonson had said in *Timber*, "can govern it with counsels, strengthen it with laws, . . . inform it with religion, and morals" (7.595), and what gives the remark its Augustan tonality, for all the tradition of Renaissance neoplatonism looming so massively in the immediate background, is the constant sense of imperiled tradition that makes Jonson the kindred spirit less of Spenser than of Dryden and Pope.

This is why, for instance, the emergence of literary Augustanism as such may be isolated in later-seventeenth-century poetry in the metaphor that Lawrence Davidow calls the Muses' Empire conceit, "with ideas like kingship, succession, legitimacy, usurpation, . . . etc., arising almost automatically to describe any relationship arising among poets" (139). One obvious effect of the conceit is to insist on the autonomy of the ideal commonwealth now existing inside poetry, but another, less generally remarked, is to transfer to the poetic commonwealth the vocabulary of a traditional society grounded in natural law, not simply kingship and divine right but, as Christopher Ricks has pointed out (221), the entire neo-Harringtonian mystique of the landed gentry associated with Country ideology. As everyone knows, the Muses' Empire conceit rises to poetic culmination in Dryden's epistle *To Mr. Congreve*, but even there, as Davidow demonstrates, it is drawing on such earlier poems as Southerne's epistle to Congreve—"DRYDEN has long extended his command, / By right-divine, quite through the Muses land"—so that its very meaning presumes the existence of the empire of which it speaks, a commonwealth of poets existing apart from the ordinary or actual world.

In the verse epistles of Southerne and Dryden we have, as well, the earliest appearance of Augustan audience. This is the epistolary audience assumed to be listening in on these private exchanges within the Muses' commonwealth, which will soon be expanded to include such exemplary souls as Dryden's kinsman John Driden and other members of the nobility and gentry driven by the forces of history, like Dryden himself, into retirement or private retreat. The Augustan situation in English poetry may be regarded as coming into existence at the precise moment of Dryden's withdrawal from the public gaze, the moment when, as James Garrison has noted (243), his poems begin to address an audience of private individuals rather than the nation as a whole. This is the situation in which poetry, having declared its autonomy from the corrupt world, will now assume the task of offering a moral choice between that world and its own ideal commonwealth.

The invisible audience to which it will offer this choice is so far, at the moment of Dryden's *To Mr Congreve*, a mere abstract implication of epistolary discourse, the "one who is absent" of Benveniste's Arab grammarians. By the time Dryden writes *To My Honoured Kinsman, John Driden* a few years later, however, the nature of this audience and the moral choices with which it is being presented have both become clearer, illustrating the usual principle according to which Augustan poetry will bring its audience into focus through the indirect means of imagining a world. For the scene in which Dryden's epistle situates his kinsman is not only the otium retreat of the virtuous soul in a corrupt age—the "love'd retreat," as Dryden says, from which his cousin is occasionally and unwillingly called to serve as an M.P., "charged with common care, / Which none more shuns, and none can better bear"—but also the ancient estate of a member of the landed gentry, the class with whose neo-Harringtonian virtues Country ideology, of which Dryden's epistle is among the first mature literary expressions, identified the highest interests of the English nation.

The mythic element already implicit in this latter idea suggests the symbolic register within which Augustan poetry will reimagine the beginnings of civil society in agriculture. The imaginary Republic of Roman poetry assumes its greatest symbolic potency in the moment of this reimagining, for now the civic mythology that attributed the early rise of Rome to the virtuous simplicity of her citizens is revealed as having its roots in an even older mythology of the earth, giving us the sense in which there lurks behind such civic parables as the return of Cincinnatus to the plow a Hesiodic sense of husbandry as the intersection of the human and divine worlds. The same notion survives in weak form in Ciceronian ethics—"In every product of earth there is an inborn power," says Cato the Elder in *De Senectute* (234)—but its great source for Augustan poetry will always be the *Georgics*, with their Hesiodic sense of divinity or natural magic. "'Twas such as these," says Thomson in the 1728 version of *Spring*,

> the rural Maro sung
> To the full Roman court, in all its height

> Of elegance and taste. The sacred plow
> Employ'd the kings and fathers of mankind
> In ancient times.

If *The Seasons* is as much a poem of the Augustan moment as Pope's later satires or *The Dunciad*, it is because the moral import of Thomson and Pope equally derives at the deepest level from a georgic mythology still present to both in a living way in the poetry of Augustan Rome.

The manner in which this mythology associates personal and civic virtue with agriculture begins in a sense of the miraculous, if by "miracle" is meant the process through which, given nothing more than sunlight and water, grain or fruit suddenly materializes where there was nothing before. An awareness of human society as sustained at the most basic level by something resembling a magical process explains the strong sense of the supernatural in Hesiod and Virgil, and a closely related idea may be heard in St. Paul's passing remark in 1 Corinthians 3.7 that, while man plants and waters, "God giveth the increase." There is thus a convergence of classical and Christian perspectives in the famous comment of Swift's King of Brobdingnag, speaking now as an unconscious exponent of both literary Augustanism and Country ideology, "that whoever could make two ears of corn . . . to grow upon a spot of ground where only one grew before" was worth more to his country "than the whole race of politicians put together" (*Gulliver's Travels* 135–36). Such notions will eventually generate the agrarian radicalism of writers such as Cobbett, but in the Augustan moment they are still strongly associated, as in Pope's *Windsor Forest*, with the ideal of a restored traditional society:

> See Pan with flocks, with fruits Pomona crown'd,
> Here blushing Flora paints th' enamel'd ground,
> Here Ceres' gifts in waving prospect stand,
> And nodding tempt the joyful reaper's hand,
> Rich industry sits smiling on the plains,
> And peace and plenty tell, a STUART reigns.

The pagan gods and goddesses Pope invokes at such moments belong to the strain in Augustan poetry that was once called neoclassicism, a term since fallen into disfavor because of its overtones of a stale or mechanical employment of classical conventions. And yet Pope's invocation of Flora and Pomona and Ceres is absolutely essential to his meaning, which is that there is in fact something miraculous about the growth of wheat or corn or roses or apples where nothing existed before, and that we recover a sense of the miracle involved whenever we remind ourselves why the ancients saw divinities at work here.[4] The classical gods are in such a context "about" a restored capacity to see the ordinary world as miraculous—what

Pope is trying to get at in the preface to his translation of Homer when he says that, though subsequent ages have come to "blame" Homer's gods from a religious or philosophical point of view, they "continue to this day the gods of poetry" (93). In general terms, the invocation in Augustan poetry of Greek or Roman deities always operates as a profound resistance to the desacralization of the world, and thus to the dark forces carrying English society into a bleak and inscrutable modernity.

In more specific terms, the origination of civic virtue in what Thomas Rosenmeyer calls the Hesiodic world of husbandry and agricultural work involves, once the sense of rootedness in the miraculous or supernatural has been established, a simultaneous sense of labor as harsh piety, human sustenance as produced only through a submission to and cooperation with processes outside human control. The central term in the Hesiodic world, says Rosenmeyer, is *ponos*, which means both grief and labor, and which he translates in its ethical sense as "self-denying labor." This is the value through which the "hesiodic code of country living" becomes "one of discipline and foresight," in turn resulting in a moral or ethical perspective that is "activist, critical, and realistic" (21), and from which—though this is not part of Rosenmeyer's argument—any more advanced stage of culture or civilization is likely to appear luxurious, decadent, or corrupt. This is why, in an ideal state of the Republic, the plow yields generals and sages, and why in such stories as that of Cincinnatus leadership and agriculture are always associated with each other.

At the deepest level of literary Augustanism, then, always visible through its more obvious grounding in a later Virgilian mythology, there lies an idea of society and of natural leadership going back to archaic Greece, the poetic or mythic form of what would emerge in the seventeenth century as Harringtonian political theory and in the eighteenth as Country ideology. The source of social regeneration in this context is a civic version of the myth of the Golden Age, involving an ancient patrician ideal still surviving in Seneca's description of the Golden Age as a time when wise men were the natural and uncontested rulers of society: "they exercised scrupulous self-control, protected the weak from the strong, . . . explained what was useful and what disadvantageous. Their foresight provided against dearth, their steadfastness averted danger. . . . To govern was to serve, not to reign" (227). This is the ideal so often invoked in Bolingbroke's political writings, one then represented in poetry by the idealized nobleman who so often serves as imaginary addressee in Pope's verse epistles.

The aristocracy begins to symbolize in this situation not simply that vision of a simpler, more virtuous past on which an imperiled traditional society always draws as a measure of present corruption, but also, in an age haunted by the specter of isolation and estrangement, a world yet coherent and whole. Thus, for instance, we hear in Garth's *Claremont* of ancient

Britons "Upright in actions, and in thought sincere," a consequence of their living in an age when, as Garth says, "Honor was plac'd in probity alone." In the following years, as a sense of modern corruption grows at once more acute and more despairing, moving toward the bitter disillusionment of Pope's last satires and the final *Dunciad*, the same idea of ancient honor is invoked with the greater moral urgency that we hear in such poems as John Brown's *Essay on Satire*—"Bid Britain's heroes (awful shades!) arise, / And ancient honor beam on modern vice: / Point back to minds ingenuous, actions fair, / Till the sons blush at what their fathers were"—until Augustan satire itself becomes a prolonged lament for an older world now barely lingering on as an ethical memory.

Within the expanded confines of the Augustan metaphor or myth that lies behind so much eighteenth-century writing, this gives us the situation of Pliny the Younger as he appears in his *Epistulae*, which thus also becomes exemplary at a certain moment in English literary Augustanism. For Pliny is a Roman acutely aware of having been born into a declining and diminished age—"every sense of modesty and reverence is broken down," he says at one point in his letters, "and all distinctions are levelled and confounded" (100)—and who in his personal relationships turns always to kindred spirits for whom the memory of a nobler past provides a kind of moral sustenance: "where indeed is the man who exceeds Cornutus in worth or virtue? or whose conduct is a more express model of ancient manners?" (287). This is a Pliny as exemplary in his way for late Augustanism as Cicero was for its emergence, or Virgil and Horace for the middle state in which the Republic has been reborn for a time within the sphere of language.

One great virtue of Pliny's *Epistulae* is that they so unmistakably dramatize, in just that elegance of style that so struck eighteenth-century readers, a transposition of civic virtue from the sphere of action to that of discourse. For though Pliny himself is immensely active in civic life, his activity, as Conyers Middleton unflatteringly points out, is meaningless, public life since the vanishing of the Republic having long since become an empty show: "all his stories and reflections terminate in private life; there is nothing important in politics; no great affairs explained; no account of the motives of public councils: . . . his honors were in effect but nominal; conferred by a superior power, and administered by a superior will" (3.316). This is Pliny as viewed from a Ciceronian perspective by a biographer who shares Cicero's own bitterness at the demise of the actual Republic, however, and what it misses is the sense in which Pliny has, within the limits of his diminished world, devoted his life to a veneration of the Republic.

That veneration explains the symbolic importance in Augustan England of Melmoth's remarkable translation of Pliny's *Letters*, in which there appears a Pliny who speaks and thinks and acts as the very model of an English Augustan gentleman. For in Melmoth's translation one sees, as the eighteenth century immediately saw, the manner in which an internalized sense of Republican virtue comes to express itself as a certain nobility or elegance of utterance, the stylistic qualities of Virgilian or Horatian poetry now finding a last fugitive home in the private sphere. "The elegance of his writings," says Vicesimus Knox about Pliny toward the end of the eighteenth century, "resulted from the habitual elegance of his mind," an elegance contemporary readers saw as having been caught by Melmoth and, to a lesser degree, by Pliny's other translator, Lord Orrery. "All the spirit, ease and elegance of original epistles enter into his translation of Pliny's," says John Mason about Melmoth in 1749 (55). "Lord Orrery and Mr. Melmoth seem to have resembled him in their manners, as well as in their style," echos Knox a few years later: "while they expressed their author's idea, they appear to have expressed their own" (2.255).

Yet Pliny's elegance of mind, as he moves among members of a circle sharing his own reverence for the lost Republic, never obscures the substratum of older magical or mythological belief from which it is continuously drawing spiritual substance. "Titianus Capito," he reports approvingly about a friend, "has placed in his house . . . statues of the Bruti, the Casii, and the Catos, and it is incredible what a religious veneration he pays them" (41). The aura of religious mystery at such moments always derives from a Roman ancestor-worship that saw the souls of the patrician class as being literally reincarnated, reborn from generation to generation within their appointed lineage. This is a sense of ancestral rebirth still very strong in Virgil and Horace—

> O noble Aelius, descended from ancient
> Lamus, father of all Lamiae
> And of your father, and
> Recorded in our oldest
>
> Annals as founder of your race,
> He who first ruled the Formian
> Walls.
>
> (Horace, Ode 3.17)

—and, as Marcel Mauss observed some years ago, one remaining vital well past the Augustan period. The Table of Lyons, signed in bronze by the emperor Claudius, "concedes to the young Gaulish senators freshly admitted to the Curia the right to the *imagines* and *cognomina* of their ancestors;" "to the very end," Mauss reminds us, "the Roman Senate thought of itself as being made up of a determinate number of *patres* representing the 'persons' (*personnes*) and 'images' of their ancestors" (17).

In Virgil or Horace or Pliny, the ancestor-idea exists at the deep level of unconscious cultural assumptions, one of the ways in which Roman civilization would remain, even in its advanced stages, close to its primitive origins in tribal society. In English Augustan poetry, the same notion is taken over from Roman writing as a myth of lineage through which the hereditary nobleman becomes an actual survivor of the virtuous past moving among the inhabitants of a diminished present. Thus, for instance, it is Dryden's awareness of the Roman ancestor-idea that governs his translation of Virgil's lines on Marcellus—"'Tis plain, that Virgil cannot mean the same Marcellus, but one of his descendants, whom I call a new Marcellus, who so much resembled his ancestor . . . that Virgil cries out, *quantum instar in ipso est!*" (6.825)—but it is the way Augustan poetry will develop that idea that has him explaining to the earl of Musgrave in the dedicatory epistle to *Aureng-Zebe* that he sees his unwritten epic on early Britain as a noble "occasion to do honor" to his king, country, and friends, "most of our ancient nobility," as he says, "being concerned in the action" (4.84).

The idealized nobleman who appears as addressee in so many Augustan verse epistles may already be glimpsed at such a moment, yet in the notion of an aristocracy that is to thus serve its country through personal example, rather than in council or on the battlefield as its ancestors had, there is nonetheless at this point the dangerous hint of an emblematic role, of a class that has awakened on the wrong side of history to find itself serving a merely ornamental purpose. This is the problem Augustanism will solve by transposing the idea of civic leadership to a new locus within the sphere of language, with patrician discourse exerting its authority as the norm for literary or poetic expression. The movement through which this comes about, leading to Bolingbroke or Bathurst or Cobham as ideal presences in Pope's epistles nearly fifty years later, begins in the late seventeenth century in a symbolic purge of the Restoration rake as a figure of the false patrician, someone guilty of an unwholesome and self-indulgent response to the crisis in aristocratic values.

Though they are ultimately closely related, it becomes essential to distinguish in this context between the exuberant bawdry of Restoration stage comedy and the "placket-rhymes," as Oldham memorably called them, written by aristocratic rakes ostensibly for private circulation. For the Restoration stage, as everyone is aware, created a nobleman intended to outrage the Cits in the playhouse audience, the local representatives of that militant Puritanism that had earlier abolished the social order in which the hereditary aristocracy were natural leaders. The attempt, as outraged critics such as Jeremy Collier and Sir Richard Blackmore were famously to demonstrate, was entirely successful; the "finished gentleman" of Restoration comedy, fumes Blackmore, is "a derider of religion, . . . a person wholly idle, dissolv'd in luxury, abandon'd to his pleasures, a great debaucher of women"—in short, "a finished libertine" (qtd. in Loftis 29). And, as was recognized then and throughout the eighteenth century, this was nothing more than a continuation of the civil war by literary means.

"Under the notion of laughing at the absurd austerities of the Puritans," Joseph Warton would say disapprovingly in the *Essay on Pope*, "it became the mode to run into the contrary extreme, and to ridicule real religion and unaffected virtue" (1.160).

Yet behind the private or placket-rhyme mode of the aristocratic rake-poet lies a darker impulse, the nihilism of a class imprisoned within a new historical order in which its own role has been rendered superfluous. The irreligion denounced by Blackmore appears in this context as the symptom of a deeper sense of meaninglessness, the sexual libertinism of the placket-rhyme mode as, in Leopold Damrosch's chilling and accurate phrase, "a kind of Hobbesian matter-in-motion, a Sisyphean struggle against the weariness of the flesh" (651). Thus, typically and depressingly, Etherege in a verse epistle to Sackville:

> The Queen of Love from sea did spring,
> Whence the best cunts still smell like ling.
> But sure this damned notorious bitch
> Was made of the foam of Jane Shore's ditch.
>
> (*Mr. Etherege's Answer*)

And Sackville in return:

> What horrid fury could provoke thee
> To use thy railing, scurrilous wit
> Gainst prick and cunt, the source of it?
>
> (*A Letter to Mr. Etherege*)

"From hunting whores and haunting play," Etherege later complains to his London friends, lamenting the fate that has sent him on a diplomatic mission to Ratisbon, he has nothing to do now but "make grave legs in formal fetters, / Converse with fops, and write dull letters." This is the community of rakes turned inward, an aristocracy given over to a nihilistic mock-celebration of its sudden historical uselessness.

The same nihilism, occurring now as a note of rage and bafflement at the meaninglessness of the universe, is what allows Rochester to rise so often from mere aristocratic versifying to genuine poetry, for in these moments his language at its most scabrous assumes a grim existential grandeur that will scarcely be heard again until the twentieth century, something belonging more to the world of Beckett than to that of Dryden and Congreve. In Rochester's usual mode of bleak raillery, as in such poems as *To the Postboy* ("I have blasphemed my God, and libeled Kings"), this is most often heard as a strain of self-mockery, but occasionally there arrives a moment of calm in which nihilism is seen for what it is, an experience of utter meaninglessness. To such a moment belongs the famous translation from Seneca's *Troades*:

> After death nothing is, and nothing, death:
> The utmost limit of a gasp of breath. . . .
> Dead, we become the lumber of the world,
> And to that mass of matter shall be swept
> Where things destroyed with things unborn are kept.

Here we are taken, as no lesser Restoration poet-rake ever takes us, to the unseen heart of the placket-rhyme mode.

This is why Rochester stands, as criticism has begun in recent years to see, as the great unacknowledged predecessor of the Augustan mode in poetry. For beyond the obvious stylistic affinities between Rochester and the Augustan poets there is the deeper sense, so admirably brought out by David Farley-Hills, in which Rochester's enterprise must be understood as an attempt to construct, "against a backdrop of metaphysical inanity," "local harmonies that defy the disharmony of the spheres" (204). Some such sense of Rochester's poetry no doubt explains the growing body of fascinated commentary that has come to surround his verse epistle *From Artemisia to Chloe*, which through the "Chinese box" effect of its three stories becomes a triumphant example of the mind's power to impose order on meaningless flux. "The stronger the forces of disruption become the further are they distanced. . . ," observes Farley-Hills in the first persuasive analysis of that extraordinarily perplexing poem, "until at the end the frightening world of the prostitute Corinna is recounted to us at three removes from the reader's actuality" (206).

In an incidental sense, the epistolary audience that floats free at the end of *Artemisia to Chloe*, having been distanced from metaphysical inanity but as yet having found no refuge in any alternative world of meaning, represents the embryo of Augustan audience. To have seen this, however, is to have grasped another sense, by no means incidental, in which Rochester in stark terms and in an ideological vacuum was inventing the Augustan enterprise itself, which would consist of nothing other than the imposition of meaning, through mind or language or poetry, on a scene of mindless anarchy. Yet the reason that no Augustan poet would be permitted to name Rochester as a precursor is precisely that Augustanism would emerge through a repudiation of the rake-aristocrat that he more superficially also was. This is the repudiation that begins in Oldham's denunciation of

> Damn'd placket rhymes,
> Such as our nobles write———
> Whose nauseous poetry can reach no higher
> Than what the codpiece, or its god inspire.

Oldham's attack is a crucial episode in the emergence of literary Augustanism, for in it he has found the point of leverage from which the English aristocracy would be impelled away from a self-destructive nihilism and toward an ideal of moral as opposed to military or civic leadership. The note that sounds in Oldham's voice is not, as in Collier's or Blackmore's, one of outraged bourgeois morality, but that of disappointed class expectation, a world of commoners who, unable to understand the crisis in aristocratic values that has driven their superiors into a frenzy of blasphemy and debauchery, knows only that it has been left leaderless. The unexpected and cutting point is that the noble rake, while doing his best to outrage the lower orders, has only managed to sink unwittingly to their level: "If ribaldry deserv'd the praise of wit," cries Oldham, "He must resign to each illit'rate cit, / And prentices, and car-men challenge it." The power of this denunciation will be felt to the end of the Augustan period, with an angry sense of class betrayal still to be heard in Pope's last satires: "Ye Gods! shall Cibber's son, without rebuke / Swear like a Lord? Or a Rich out-whore a Duke?" (*Epilogue to the Satires*).

The rake-aristocrat thus becomes in the Augustan moment the symbol of the false patrician, whose sins are blacker than those of plebeian souls precisely because he has betrayed a higher ideal. This is the context in which the nobleman who lives up to hereditary expectation becomes a living embodiment of the virtuous past—"O if true virtue fires their gen'rous blood," cries William Whitehead in *On Nobility*, "We hear the rattling car, the neighing steeds, / A Poitiers thunders, and a Cressy bleeds!"—which then becomes the measure of the disgrace involved

> If, from the breathing walls, those sires behold
> The midnight gamester trembling for his gold:
> And see those hours, when sleep their toils repair'd,
> (Or, if they wak'd, they wak'd for Britain's guard,)
> Now on lewd loves bestow'd, or drench'd in wine.

Thus Augustan poetry, committed through its myth of civic origins to an aristocratic ideal, simultaneously becomes the most uncompromising censurer of aristocratic misbehavior. All the foolish or vicious noblemen of Pope's poetry are caught in Henry Fielding's remark that mere nobility of birth "is a poor and mean pretence to honor, when supported by no other": "persons who have no better claim to superiority, should be ashamed of this; they are really a disgrace to those very ancestors from whom they would derive their pride" (1.141).

The idealized nobleman who presides symbolically over the emergence of the Augustan mode, and does so specifically because his career could be read as an allegory of aristocratic values transposed to the sphere of discourse, is the Earl of Roscommon. The occasion of his coming to be seen as an exemplary figure, a few somewhat halting lines in the *Essay on Translated Verse*, is innocuous enough: "Immodest words admit of no defense," says Roscommon there, "For want of decency is want of sense. / What moderate fop would rake the Park or stews, / Who among troops of faultless nymphs may choose?" Yet contemporaries immediately glimpsed in these lines the new patrician ideal only indirectly or inversely demanded in Oldham's attack on placket-rhymes, and Roscommon was just as immediately proclaimed, as in Chetwood's epistle to him, a paragon of "wit, reading, judgment, conversation, art": "No fame you wound, give no chaste ears offence, / Still true to friendship, modesty, and sense." Or, as in an epistle by Dryden in which one feels the lingering prestige of an older ideology of civic and military leadership, as a paragon of "both court and camp": "Roscommon first in fields of honor known, / First in the peaceful triumphs of the gown."

Epistolary audience in Restoration commendatory verse is normally projected as a public still finding its way into a new system of neoclassical conventions, but in verses such as these it becomes instead an audience to whom a shift in the symbolic coordinates of English poetry is being announced. For Roscommon as he is being celebrated now by Chetwood and Dryden will be remembered by Samuel Johnson nearly a century later in exactly the same terms; aside from being "perhaps the only correct writer in verse before Addison," Johnson will remark, Roscommon has a higher praise, "for Mr Pope has celebrated him as the only moral writer of king Charles's reign" (1.235). And so Pope had, in terms at once suggesting his role in the suppression of the Rochesterian rake-poet—"In all Charles's days, Roscommon only boasts unspotted bays" (*Imitations of Horace* Epistle 2.1)—and his positive significance as a new type of the ideal patrician: "Such was Roscommon—not more learned than good, / With manners gen'rous as his noble blood" (*Essay on Criticism*). Thus Restoration poetry in the Rochester-Etherege mode becomes for the Augustan poet a deviant episode, its immorality a "deadly worm" eating away, as John Brown will put it in an eighteenth-century epistle to Viscount Lonsdale, at the root of poetic genius: "Quick as autumnal leaves, the laurels fade, / And drop on Rochester's and Otway's head."

The symbolic center of literary Augustanism as it emerges from this episode will be occupied not by an idealized aristocracy but by aristocratic speech, a mode of discourse through which the listener comes into immediate contact with an otherwise vanished world of traditional values. "That easiness and handsome address in writing which is hardest to be attained by persons bred in a meaner way," says Henry Felton to the young Marquis of Granby in 1713, "will be familiar to your Lordship. And if ever you do write, you will write as you speak, with all the civility and good breeding in the world" (qtd. in Irving 167). The same sphere of discourse as looked in on from the outside is captured with a certain poignancy in Robert Dodsley's epistle to Mr. Wright—

> I hear and mark the courtly phrases,
> And all the elegance that passes;
> Disputes maintain'd without digression,
> With ready wit, and fine expression: . . .
> Where all unanimously exclude . . .
> The fluttering, empty, noisy, vain;
> Detraction, smut, and what's profane.

—the poignancy arising because this is one of the poems that Dodsley wrote while still a footman, so that he is here, as a servant waiting at table, a presence invisible to the elegant conversationalists.

More normally, aristocratic speech as the discourse of an otherwise vanished world will be taken as the governing stylistic norm of Augustan poetry itself. This is a situation in which the aristocrat-as-poet retains a certain exemplary status, as in Addison's lines on Halifax—"How negligently graceful he unreins / His verse, and writes in loose familiar strains"—but in which a more generalized notion of elegance or civility becomes the criterion of genuine poetic expression. "None have been with admiration read," says James Dalacourt in *A Prospect of Poetry*, itself an epistle to the Earl of Orrery, "But who, beside their learning, were well-bred": "While art and nature equally unite, / Sound smooth the sense, and grace make wit polite." "It is, says Melmoth in his translation of Pliny's *Letters*, now looking back on nearly half a century of writing governed by the same stylistic ideal, "the *propie communia dicere*, the art of giving grace and elegance to familiar occurrences, that constitutes the merit of this kind of writing" (97).

The moral dimension of aristocratic discourse derives from its power to dispel, during the magical moment of its duration, the raw vulgarity and teeming bustle of an importunate modernity; this is what Dodsley is witnessing when he hears conversation at a patrician dinner table as excluding all that is "empty, noisy, vain," and it is what lies behind the Augustan vocabulary of elegance, ease, civility, politeness, or "correctness" when applied to poetry. This in its emergent form is what explains Dryden's appeal in his *Essay on Dramatic Poesy* to the "gallantry and civility" of the present age as the source of stylistic or aesthetic superiority in contemporary writing, and it is what motivates Congreve, addressing the Earl of Montague in his dedication to *The Way of the World*, to attribute whatever "correctness" he may have attained to in his writing specifically to "your Lordship's admitting me into your conversation" in "your retirement last summer from the town." And this, in turn, especially in its strong overtones of the *otium* ideal, gives us the internal dramatic situation in which Pope addresses Bolingbroke in *The Essay on Man*:

> Come then, my friend, my genius, come along,
> Oh master of the poet, and the song! . . .

> Form'd by thy converse, happily to steer
> From grave to gay, from lively to severe;
> Correct with spirit, eloquent with ease,
> Intent to reason, or polite to please.

Bolingbroke as a symbolic presence in the *Essay on Man*, both as representative of a vanished social order and master of a mode of discourse with power to make that vanished world come alive again in the mind or imagination, may thus be taken to represent all the idealized noblemen to whom Augustan poetry addresses its verse epistles. And Pope as epistoler, drawing from aristocratic speech the expressive power that will allow him to create in poetry a redeeming glimpse of the vanished world, a last besieged outpost of the virtuous past yet lingering on in an age otherwise engulfed by a noisome modernity, stands forth as well as the representative Augustan poet. This is a situation in which, as contemporary readers well understood, qualities that we now tend to consider "merely" aesthetic or stylistic were inseparable from morality. "Made wise by thee, whose happy style conveys / The purest morals in the softest lays," says William Somerville in an epistle to Pope, poems such as the *Essay on Man* "In Virtue's cause shall gloriously prevail, / When the bench frowns in vain, and pulpits fail."

To see the aristocracy as survivors of an otherwise vanished world is to grasp the deeper significance of Augustanism as, in Raymond Williams's terms, a retrospective radicalism. For the idea of Augustanism as a critique of emergent capitalism is not new. The real affinities of such writers as Pope and Swift and Gay, Paul Fussell could argue twenty-five years ago, are with such writers as Brecht in our own century, in which the true Augustan voice belongs to a character like Paul in Brecht's *Aufsteig und Fall der Stadt Mahagonny*—who, in response to claims that the world as now given is a wonderful place, will only say, repeatedly and bemusedly, "Aber etwas fehlt." "This sense of human incompleteness," observed Fussell in *The Rhetorical World of Augustan Humanism*, is enlisted by Brecht "on behalf of a scathing critique of the economic basis of contemporary society" (30), and this is just what the Augustan poets, moved two centuries earlier by an identical sense of historical dismay, had done before him. It would remain for Williams, however, to demonstrate the degree to which moral leverage in Augustan writing is always provided in this situation by "celebrations of a feudal or aristocratic order": "The emphases on obligation, on charity, on the open door to the needy neighbor, are contrasted, in a familiar vein of retrospective radicalism, with the capitalist thrust, the utilitarian reduction of all social relationships to a crude moneyed order" (34).

The sense of cosmic or universal struggle in Augustan poetry thus always emerges from an uneasy sense that the society of stockjobbers and speculators symbolized by Walpole is in its way unreal, only the visible emanation of a deeper crisis at the level of material or property relations. Already, says Bolingbroke's Caleb D'Anvers in tones of some urgency early in the eighteenth century, money has become "a more lasting tie than honor, friendship, consanguinity, relation or unity of affections" (1.125). And in the background of this warning is Bolingbroke's steady sense of a historical crisis in which the landed class has become the symbolic victim of the new speculative or finance capitalism: "A new interest has been created out of their fortunes, and a sort of property which was not known twenty years ago is now increased to become almost the terra firma of our island. . . . the landed men are become poor and dispirited. . . . In the meanwhile those men are become their masters, who formerly would with joy have been their servants" (Holmes and Speck 135–36).

The voice of this new class as heard by the Augustan poets is, notoriously, Davenant's Tom Double, the modern Whig who had not a pair of shoes to his name in 1688 but is now worth 50,000 pounds. "It is our interest," says Double to his brethren, "to humble the ancient gentry, because they know our originals and call us upstarts and leeches that are swollen big by sucking up the nation's blood" (*Tom Double Returned* 32); "detract from and asperse all the men of quality," he urges them, "of whom there is any appearance that either their high birth, or their great fortunes, or their abilities in matters of government should recommend them to the future administration of affairs" (*True Picture* 63). Yet for all its malevolence toward the nobility and gentry, the sin of the upstart class is in Augustan eyes not that it represents the vanguard of some party of progress, but precisely that it represents no theory or ideology at all: the Tom Doubles of the eighteenth century are creatures of weak moral character who, simply out of greed or narrow self-interest, have placed themselves at the disposal of a blind historical contingency that works by allowing private advantage to a few while undermining society as a whole.

The reason that the stockjobbers and money managers of Walpole's England are perceived this way by Augustan satire, as mere puppets of an implacable historical process carrying English society toward ruin, has been brilliantly explicated by Pocock as a consequence of ideological collapse. "The universe of real property and personal autonomy now seemed to belong to a historic past," says Pocock in *The Machiavellian Moment*, and "new and dynamic forces, of government, commerce, and war, presented a universe which was effectively superseding the old but condemned the individual to inhabit a realm of fantasy, passion, and *amour-propre*. He could explain this realm . . . but he could not explain himself by locating himself as a real and rational being within it" (466). The same situation is one in which the nobility and landed gentry, while losing more actual power with each passing year, retain a virtual monopoly on the ideological resources of their culture: "Far from seeing himself as a mere product of historical forces, the civic and propertied individual was endowed with an ethic that clearly and massively depicted him as a citizen of classical virtue, the inhabitant of a classical republic, but exacted the price of obliging him to regard all the changes transforming the world of government, commerce, and war as corruption—corruption essentially the same as that which had transformed Rome from a Republic into an empire" (466).

This is the situation in which the Roman analogy, with its story of luxury and corruption and cultural decline, will come to dominate the English cultural imagination for well over half a century, and in which the otium ideal will become synonymous with aristocratic exile from public affairs, the refuge of a class dispossessed by history, as in Pope's epistle to the Earl of Oxford, in which poetry follows the statesman into retirement: "The Muse attends thee to the silent shade: / 'Tis hers, the brave man's latest steps to trace, / Re-judge his acts, and dignify disgrace." A sense of the world outside the otium scene as a fallen social reality will then always insistently recall the similar periods of classical history during which philosophers, as Sir William Temple had invoked their example amid the upheavals of the late seventeenth century, "would have no part in the faults of a government . . . and therefore thought all the service they could do to the state they lived under, was to mend the lives and manners of particular men that composed it" (3.90–91).

The mythic dimension of aristocratic retreat derives in this situation, we have seen, from a georgic or Hesiodic conception of rural life as the moral basis of republican virtue, so that the nobleman living in seclusion inhabits a scene in which, as Virginia Kenny has said, "one derives strength for participation in active life from close communion with the origins of civil society in the productive processes of agriculture" (190). The deeper meaning of the otium ideal thus draws on the phenomenon that Ernst Bloch named *Ungleichzeitigkeit*, a notion of social formations as temporal composites always incorporating into themselves the earlier stages of their own development. As a Roman visiting his country estate could see himself as moving not only among fields and vineyards but as involved in a sort of time travel carrying him back to the early Republic, the Augustan gentleman in otium retirement could think of himself as having returned to an earlier England in which the raw energies of a nascent capitalism had not yet begun to disrupt traditional values.

In eighteenth-century England, however, there is in addition to a Roman or classical sense of cultural decline the new terror of history as something driven by implacable social and economic forces, a sense of the emergent order symbolized by Tom Double or Sir Robert Walpole as an impersonal system obeying its own laws and moving toward ends mysterious to human intelligence. This is the situation in which the Augustan writers become very nearly obsessed, as J. W. Johnson demonstrated some years ago (58–63), with the Greco-Roman paradigm of cyclical history, the rise and fall of civilizations due to an inner imperative of growth and decay from which no society is exempt. For the great comfort of the cyclical theory is that it permits the illusion of having reimposed conceptual control on the demonic energies of the Walpole-order, allowing for history as impersonal process while speaking at the same time of known causes working toward known ends:

> Lo! the revolving course of mighty Time,
> Who loftiness abases, tumbles down
> Olympus' brow, and lifts the lowly vale.
> Where is the majesty of ancient Rome,
> The throng of heroes in her splendid streets,
> The snowy vest of peace, or purple robe,
> Slow trailed triumphal?
>
> (Dyer, *The Fleece*)

This is the situation in which the ricorso of Machiavellian political theory becomes a way of bargaining with what is mysterious or implacable in the new world of Walpole and finance capitalism. For Machiavelli had himself thought of history as a cyclical process, making due allowance for those impersonal laws of growth and decay that put the ultimate fate of civilizations outside human control, and his theory of the ricorso or *ritorno ai principii* is a carefully limited theory of moral regeneration, the project of bringing history back under human control only to the degree that this is permitted by what Dyer calls the revolving course of mighty time. The heart of the Augustan enterprise thus becomes, as Kramnick and Pocock in particular have shown, ricorso as an idea of reconstituted balance that neutralizes the forces of corruption and decline by returning a society, for whatever time is permitted, to its moral origins. The hope of a society entering into the stage of decline lies, as Moyle would put it in his *Essay upon the Constitution of the Roman Government*, in "restoring the ancient virtue and disciplines or by a thorough reformation of those corruptions and disorders which the depravity of human nature will introduce" (qtd. in Kramnick 165).

The enormous burden of reimposing conceptual order on a history otherwise spinning out of control comes to rest on the classical notion of luxury, that too-great indulgence of material prosperity that, in the Greco-Roman paradigm of rise and fall, always signals that a civilization has entered into the stage of enfeeblement and ultimate decline. So great is the anguish about luxury in eighteenth-century poetry and prose that it is easy to miss the sense in which, silently but nonetheless massively, it is simultaneously providing a kind of spiritual comfort, a known conceptual category within which to deal with the social upheaval being brought about by otherwise incomprehensible forces. The reassurance provided by Luxury as studied by J. W. Johnson and more recently John Sekora is that it allows the unfathomable energies of the new financial and industrial capitalism to be located within a timeless scheme of historical revolutions. Thus, for instance, *Craftsman* 56: "This was the case of the Roman commonwealth of old. . . . luxury and profuseness led the way to indigence and effeminacy; which prepared the minds of the people for corruption; and corruption for subjection; as they have constantly succeeded one another, and will do so again, in the same circumstances, in all countries, and all ages" (2.73).

At an even deeper level, the reassurance provided by cyclical theory lies in the way it has come to be invisibly sustained, between the time of Virgil and Horace and that of Dryden and Pope, by the entire metaphysics of an Augustinian tradition in theology. For as Walter Moyle's talk about corruptions and disorders in the body politic as something introduced by "the depravity of human nature" makes clear, the Augustan response to historical decline always possesses a theological dimension. It is the very nature of the fallen world, claims Earl Nugent, echoing in an epistle to Viscount Cornbury a thought long before given currency by Milton, that lies behind political corruption and anarchy, making kings the necessary curse of heaven:

> The darkling soul scarce feels a glimm'ring ray,
> Shrouded in sense from her immortal day. . . .
> Now grosser objects heav'n-born souls possess,
> Passions enslave, and servile cares oppress.
> Fraud, rapine, murder, guilt's long horrid train,
> Distract'd nature's anarchy maintain.

The social middle state of the Roman poets, that moment suspended between past virtue and future corruption, thus comes to be defined in Augustan poetry as Pope's "isthmus of a middle state" between the world of God and angelic intelligence and the insensate world of brute matter. The halo of cosmic implication surrounding every particular in Augustan poetry derives ultimately from this Augustinian perspective, for within the local limits of Walpole's England, we are always aware, this is the war in Heaven being fought all over again. Here again is a situation in which William Law, responding to the same sense of cultural crisis as Pope and Swift and Gay, may be taken as the theologian of literary Augustanism. For the whole impulse of Law's theology, which enters Augustan poetry as versified by his admirer John Byrom, is toward a reinterpretation of Scripture as a drama of the here and now. The death suffered by Adam was not physical death but a loss of the sense of dwelling with God in a divine reality; "he died to Paradise"—"Naked, asham'd, confounded, and amaz'd, / With other eyes, on other scenes he gaz'd." The world into which Adam fell is the world of Pope and Swift and Walpole, which thus stands revealed as an abstract middle state between Heaven and Hell: "this state of time and place, / Where, tho' his outward system must decay, / His inward ripens to eternal day" (*Epistle to a Gentleman of the Temple*).

Only against the background of an Augustinian metaphysics are we fully able to grasp why the Augustan writers are so ready to envision a literary solution to social or political crisis, granting to poetry, in particular, the power once attributed by Milton to education, "to repair the ruins of our first parents by regaining to know God aright" (4.277). In the Augustan context, this becomes the aim of creating a moral community through art—"the great design of arts," says John Dennis, "is to restore the decays that happened to human nature by the Fall" (1.336)—specifically by educating an audience in a mode of moral penetration that ceaselessly pierces the veil of illusion or unreality by which ordinary souls are taken in; "True, all men think of course, as all men dream," observes Edward Young in one of his epistles to Pope, "And if they slightly think, 'tis much the same." In universalized form, this notion of moral penetration will survive as the "Augustan" premise of Johnson's *Rambler* and *Idler* essays, but in the earlier eighteenth century its major role is in the war between Augustan poetry and the rising corruption of Walpole's England.

This is the moment at which the grand analogy between eighteenth-century England and Augustan Rome becomes a lesson about what it means to learn from history. For the truth of the Roman analogy will now be seen to lie less in tales of corruption and historical decline than in the thought that certain things must be permanently true about human nature and the world for one society to learn anything at all about itself by pondering the fate of another. This is Augustan moral penetration as a mode of historical awareness, where it appears, as in Rollin's influential remarks on the study of history, as the antidote to a kind of cultural solipsism: "Confined without it to the bounds of the age and country wherein we live, and shut up in the narrow circle of such branches of knowledge as are peculiar to us, and within the limits of our own private reflections, we remain ever in a kind of infancy, which leaves us strangers to the rest of the world, and profoundly ignorant of all that has gone before us, or even now surrounds us" (3.1).

The great lesson to be learned from history is that actual societies are themselves to a great degree unreal, shifting and illusory composites of opinion and belief having no real existence except in the minds of those dwelling inside them for a brief historical moment. To mistake the illusory for the real is thus, as Rollin says, to remain in a kind of infancy, staring with a child's credulous eyes at a world composed mainly of false appearances. To learn the lesson of history, on the other hand, is to begin to dwell in an ideal society more real than any actual one, the imaginary commonwealth inhabited by those whose lives have answered to the imperatives of a permanent realm of natural or universal law. This is, in Rollin's view, the moral use of historical study by younger students: "To heal or preserve them from the contagion of the present age, we must carry them back into other countries and other times, and oppose the opinions and examples of the greatest men of antiquity . . . to the false principles and ill examples, which carry away the greatest part of mankind" (1.17).

The audience posited by Augustan poetry is one that has grasped the truth glimpsed by Rollin's young students of history, but has done so in the immensely more complex way implied by poetic imitation as a literary mode. A great deal has been written about the movement that carries Augustanism from its first tentative translations of classical authors in the later seventeeth century to the triumphant moral resonances of Pope's Horatian imitations, but the essential point remains that imitation became the major Augustan poetic mode because it posits an ontology: "if the story we treat be modern," says Dryden in his preface to the *De Arte Graphica*, "we are to vary the customs according to the time and country . . . ; for this is still to imitate nature, which is always the same, though in a different dress" (17.317). This is a vision of literary reality in relation to which distinctions between Rome and England dissolve and even translation can be seen, as in Addison's epistle to Dryden, as original poetry:

> Thy lines have heighten'd Virgil's majesty,
> And Horace wonders at himself in thee.
> Thou teachest Persius to inform our isle
> In smoother numbers, and a clearer style;
> And Juvenal, instructed in thy page,
> Edges his satire, and improves his rage.

By the time Johnson gives it final expression in *Rambler* 60 the Augustan universal will have taken on the status of a disembodied ideal, a poetic or literary ontology appearing to have remained constant from the time of Dryden and Pope to the last writings of Johnson himself. Yet as expressed by Dryden in nearly identical terms half a century before—"mankind being the same in all ages, agitated by the same passions, and moved to action by the same interests, nothing can come to pass but some precedent of the like nature has already been produced" ("Life of Plutarch" 17.270)—the same idea must be understood as having originated in the Augustan battle against modernity, as a singularly powerful means of combating the glittering unrealities thrown up by a ceaseless maelstrom of social change. For to have glimpsed the unchanging background against which particular human societies live out the evanescent span of their historical existence is to have gained power over the illusions continuously produced within one's own society. The power of what Raymond Williams calls retrospective radicalism thus ultimately derives not from its appeal to an imaginary and ideal past, but from the manner in which that appeal operates as a basis of demystification, an endless stripping away of the veils of illusion that ideology seeks to draw over a hidden world of raw power and naked self-interest.

The ideal commonwealth of Augustan poetry becomes in this situation the very measure of the real. For the attack of the Augustan poets on emergent capitalism will always take the form of an attack on its unreality: the unreality of the wealth engendered by "paper credit" and financial speculation, with huge sums of money created out of nothing on one day and disappearing just as mysteriously the next; the unreality of the social claims made by the new class of wealthy speculators and rich tradesmen conjured into existence by the same invisible forces; and the unreality of the whole crazed and haphazard structure of government erected by Walpole on the shifting foundations of that same unreal treasure. From the Augustan perspective, the visible enemies in the war against modernity—Walpole and his lieutenants, the stockjobbers and speculators whose interests they serve, the bad poets and hireling pamphleteers who write their propaganda—will never be more than emanations of the same underlying system of economic relations that produced this imaginary wealth.

The ideal commonwealth of the poets takes on a paradoxical solidity in this situation precisely because it represents a system of values rooted in the real: the real wealth represented by ownership of the fields and orchards from which actual human beings derive their real sustenance; the real authority of the landed class whose ancestral claims derive from such ownership; the real weight of custom and tradition in an agrarian society in which higher and lower orders are bound to one another through ancient ties of mutual responsibility. This is the vanished world of traditional English society as it lives on in poetry, and from its vantage point the teeming and disorderly world of Walpole's England, dominated by stockjobbery and political corruption, seems a society dissolving into unreality:

> Tag, rag, and bobtail to Sir Harry's run,
> Men that have votes, and women that have none;
> Sons, daughters, grandsons, with his Honor dine;
> He keeps a public-house without a sign.
> Cobblers and smiths extol th'ensuing choice,
> And drunken tailors boast their right of voice.

The vulgar populace endlessly pilloried in Augustan satire, as here in James Bramston's *The Art of Politics*, is, as much as Walpole's corrupt parliaments or the speculators whose new wealth circulates through boroughs increasingly rotten, a product of the same underlying system of invisible forces that have produced the joint-stock companies and the National Debt, and what makes it objectionable is that it is, like them, unreal. The sin of Bramston's "rag, tag, and bobtail" is that it has deserted a world of honest work and genuine value for a realm of false or illusory appearances, and that in doing so it has unwittingly lent an impetus to the process of historical decline. Dimly visible in the background of Bramston's boisterous election scene is another world where tailors spent their days at work on clothes and cobblers on shoes for the men and women of their community, and the smith could be found at his forge producing this or that simple implement demanded by life in an agricultural society. The picture is idyllic, but it is nonetheless rooted in the real, and that is its virtue in an age of increasing unreality.

The manner in which Augustan poetry portrays its vulgar populace ultimately derives, as Bernard Schilling demonstrated many years ago (39–43), through Horatian satire from Greek philosophy, in which it represents the collective mentality of those within a society who, out of perversity or sloth or simple incapacity, are strangers to rational deliberation. Aristotle's roster of these creatures of mere appetite and whim, headed by women and slaves, is especially notorious. Yet in the new world of social mobility projected by *Absalom and Achitophel* or the *Dunciad*, the same idea carries a quite different burden of implication: the mob in Augustan writing is a moral rather than a social category, and one becomes a member not by thinking wrongly but by refusing to think, yielding to a world of illusion and false appearances to the degree that one becomes its unreal creature. The Augustan mob has less to do with Aristotelian rigidities of social exclusion than with the phenomenon that modern theorists, struggling with the paradox of populations who seem eagerly to embrace every new source of their own debasement produced by a culture of commodification and lies, have labeled false consciousness. The faceless members of the Augustan multitude have, as in Aristotle or Horace, foregone rational deliberation, but their sin is the more modern one of having thus become puppets of a blind process of social deterioration.

As the idealized nobleman of Augustan poetry already symbolizes an otherwise vanished world of traditional values, the mob or multitude comes to symbolize a world in which even the lingering memory of those values has been utterly extinguished. For the reason that the vulgar populace provides the crowded and indistinct background against which Augustan poetry will attempt to carry out its project of social regeneration is precisely that it has come to represent an irrationality unknown to Aristotle and Horace, not turbulence or anarchy but the inert mindlessness that Pope called dulness, the drugged sleep of an obliviousness to history. The solitary patrician and the mob represent the opposing limits of moral choice for Augustan audience, and the consequence of either a mistaken choice or a refusal to choose is not banishment to some outer darkness but a simple reabsorption into the faceless multitude, a loss of moral identity or individuality as one is pulled back down into the blind current of impersonal historical process.

Augustan audience is thus always imagined as a reader or readers who are drawn out of the vulgar and into the patrician world. The mob is in this context the busy, bustling urban population for which the playhouse audience, throughout the eighteenth century, will serve as the usual synecdoche:

> Do thou, my Muse, describe the bright abodes
> Of wits, of cits, of critics, beaux, and bawds. . . .
> The pit they fill, the pit where punks patrol,
> These look a luring leer, and those a gloomy scowl;
> Footman and 'prentice bawl in upper air,
> Bright in the middle sits enthron'd the fair.
>
> (Mr. Webster, *The Stage*)

The democracy of the playhouse will remain a favorite Augustan metaphor for modern society, the audience here being, roughly speaking, the same populace that will read Defoe's novels and the rogue biographies of Curll, the same readership into which Addison and Steele will so brilliantly attempt to inculcate a new bourgeois sensibility in *The Spectator*. This is the imaginary public in opposition to which Augustan poetry will define its own more rigorous and selective notion of audience. The audience of the Augustan verse epistle may be taken to be, from this perspective, the reader who has deserted the teeming world of the playhouse for the quieter companionship of Dryden's *Aeneid* or Pope's Homer, and thus for entrance into a world of classical values already containing those implications of moral choice posed in direct terms in Pope's *Epistle to Arbuthnot* or the Horatian poems.

The idealized nobleman of Augustan verse emerges in this context as the symbolic antagonist of the new world of alienation and estrangement represented by Walpole, the ricorso envisioned by Country ideology as a return to what C. B. Macpherson calls customary or status society, a world in which members of a community are bound to one another by relations of mutual obligation and the notion of the individual as isolated or separated from the social whole is simply meaningless. The return to aristocratic governance demanded by Bolingbroke would be on this account less a political event than a moral revelation, a situation in which the counterfeit social claims of Walpole and the Robinocracy would be exposed in all their tawdry fraudulence, and power would pass once again back to the landed class. It would be a situation, in short, in which the tailors and cobblers and smiths of Bramston's election scene would cheerfully resume their places in a world of real work and actual value, the gentry would resume their roles as overseers of their country estates, and Walpole and the Robinocracy would pass from the scene of English history like a troubled dream.

This is precisely the point at which Augustan audience begins to pose a problem for which Augustan poetry has no solution. For the role of traditional society in this drama of moral choice has until now been wholly imaginary or symbolic. In the teeming world of Walpole and Change Alley the picture of a lost agrarian society has the status of a metaphor or parable, a story told to the modern age about its origins in a simpler, nobler, more virtuous time: *moribus antiquis res stat Anglicana virisque*. It is moral response to this story that determines one's ultimate allegiances, with vulgarity of mind implying less about social class or status than about habits of self-interest and narrow expediency, the moral solipsism of a shrunken world in which isolated egos do battle in the Hobbesian or Mandevillian warfare of an emergent market society. To be drawn toward the sphere of patrician sensibility, on the other hand, is simply to honor the ideal of civic virtue, subordination of self to the interests of the community as a whole, embodied in the idealized aristocracy of an earlier age. "None but the virtuous," says Garth in *Claremont*, thinking of just this notion of civic virtue, "are of noble blood."

The problem of Augustan audience may thus be seen to arise in the end from the logic of ricorso itself, for which the notion of traditional society had never been metaphor or parable but the very object of social transformation. To speak the language of classical republicanism, as Augustan poetry does from the moment of its origin, is not to demand some future state of genuine community for which the story of a lost organic society serves as a convenient myth, but to demand an actual return to that organic or traditional order, a recovery of the world one has lost. And in this moment of ricorso, one sees, the opposing metaphors of vulgar and patrician sensibility would in an instant collapse back into a sociological literalness of status and class and birth, leaving homeless and forlorn an audience created in the image of patrician values. For at the heart of Augustanism as a symbolic system there will always have lain that genealogy of morals on which Nietzsche would put so unerring a finger in the next century: "I saw that the terms for 'good' in different languages were all transmutations of a single root idea—'aristocratic,' 'noble,' 'of high or superior rank'—and that 'good' had everywhere developed, as though by a kind of necessity, out of an earlier sense of 'aristocratic in soul or spirit' [*seelische-vornehm*]" (2.774). As we shall see, it is the creation of an audience with aristocratic soul or spirit and indeterminate social origins that will return to haunt the Augustan verse epistle.

THREE

SATIRE AND EPISTLE

THE IMAGINARY Republic held out by Augustan poetry as a moral alternative to the corruptions of Walpole's England has its remote origins, as Maynard Mack suggested in *The Garden and the City*, in the ideal polis of Plato's political philosophy: "'But the City whose foundation we have been describing,' protests Glaucon in the ninth book of the *Republic*, 'has its being only in words; there is no spot on earth where it exists.' To which Socrates replies: 'No; but it is laid up in heaven as a pattern for him who wills to see, and seeing, to found the City in himself. Whether it exists anywhere, or ever will exist, is no matter'" (231). The aim of literary Augustanism is in one sense simply to enable its audience to behold this ideal commonwealth, to dispel the mists and fogs of delusion thrown up by the new money or credit society and to lay bare the imaginary Republic that will restore the nation to itself. The means through which it proposes to accomplish this is satire, an unmasking of the deceptions of the new society so uncompromising that delusion will ultimately evaporate and the commonwealth emerge into visibility.

The underlying relationship between epistle and satire in Augustan poetry comes to light here, for satire at just this point enters a competition for the moral allegiance of the imaginary audience projected by the verse epistle. This is audience as, once again, the site of Laclau's "struggle in ideology," that war of interpellations through which an abstract audience may be imagined as taking on body in the world of actual readers, which now is what must occur when any actual reader is taught by satire to gaze through the delusions of the new money society to the ideal commonwealth embodied in Augustan poetry. That commonwealth is, as Socrates says, laid up in heaven as a pattern for him who wills to see, but in eighteenth-century England it is assumed to have been preserved as well in Virgil and Horace and Livy, and to be recoverable by contemporary Englishmen through the writings of Swift and Gay and Pope, whose purpose is to bring their readers, as Socrates also says, to found the commonwealth in themselves.

The metaphor controlling the relation between poet and audience in this situation, one running as a major theme through Augustan poetry and attaining ultimate expression in Pope's *Epistle to Arbuthnot*, is that of the satirist as moral physician. The force of the metaphor arises from the assumed benignity of the idealized physician, which gives us, in nonsymbolic or literal terms, such figures as Johnson's Dr. Levet or Dr. Downman in Richard Polwhele's *Epistle Written During a Violent Illness*: "Strenuous to chase from man each brooding ill, / Thy social kindness, or thy healing skill, / Through all the tenor of that life appears, / And brightens up a gloomy vale of tears." Yet the whole point of the metaphor is then to justify the wholesome bitterness of the satiric medicine, a notion already long established when Seneca, in one of his epistles to Lucilius, imagines an orator justifying himself to his listeners: "Medicine is beginning to take effect when the distempered body twitches at a touch. What I say will benefit you even if you don't like it. . . . because you do not wish to listen to the truth individually, hear it as an audience" (224).

The metaphor of the poet as moral physician may be glimpsed in Augustan poetry as early as Dryden's epistle to Dr. Charleton, in which the worlds of writing and medicine have already begun to merge in symbolic terms—"Such is the healing virtue of your pen," says Dryden to Charleton, "To perfect cures on books as well as men"—and it then underlies the distinctively Augustan cultural role played by such physician-satirists as Garth and Arbuthnot, but its main purpose is always to establish the bitterness of the medicine as an inversely proportional measure of the real good nature of the satirist. The potency of the moral physician metaphor explains why Augustan satire was so long able to insulate itself against the massive counterattack on satire as an expression of simple malevolence or ill nature, and it explains as well why Pope, in his poems and letters equally, was able to sustain without apparent contradiction that mythologizing of his own life that revolved so steadily around his own posture as *vir bonus*.

Pope comes to occupy the center of literary Augustanism by transforming himself and Twickenham into compelling symbols of the attempt to draw souls away from the realm of delusion that was Walpole's England and toward the ideal commonwealth embodied in Augustan poetry. The degree to which contemporary readers were conscious of this aim, especially as it involved a ceaseless unmasking of the world of illusion being thrown up by the forces of money and mystification, is splendidly captured in John Brown's image of Augustan satire as the spear of Ithuriel, the Cherub sent by God in *Paradise Lost* to locate Satan, a touch of which compels Satan to assume his true shape:

> Her magic quill, that like ITHURIEL's spear
> Reveals the cloven hoof, or lengthen'd ear:
> Bids Vice and Folly take their natural shapes,
> Turns duchesses to strumpets, beaux to apes,
> Drags the vile whisperer from his dark abode,
> Till all the demon starts up from the toad.

The occasion of Brown's *Essay on Satire* is the death of Pope, and the poem always makes clear that Pope's near-mythic status as the greatest Augustan satirist derives from his having possessed a greater power of demystification than other poets. "Each Roman's force adorns his various page," exclaims Brown: "Despairing Guilt and Dulness, loathe the sight, /As spectres vanish at approaching light." Yet the *Essay* is also a poem about Pope's relation to his imagined audience, and in particular about his satire as posing a moral choice between the realms of illusion and truth, corruption and virtue: "Here Vice, dragg'd forth by Truth's supreme decree, / Beholds and hates her own deformity, / While self-seen Virtue in the faithful line / With modest joy surveys her form divine." The choice is not an easy one—the bitterness of the satiric medicine is precisely that it involves admitting that one has been taken in by the world of false appearances—but its reward, when made rightly, is both a recovery of moral health and a welcome into the imaginary commonwealth or kingdom of the Augustan poet.

When the ideal commonwealth is imagined in Augustan poetry as a kingdom, the point almost always concerns the autonomy of poetry, its power to create an alternative moral reality in the midst of cultural decline, and the related power of a satirist such as Pope to compel a choice between the world revealed in poetry and the actual world of lumpish monarchs and corrupt statesmen. The actual world is a realm of illusion not least because its panegyrists, out of venality or mere moral shortsightedness, so often celebrate it in ideal terms. Thus, for instance, Ambrose Philips's epistle to Lord Halifax on the arrival of George I in England: "Lost in the sailors' shouts the cannons' roar: / And now, behold, the sovereign of the main, / High on the deck, amidst his shining train, / Surveys the subject flood." The symbolic language of this entire order of political reality is being contested in poems that, as in Gay's epistle to Pope on the completion of his Homer—in Gay's conceit, Pope's "return from Greece"—portray the poet as himself a monarch:

> Hark how the guns salute from either shore
> As thy trim vessel cuts the Thames so fair:
> Shouts answering shouts from Kent and Essex roar . . .
> Bonfires do blaze, and bones and cleavers ring
> As at the coming of some mighty King.

Such images mark the moment at which Pope's mythologizing of his own life, a steady insistence on the symbolic value of his role as Twickenham satirist, may be seen to have assumed the status of an autonomous cultural myth. This is the moment, as Stanford Budick remarks, when Pope's portrayal of Hanoverian England as a declining world comes to be balanced by a new myth of political authority in which the satirist becomes the spokesman for a higher secular power; Pope, in short, "will be the poet of a shadow authority that is pristinely Roman and Greek. He will create its empire, or 'court,' *in his words*" (128). This then gives us not only the essential Augustan movement through which the Republic vanishes from history to be reborn in imaginary or ideal terms in poetry, but also the beginnings of a related movement through which the interior landscape of the Augustan verse epistle, within which the otium scene of Pope's Twickenham villa and garden represents simply one prominent locale, will emerge as a fully worked-out moral topography. The complication introduced by satire is that the choice demanded of epistolary audience is no longer simply between a corrupt actual world and an ideal poetic one, but then, within the poetry, between corruption and virtue all over again.

This is the choice posed in terms of topography. The interior landscape of the Augustan verse epistle is given its essential shape, as has always been recognized, by a strong controlling tension between country and city, the symbols respectively of an older, simpler, more virtuous agrarian society and a modern order of mercantile energies and fluid social distinctions. More recently, in light of arguments made by Carole Fabricant, Alistair Duckworth, and others, we have begun to see this same country-city opposition as part of an Augustan ideological warfare in which victory consists of gaining control of the poetic landscape. That warfare is the background against which symbolic topography, by translating into concrete terms the moral choice demanded of epistolary audience, reintroduces the dilemma of an audience excluded by Augustan premises from its restored world. The problem of epistolary audience here becomes the problem of imaginary readers invited to gaze inward upon a landscape they may in principle never come to inhabit.

Twickenham assumes an enormous symbolic importance in this topography because, as a still-rural village located on the margins of a burgeoning metropolis, it occupies an imperiled intermediate ground between the older England of the agrarian past and the urban bustle of an emergent capitalism. The London from which impoverished Grub Street writers walk out on Sunday to catch Pope just at dinnertime exerts its pressure as a locus of social derangement and raw commercial energies because these are the demonic forces against which Augustanism has ranged itself in symbolic combat, but equally important is the quieter strength that Twickenham is continuously drawing from another portion of the landscape lying beyond its immediate perimeters, the English countryside through which Pope makes his annual summertime jaunts to visit the country houses of his aristocratic friends. In the Horatian poems, particularly, the urban clamor of an importunate London is always balanced by the deeper silence, meaningful to those who hear it, of the peaceful landscape of country house and hedgerow and hamlet, an England so far largely uncontaminated by the corruptions of Walpole and modernity.

The landscape of this older England is also a poetic topography, for this is where the Augustan verse epistle incorporates into its own interior scene the timeless rural setting of the country-house poem as it had developed from Jonson's *To Penshurst* to Garth's *Claremont*. The common denominator of these poems, as G. S. Hibbard argued in a well-known essay, is their agreement "that the proper aim of the individual should be the subordination of himself to the service of the community, not exploitation of the community for his own personal ends" (174). The locus classicus is *To Penshurst*:

> And though thy walls be of the country stone,
> They are reared with no man's ruin, no man's groan;
> There's none that dwell about them wish them down,
>   But all come in, the farmer and the clown,
> And no one empty-handed....
> But what can this, more than express their love,
>   Add to thy free provisions, far above
> The need of such, whose liberal board doth flow
>   With all that hospitality doth know?

The country house as the center of an ancestral estate is then taken over into the interior landscape of the verse epistle as the symbol of restored organic or traditional society. This is the ancestral setting surrounding John Driden in Dryden's epistle to his kinsman, or the estate of the Earl of Burlington in Gay's *Journey to Exeter*: "While you, my Lord, bid stately piles ascend, / Or in your Chiswick bowers enjoy your friend, / Where Pope unloads the bough within his reach . . . / I journey far." Yet even the most idyllic of such moments does not exclude the sense of moral and ideological crisis out of which Hibbard sees the country house emerging as a symbolic locale, giving us the contrary logic through which the country house simultaneously becomes, the more Augustan poetry insists on its status as a symbol of traditional values, the symbol of a cultural upheaval that threatens to sweep all such values away. Thus the Augustan critique of emergent capitalism as Raymond Williams analyzes it: "a moral order is abstracted from the feudal inheritance and break-up, and seeks to impose itself ideally on conditions which are inherently unstable. A sanctity of property has to co-exist with violently changing property relations, and an ideal of charity with the harshness of labour relations in both the old and new modes. This is then the . . . source of the idea of an ordered and happier past set against the disturbance and disorder of the present" (45).

The distinction between the otium scene and the country house as symbolic locales in Augustan poetry lies in the degree to which they register an awareness of the submerged crisis that Williams describes, for the country house remains the symbol of an ancient stability not least because it has so far been allowed to remain in a state of blessed obliviousness to historical change. Thus, while there are strong elements of otium retirement in

Gay's description of Burlington's estate at Chiswick, and especially in the note of literary and ethical friendship arising from Pope's imagined presence there, the meaning of such scenes derives from the sense of an older England, very often geographically remote from London and its raw commercial bustle, that represents an unbroken continuity with the world of traditional values presumed to have existed up to the civil war. The otium scene as such, on the other hand, is always born out of an acute and dismayed consciousness of historical change, an effort to create a moral sanctuary through private retreat from what Williams calls the disturbance and disorder of the present.

At the same time, the otium elements in Gay's description of Chiswick arise precisely because, with the imagined presence there of the greatest Augustan satirist, the country house has for the moment become a conscious refuge from modernity and change, reminding us that the distinction between the two locales is always felt as a matter of relative moral urgency rather than geography as such. Thus it is that the country estate of John Driden in Dryden's epistle is undergoing transformation into an otium scene before our eyes, and thus it is too, as Maren-Sofie Røstvig showed some years ago in her monumental study of English retirement literature, that the origins of English otium poetry in the seventeenth century were closely related to the retreat of the royalist gentry to their ancestral domains in time of civil war. The celebration of otium by a poet such as George Daniel of Beswick—"The trumpet's clangor, nor the rattling drum, / Noises of war.... / Nor all the plunge / Of apprehension, shakes, or enters on / The temper of that true complexion"—may thus be taken to presage Pope's subsequent retirement to Twickenham in the age of Walpole and the South Sea Bubble.

Yet the mere notion of private retirement, though in some sense it perhaps always implies a critique of contemporary society, to this point gives no hint of the relentless satiric attack on modern corruption that Augustan poetry will subsequently launch from the secluded precincts of the otium scene. For the manner in which the otium perspective generates this attack has less to do with any direct moral contrast between private and public existence than with the idea of otium not simply as retirement from the world but as learned or studious retirement. This is the idea lying behind Scipio's famous remark, "Numquam minus solus, quam cum solus," which Cowley in his essay on solitude moralizes thus: "he found more satisfaction to his mind, and more improvement of it by solitude than by company; and to show that he spoke not this loosely or out of vanity, after he had made Rome mistress of almost the whole world, he retired himself from it by a voluntary exile, and at a private house in the middle of a wood near Liternum, passed the remainder of his glorious life no less gloriously" (2.311).

The ennobling thought that one is never less alone than when alone, as Scipio's apothegm has it, assumes not only that one has in retirement one's books, but that through those books lies entry into a timeless company. This is reading as, in Thomson's phrase, "high converse with the mighty dead," an ontology of the written word already understood as such in classical times—"No age is forbidden us," Seneca said about reading: "we have admittance to all, . . . there is a vast stretch of time for us to roam. We may dispute with Socrates, . . . repose with Epicurus. . . . Since nature allows us to participate in any age, why should we not take ourselves in mind from this petty and ephemeral span to the boundless and timeless region we can share with our betters" (65–70)—and in the eighteenth century lying at the very heart of the Augustan otium ideal, as in Edward Young's epistle to Lord Lansdowne:

> When you, my lord, to sylvan scenes retreat,
> No crowds around for pleasure, or for state,
> You are not cast upon a stranger land . . .
> But unconfined by bounds of time and place,
> You choose companions from all human race;
> Converse with those the deluge swept away,
> Or those whose midnight is Britannia's day.

Within the larger setting of the otium scene—either the country house of the nobility and gentry or the simpler retreat of the poet or clergyman—this gives us the library as the privileged scene of converse with the mighty dead, a magical sanctum existing, for all its solidly physical aspect as an arrangement of shelves and chairs and fireplace, outside the flow of historical time. The very notion of the library as a timeless setting arose as a response to the modern sense of historical time born in the Renaissance—it is traceable to the letters Petrarch writes from his retreat at Vaucluse, and the study in Montaigne's tower remains its permanent symbol—but by the eighteenth century it has become the moral center of the otium world. "Whilst thus within these magic walls I stray," writes Soame Jenyns in his lines *Written in the Earl of Oxford's Library*, "At once all climes and ages I survey: / On fancy's wings I fly from shore to shore, / Recall past time, and live whole eras o'er." "Selected shelves shall claim thy studious hours," we find Samuel Rogers writing half a century later in an epistle to a friend. "There, while the shaded lamp's mild luster streams, / Read ancient books, or woo inspiring dreams."

The library thus becomes the symbolic center of Augustan satire, the unseen sanctum within which abides the timeless or universal community of souls in which Augustanism and its intended audience have their hearts' being and home. In theological terms, as we have seen, this is the universal humanity-in-God of St. Paul's epistles or Augustine's *De Civitate Dei*, the radiant positive vision that gives meaning to satire's grimly negative estimate of the present or actual world as a sphere of moral unreality. In epistemological terms, it is the Augustan universal, the notion of a permanent human nature remaining eternally the same beneath what Dr. Johnson calls the separable and adventitious disguises of nation and age and social class; this is the universal humanity to which both reading and introspection give access, providing not only the indispensable standard of all satiric judgment but the principle of moral intelligibility to which Augustan satire constantly appeals against the new empiricist epistemologies of mental association. In literary terms, it is the ideal commonwealth that, having earlier vanished from history, now dwells in poetry.

The meaning of the library or study as a symbolic locale thus derives not simply from a notion of reading as escape to, as Seneca puts it, the boundless and timeless region where dwell Socrates and Epicurus, but also of the library itself as the very location on earth of that timeless realm. There is, in short, a complex reflexivity at work in the image of the library as the magical inner sanctum of the otium world, one that begins as the imaginary reader of the Augustan verse epistle is drawn out of the corruption and sham of Walpole's England and into the interior landscape of the poem, and then, within that landscape, toward the otium world inhabited by the poet and his friends in their rural setting, and then, within that setting, into book-lined surroundings in which one settles down and enters through reading into a timeless realm that includes not only Socrates and Cicero and Seneca but—the shock of reflexive awareness—Pope and Swift and Gay and oneself as their reader, and specifically as reader at *this* moment of *this* verse epistle in *this* setting, which becomes, as a location in the world but outside ordinary space and time, at one with the imaginary library inside the poem.

The verse epistle thus aims to expand the otium community at its center, that tiny remnant of traditional society represented by the poet and his circle of literary companions and aristocrats exiled by history, through a dynamics of moral and literary response that subtracts souls from the crowded world of Walpole's England—that is, from the delusion that the world of bustling actuality presided over by Walpole is real—and permits them to reside instead in the ideal commonwealth to which reading and classical values and genuine introspection give access. The initial effect is to make the entire otium setting, rather than simply the library as its magical inner sanctum, a timeless scene—thanks to his "ancestors and Heav'n," says John Gilbert Cooper in one of his Aristippus epistles, he lives in literary ease: "Caesar and Tully often dine, / Anacreon rambles in my grove, / Sweet Horace drinks Falernian wine / Catullus makes on haycocks love"—but this then sets off the otium world, even within its own interior or poetic landscape, from that world beyond its perimeters still implicated in time and historical change. Here originates the moral tension between country and city that gives shape to the Augustan landscape as a whole.

So greatly does the tension between country and city dominate Augustan poetry that any sense of an intervening landscape, a world of village and field and copse lying between the remote country house and the burgeoning modern metropolis, seems at times to have been altogether erased. Yet this collapse of distance between the center and the remotest corners of the kingdom is itself one of the major themes of the verse epistle—even, so far as letters are now written in a world where mail travels rapidly and easily along modern roads, something increasingly assumed by epistolary address itself—and the very subject of its deeply ambivalent meditation on an England being carried toward a state of advanced civilization. There is no ambivalence, of course, about the evils of an encroaching modernity, for the symbolic value of the country house has been precisely that it has so far remained inside its own temporal medium, a reminder of the age when great estates were agriculturally self-sufficient, when both squire and tenant thought rather in terms of locality than of nation, and where wars and great events passed virtually unnoticed at a distance incalculably remote from the peasant in the fields. The system of modern transport and communication that is even now eliminating this sense of an older, slower, all but timeless order of enclosed local societies belongs to the new world of emergent capitalism that has also produced Walpole and Exchange Alley and the National Debt.

At the same time, a system of roads bringing the distant points of an extended empire into nearly simultaneous communication had been one of the great achievements of Rome as a classical civilization, and eighteenth-century English poetry is always aware of Roman roads not simply as a curious feat of ancient engineering but as part of the interior landscape of Roman writing itself, something taken over into poetry in epistles such as that in which Horace recounts his journey to Brundisium, and into Roman epistolography in the constant movements between metropolis and country villa in the letters of Cicero or Pliny. Thus, for instance, it is really the idea of Roman roads as symbols of advanced civilization that prompts a footnote by Melmoth in his translation of Pliny: "These roads extended to a great distance from the city on all sides, the most noble of which was the Appian, computed to reach three hundred and fifty miles. Mr. Wright in his travels speaking of this road observes, that 'tho' it be much broken in several places . . . in others it is wonderfully well preserved, notwithstanding it be computed near two thousand years old. They are paved with such hard stones, that they are rather polished than worn'" (287).

The movement toward an Augustan awareness of Rome as a civilization in some sense brought into being by such roads may be traced in earlier English poetry as a consciousness that England, for all her rising glory as a modern nation, still sadly and anomalously lacks them. This, too, is a matter of interior landscape, an awareness among classically educated Englishmen that their own countryside remains primitive in relation to the world they enter when reading Horace or Cicero or Pliny. Thus, in 1636, the Reverend Richard James in his *Iter Lancastrense*:

> Our ways are gulfs of dirt and mire, which none
> Scarce ever pass in summer without moan;
> Whilst theirs through all the world were no less free
> Of passage than the race of Wallisee,
> O'er broken moors, deep mosses, lake and fen. . . .
> So did their business speed, and armies fly
> From east to west like lightning in the sky.

In the eighteenth-century verse epistle, a similar thought most often occurs when the epistoler, journeying over an actual stretch of surviving Roman road—"rough, tho' truly Roman ground," as Francis Fawkes once calls it—suddenly recalls the time when Britain was a remote and inconsiderable province of Rome. "Now o'er true Roman way our horses sound," says Gay in his *Journey to Exeter*. "Graevius would kneel, and kiss the sacred ground."[1]

Such moments as these, reminders of the attempt of Augustanism to come to terms with an emergent capitalism through the analogy with Roman civilization, remind us as well that Augustan landscape is to a very great degree a landscape of modern transformations being grasped in classical terms. Thus the increasing excellence of English roads—"O'er finest turnpike-road we bowl," exults Francis Fawkes, proving his point by writing in the moving coach, "The wheels, the numbers, gently roll"— simply suggests that England is now approaching the state of civilization long ago achieved by Rome, and thus the inns along Gay's route, though outposts of the new money society set down in an otherwise rural landscape—"The ready ostler near the stirrup stands, / And as we mount, our half-pence load his hands"—seem not dissimilar to the inns of Horace's journey to Brundisium. And even signs that the contagion of London is spreading into the countryside, as when Gay's company rides along in fear of an attack by highwaymen—"Prepared for war, now Bagshot-heath we cross / Where broken gamesters oft repair their loss"—need remind us of nothing more than the sharpers and ruffians of Horace's and Juvenal's Rome.

A sense of disruption occurs within the Augustan landscape only when there are disturbing hints of a transformation at work for which classical civilization provides no reassuring parallels, energies that exceed or escape the ancient paradigm of decline due to luxury and corruption. Within the interior scene of the verse epistle, the major symbol of these new energies, what we retrospectively identify so readily as the emergence of a modern social and economic order, is the dark cloud of smoke visible first over

London, then subsequently over other English cities as they grow in population, from the seventeenth century onward. As a symbol of change, what matters is less the cloud itself—which, as Evelyn saw, was mainly due to the coal used for fires—than the way it was immediately taken, as a troubling sign of submerged forces at work in English society. "I see the city in a thicker cloud / Of business, than of smoke," says Denham in one of those moments that give *Coopers Hill* a claim to being the first genuinely Augustan poem, "where men like ants / Toil to prevent imaginary wants."

The smoke of the metropolis, Ruskin's storm-cloud of the nineteenth century as it earlier overhung an emerging eighteenth-century urban and industrial scene, is wherever we encounter it in Augustan poetry evidence of an uneasy awareness that English society is undergoing changes unknown to Horace and Virgil, unsuspected by Juvenal even in his deepest moments of angry despair. Thus, though there are routine attempts to classicize the urban cloud—"Full swelling to the sight," says John Dalton, pausing on a journey to look back at London from its outskirts, "I found / First holy Paul's majestic round, / Thro' wide Augusta's smoke"—there is also a steady counterpoint of something very like modern dismay. "We left dull Norwich smoke behind," says John Whaley at midcentury, breathing a sigh of relief when he again finds himself moving along through "a fair verdant water'd vale." "We cast a parting look behind," echoes Francis Fawkes, leaving London on his journey to Doncaster, "Pleas'd to'have left yon sable cloud, / That buries millions in its shroud; / Alas! they toil, the sons of care! / And never breathe the purer air."

The metropolis over which the shroud of smoke and care impends, in turn, is no actual city but the imaginary London of Augustan satire, the busy, bustling, corrupt, crowded symbol of that new commercial or money society whose demonic energies proved so difficult to explain entirely away within a classical paradigm of luxury and corruption. This is the London of *The Dunciad* or Gay's *Trivia* and *Rural Sports*, the city as it exists within the consciousness of those who

> Long in the noisy town have been immur'd,
> Respir'd its smoke, and all its cares endur'd,
> Where news and politics divide mankind,
> And schemes of state involve th'uneasy mind;
> Faction embroils the world, and ev'ry tongue
> Is moved by flatt'ry, or with scandal hung.

In every such description, it is the sense of barely contained energies of social transformation, especially as conveyed through a vocabulary of electoral or parliamentary corruption—Gay's "politics" and "faction" and "schemes of state"—that accounts for the disruptive powers of the metropolis within the Augustan poetic landscape, and for London as the source of a moral contagion only perilously held at bay through the opposing power of Augustan satire.

The metropolis appears in such poems as *Trivia* less as a symbol of the new money society, however, than of something even more dangerous, an ideological shift within English society in favor of trade or commerce. For though the profit motive or lust for wealth that so unsettled Hesiod and Virgil is always duly acknowledged as a danger in Augustan writing, the greater danger is moral enfeeblement, a signal that the energies that have so far carried the nation upward toward prosperity and political dominance have now begun, precisely through the temptations of its new wealth and power, to bring about its eventual decline. This is the cyclical theory of history as it dominated ancient thought from Herodotus to Virgil and beyond, the paradigm from within which Davenant is still writing about trade early in the eighteenth century. Davenant gives to the temptations of wealth and power and the moral decay induced by them the name Luxury, recently and perceptively studied by John Sekora as the master term encompassing all the depredations of modernity: "Trade, without doubt, is in its nature a pernicious thing; it brings in that wealth which introduces luxury; it gives rise to fraud and avarice, and extinguishes virtue and simplicity of manners; it depraves a people, and makes way for that corruption which never fails to end in slavery, foreign or domestic" (qtd. in Sekora 79).

For all his steady commitment to the classical paradigm of corruption through luxury, however, Davenant always has an uneasy sense that he is dealing with forces unknown to the ancient historians, which allows him on the one hand to give in *The True Picture of a Modern Whig* what Pocock calls his bloodcurdling caricature of the new class of credit managers, and on the other to see that the invisible power that has conjured this upstart class into existence and dressed it in fine clothes and permitted it to drive through the streets in coaches is something called credit. This is Pope's "paper credit," a force at once real and unreal, as insubstantial as human opinion but at the same time tremendously powerful in the world of the actual, able to create real coaches and real houses where none existed before. "Of all beings that have existence only in the minds of men," says Davenant, "nothing is more fantastical and nice than credit; . . . it hangs upon opinion, it depends upon our fashions of hope and fear" (qtd. in Pocock 439).

In a purely neutral sense, Davenant is at such moments simply glimpsing and attempting to analyze, as Pocock observes, "the epistemology of an investing society" (440), but from the Augustan perspective what he is seeing is that same epistemology in its demonic aspect. If we understand now that Davenant is glimpsing the workings of emergent capitalism grasped as a system, it is because modern scholars like Kramnick and Raymond Williams, writing with a Marxist attentiveness to social systems as they work implacably toward ends unforeseen by those inside them, have alerted us to this dimension of Augustan dismay. Yet this was precisely what was not understood by the Augustan poets, who knew only that they were living inside a history that had gotten out of control, and that this had somehow to do with commerce or credit or trade. Similarly, an awareness of the transforming powers of nascent capitalism gives us, later in the century, moments like that in which Cowper tries to understand exactly how "burghers" or members of the new bourgeoisie, "men . . . immaculate in all their private functions," become a "loathsome body" when they enter into commercial combination, and in particular why "merchants, unimpeachable of sin / Against the charities of domestic life, / Incorporated, seem at once to lose / Their nature; and, disclaiming all regard / For mercy . . . / Build factories with blood" (*The Task* 4.671–83).

The curious note of fatalism in Cowper's lines occurs because he is looking at the world as it would come to exist after the Augustan collapse, the failure of poetry and polemic to bring about the restored traditional society envisioned by Bolingbroke and Pope and Swift and their friends. It was in the long moment before that collapse had come to seem inevitable that a mounting sense that Augustanism was contending against energies of social transformation only imperfectly grasped within its classical paradigm of luxury and corruption led increasingly to a demonization of the opposing forces, a sense that the new social and economic order, whatever else it might turn out to be, was something monstrous, irrational, gigantic, implacable, and above all inhuman. The great symbol of modernity in this monstrous aspect was Walpole, who is seen more and more in Augustan satire, as in a typical epistle from Swift to Gay, as "a bloated Minister," a creature more resembling Spenser's beasts of sin and error than anything in the mundane world of actual parliamentary politics:

> Two rows of teeth arm each devouring jaw;
> And, ostrich-like, his all-digesting maw. . . .
> Of loud un-meaning sounds, a rapid flood
> Rolls from his mouth in plenteous streams of mud;
> With these, the court and senate-house he plies,
> Made up of noise, and impudence, and lies.

The portrayal of Walpole during the later years of his political reign draws continuously on this symbolism of monstrosity and mindless malevolence, not just Augustan satire but Opposition journals like *The Craftsman* and, as Vincent Carretta has shown, the satirical prints that flooded the streets of London along with the ballads and broadsides that pursued the theme of Walpolian monstrosity on the popular level.[2] This is Walpole not as politician or prime minister but as bogeyman, the "loathsome body" of Cowper's incorporated capitalism stalking the nether regions of an emergent modern consciousness as a creature out of folklore or fireside tale. The role of Walpole-as-bogeyman is to give a name and shape to forces otherwise nameless and terrifying, and in the climactic years of the Augustan enterprise the unceasing calls for Walpole's overthrow have less to do with politics or party than with a last desperate hope of exorcising the demon of modernity itself. The ricorso of literary Augustanism and Country ideology would be, from this perspective, not simply a return to traditional society but an awakening from the nightmare of Walpolian modernity into a restored world of sunlight and rationality.

This is the moment at which the dilemma of an audience at once created by Augustan discourse and excluded by its ideological coordinates begins to be felt by Augustan poetry as a source of unease. The dilemma is most easily understood, as we have seen, as a problem in the way Augustanism imagines its ricorso. For the triumph of Augustan satire would consist not simply in the overthrow of Walpole but in the recovery of the status quo ante; it is in that shining instant, as Bolingbroke's Caleb D'Anvers puts it at a time when he is still able to believe in the possibility, that "the old Country interest of the best families in the kingdom (which hath lately been almost swallowed up by stockjobbers and monied upstarts) will return to its normal channel" (*Craftsman* 5.5). The problem of Augustan audience is embodied not so much in D'Anvers's talk of best families and monied upstarts as in his utter lack of constraint in speaking of such things, revealing a mind so wholly intent on the restoration of a hierarchical society grounded in natural law that it has never grasped the paradox that the audience it is creating through its discourse would have no place in such a world.

This is the moment at which Augustan poetry, having located at its symbolic center the figure of the idealized aristocrat, having founded its own discourse on the presumed moral authority of aristocratic speech, and having created an interior landscape in which the country house and the otium scene operate as objectifications of aristocratic values, summons an audience now endowed with aristocratic sensibility out of the timeless world of a universal human community and into a poetic world that, for all its own ideality, is governed by an uncompromising system of social or class distinctions. So far as the ricorso envisioned by literary Augustanism has never yet occurred, of course, the contradiction of an audience aristocratic in sensibility but not by right of birth, and thus excluded from a world in which right of birth lies at the very center of a divinely ordained order of things, is felt as an abstract or unvoiced source of unease. Yet the contradiction haunts Augustan poetry almost from the beginning, producing pressures and dislocations within its interior landscape.

The paradox of excluded audience lies at the heart of the Augustan collapse, the last despairing sense of the Augustan satirists that their campaign against Walpole and modernity has been in the end an inglorious failure. "This was the last poem of the kind printed by our author," says Pope in the famous endnote to the *Epilogue to the Satires*, announcing his permanent withdrawal from satiric combat, "with a resolution to publish no more, but to enter thus, in the most plain and solemn manner he could, a sort of PROTEST against that insuperable corruption and depravity of manners, which he had been so unhappy as to live to see. Could he hope to have amended any, he had continued those attacks, but bad men were grown so shameless and so powerful, that ridicule was become as unsafe as it was ineffectual." This is Pope's goodbye as well to epistolary verse, and in it we may hear echoes of his belated and unhappy conviction that epistolary audience, that imaginary readership that was to have taken on body in the world of the actual, had never been more than a figment of Augustan discourse after all. Pope's valedictory endnote represents the return of solipsism from its long Augustan banishment, for at the heart of these unhappy mutterings about the ineffectuality of satire lies a gloomy sense that Augustan poetry had all along been talking only to itself.

Yet this is an error, for Augustan poetry, though it had not proved able in the end to alter the course of Walpolian modernity, had nonetheless been supremely successful in creating an audience in the image of its own values. This is why the audience posited by Pope's epistolary verse is able, as we have seen, to survive his own death to become the locus of poetic address in such poems as John Brown's *Essay on Satire*, and it will then persist, though as a steadily diminishing presence, in later-eighteenth-century poetry until the last brief satiric revival associated with the *Anti-Jacobin*. What Pope perceives as a failure of audience—and specifically as the failure of audience to, as we should now say, assume an autonomous existence in the sphere of ideology—has in reality been the problem of an audience excluded from the ideological domain whose values it embodies. This is the problem of an audience with aristocratic soul, to borrow Nietzsche's phrase once again, doomed first to exist as an anomalous presence within its own poetic world, where it inevitably proves an empty resource in the wars against Walpole and corruption, and then subsequently, after the Augustan collapse and the death of Pope, as an audience floating free of its original literary context to work out its own terms of survival within a changed cultural reality.

In just the same way, the interior landscape created by Augustan poetry survives the collapse of the Augustan enterprise to persist as a recognizable scene in eighteenth-century writing. When this landscape is haunted by a sense of failure and irreversible decline, we have, properly speaking, the last elegiac moment of Augustanism itself. This is the context in which the half-melancholy mood of otium retirement in *The Task* should be taken as bespeaking Cowper's sense of himself as a poet who has lingered beyond his time, and in which Goldsmith should be taken in *The Traveller* not as denouncing current ills but as ruefully acknowledging the forces that have brought about the Augustan collapse—"As nature's ties decay, / As duty, love, and honor fall to sway, / Fictitious bonds, the bonds of wealth and law, / Still gather strength, and force unwilling awe"—and in *The Deserted Village* not to be uttering a lament for any actual England but for the Augustan poetic landscape as it had existed before the hope of a restored organic or traditional society had met with extinction.³

The poetic revival associated with the Wartons and their school becomes possible at just the moment the imaginary audience and poetic landscape that survive the Augustan collapse are redefined in relation to each other, something that occurs when Augustan audience belatedly and unexpectedly discovers in Shaftesburian moral sympathy a justification for its own claims to aristocratic sensibility. The justification is necessary, we have seen, precisely because Augustanism had originally defined itself through symbolic opposition to Bolingbroke's class of "monied upstarts"—people, as John Dennis scornfully says early in the century, "who from a state of obscurity, and perhaps of misery, have risen to a condition of distinction and plenty." From the Augustan perspective, this is a class that had always betrayed in its attitudes and tastes the vulgarity of its origins; "not many will wonder," says Dennis, "if these people, who in their original obscurity, could never attain to any higher entertainment than tumbling and vaulting and ladder-dancing, should still be in love with their old sports" (1.293).

Yet as it feels itself to be an excluded audience, besought to honor the values of a traditional order and yet given no place within traditional society, the same class is one that during the Augustan moment comes to aspire to the condition of *otium* retreat and landed status. This gives us, for instance, the crucial moment in *The Spectator* when Sir Andrew Freeport retires from commerce to his country estate, and in the *Tour of Great Britain* Defoe's celebration of domiciles that are not, as he says, "the ancient residences of ancestors," but "citizens' country houses, whither they retire from the hurries of business, and getting money, to draw their breath in a clear air." The symbolic tendency of setting in Defoe's *Tour* is thus always, as Alistair Duckworth puts it, "to naturalize the citizens in the landscape," "bringing the city into the country and enfranchising citizens into the rights and privileges of landed ownership" (455). To the rudimentary extent that the new class possesses an ideology, its expression may be heard in a bourgeois wish-fantasy like Pomfret's *The Choice*, the otium ideal of Horace or Pope as dimly grasped within the consciousness of one of Defoe's successful tradesmen.

Yet the crucial point about the parvenu class, what allows Defoe's solid "citizens" to be scorned as monied upstarts by Bolingbroke, is precisely that it is so far largely naked of a sustaining ideology, remaining exposed to

Augustan contempt because it has asserted its claims to a higher status entirely in terms of external symbols like fine clothes and coaches and estates in the country. This is why Augustanism was able so unwaveringly to regard the new class as the very emanation of the new speculative or money economy ushered in by William of Orange in 1688, and why the pretensions of Defoe's admired citizens to landed or patrician status appeared to Augustan eyes a macabre social masquerade being danced on the ruins of traditional society. A contemporary newspaper account quoted by Kramnick beautifully captures the sense that, with the first great crash of the new speculative economy, the pricking of the South Sea Bubble, the unreal music seems to have stopped and the masquerade, for the moment at least, to have ended:

> You may see second-hand coaches; second-hand gold watches, cast off diamond watches and earrings to be sold; servants already want places who were, but a little while ago, so saucy and insolent, no wages and no kind of usage could oblige them. The streets are full of rich liveries to be sold, nay, and full of rich embroidered petticoats, rich embroidered coats and waistcoats; in a word every place is full of the ruin of Exchange Alley. (68)

When Defoe's solid citizens are stripped of their gold watches and embroidered waistcoats, in short, one sees precisely their ideological nakedness, that state of disequilibrium described by Pocock in which an emergent class has grown enormously in wealth and power while its ability to develop a sustaining cultural mythology has been blocked or neutralized. This is the point at which members of the new class, already excluded by their obscurity of birth from any honorable place in the Augustan scheme of things, are at the same time prevented by their own eager embrace of Augustan values from turning to some alternative ideology of individual enterprise or self-interest. For though the lineaments of such an ideology may be glimpsed in writers such as Defoe and Mandeville—"every individual is a little world by itself," said Mandeville, "and all creatures, as far as their understanding and abilities will let them, endeavour to make that self happy: this in all of them is the continual labor, and seems to be the whole design of life" (2.178)—any more positive expression of a doctrine of self-interest will always be blocked by the power of Augustan satire to discredit such notions as a glorification of human pride, the swollen self-delusion of beings cut off from God and mistaking the earthly realm as their home.

This is the moment at which William Law emerges as the theologian of literary Augustanism, and the verse epistles of John Byrom, which form a fugitive and remarkable branch of Augustan poetry, as laying bare the assumptions common to Law and satirists like Pope and Swift. As we have seen, Law's most important move would always be to insist on scripture, which was increasingly being demoted even by such orthodox divines as

Warburton to the status of mere historical record, as being in the strictest sense about the inward life of the individual: "it is only the description," says Law of the story of Adam and Eve and Exodus and Jesus of Nazareth, "of that which passes within you. It is the book of yourself" (qtd. in Sitter 67). This is the context in which sin, as a self-willed alienation from God, becomes a form of moral or spiritual solipsism. Thus, as in Byrom's *Epistle to a Gentleman of the Temple*, the rebellion of Satan against God becomes the very moment of the fall into separate consciousness: "Then self, then evil, then apostate war / Rag'd through their hierarchy wide and far." And thus imprisonment within a separate consciousness becomes, quite literally, Hell: "when a selfish separating pride / Will break all bounds, and good from good divide, / 'Tis then extinguish'd, like a distant spark, / And pride self-doom'd into its joyless dark."

Solipsism as the Augustan verse epistle combats it on the spiritual level is always something nearly related to sin viewed in this Augustinian manner, as the joyless dark of a self-imposed isolation from God and the humanity that moves and has its being in him. From the same Augustinian perspective, the mystifications of the new money society are immediately recognizable as nothing more than the oldest and most gigantic sin in its newest disguise, attempts to dress what Byrom calls a selfish separating pride in the garb of an innocent self-interest. This is the perspective from which all the varieties of modern freethinking themselves become simply grandiose examples of the same sin of pride—"Detested names!" John Brown will cry, excoriating "Th'envenomed stream that flows from Toland's quill, / And the rank dregs of Hobbes and Mandeville"—and from which Augustan poetry will always make its ultimate appeal to that timeless inward scene of Augustinian introspection in opposition to which the outward world and its unreal creatures stand revealed as a mere passing shadow show. The central scene of Augustan poetry is the one glimpsed in the instant when, as Byrom has it in his epistle *Enthusiasm*, human beings have met and conquered their own pride:

> Led by this faith, when man forsakes his sin,
> The gate stands open to his God within:
> There, in the temple of his soul, is found,
> Of inward central life, the holy ground;
> The sacred scene of piety and peace.

The inward temple of the soul becomes at such moments the very ground of moral intelligibility in Augustan writing, permitting both satire and epistle to lay claim to the massive authority of a tradition running back through Augustine and Plotinus to Plato and the *Nosce teipsum* of Socrates; "they alone, who in themselves oft view / Man's image," says Benjamin Stillingfleet, giving late expression to the imperative that had guided

Augustan poetry since Dryden, "know what method to pursue." In Byrom's homely lines may be felt the full majesty of the vision that Augustan satire was to summon against the vanity and folly of its age, and the seriousness of the obstacle this then posed to any assertion of individual self-interest as an honorable stimulus to human happiness. The manner in which Augustanism was able so triumphantly to block or discredit ideologies of self-interest then explains the rise of the alternative movement now generally referred to as eighteenth-century Pelagianism, the name recalling the great controversy fought out between Augustine, the uncompromising theorist of earthly life as a gloomy state of alienation from the divine, and the fifth-century heretic Pelagius, promulgator of the infinitely more cheerful doctrine that human beings in their moral nature were innately good and that Adam, far from dooming humankind to a perpetual share in his own guilt, had merely set a bad example to posterity.

The evolution of a bourgeois ideology adequate to the demands of a new social and economic order begins, as we have some time since come to realize, not in such works as *The Fable of the Bees* but in the pages of Shaftesbury's *Characteristics*. For while Augustanism was fully engaged in a struggle with Hobbesian or Mandevillian egoism, it was Latitudinarian theology and the tradition of Shaftesburian ethical theory running through Hutcheson and Butler to Smith's *Theory of Moral Sentiments* that would emerge, nearly unnoticed in its more momentous implications, as the alternative wellspring of bourgeois progressivism. The uncontroversial root assumption shared by all these positions, endlessly troublesome to orthodoxy precisely because it was its own first tenet, is the goodness of God; this is Byrom's "he is all glory, goodness, light, and love" as it would be echoed by innumerable deists and benevolists down to the end of the century. The radical second assumption, however, the move of the original Pelagius now reintroduced by the new Pelagians of the eighteenth century, was that human beings, as the creation of an infinitely good Creator, must themselves be innately good; "this self of mine . . . ," as Shaftesbury's Theocles would serenely put it, "is a real self, drawn out from and copied from another principle and original self (the Great One of the World)" (2.105). From this arises the notion that only through some deviltry or brainwashing could human beings have come to believe in their own sinfulness or depravity, the prime example being the doctrine of Original Sin.

Shaftesbury stands out as a revolutionary thinker not least because there arose, among the unsystematic musings of his philosophy, an idea that, as well as providing an immediate metaphysical basis for eighteenth-century benevolist thought, was then to exert an influence that may yet be felt in our own century. This is the notion of a universal humanity, the eternal mankind-in-God of St. Paul or Augustine, taken out of its timeless realm and relocated within the here and now of a present temporality and an evolving secular history. In its distant transmigrations, Shaftesbury's temporal community of man would become both the universal humankind of European liberal thought and the notion of an abstract "totality" running through Hegel and Marx to modern radical social theory, but at the moment of its origin it was something altogether more modest, a theory of natural sociability holding that human beings, in addition to being innately virtuous—the general Pelagian principle that appears in Shaftesbury as "intire affection"[4]—are also naturally or innately benevolent in their relations to one another.

The notion of humankind as a universal and mutually benevolent temporal community simply follows, it will be seen, in immediate logical terms from the Pelagian premise of an innate human virtue. For it was the fallen condition of man, that sense of alienation and deranged will for which the Fall serves as central myth, that had explained the separation of men from God and from one another: abolish Original Sin and we are all of us, except for some minor evils introduced by the physical environment and misguided custom, already companions in a celestial company. The revolutionary force of the idea as Shaftesbury developed it lay in his steady insistence that even vice and folly are no more than disguised modes of natural sociability: "Of this, vanity, ambition, and luxury, have a share; and many other disorders of our life partake.... Out of these two branches (viz. *community or participation in the pleasures of others*, and *belief of meriting well from others*) wou'd arise more than nine tenths of whatever is enjoy'd in life. And thus in the main sum of happiness, there is scarce a single article, but what derives itself from social love, and depends immediately on the natural and kind affections" (1.299).

The immediate consequence of natural sociability as Shaftesbury developed the idea was to turn even vice and criminality into moral phantoms, for even the vicious and the criminal are under the sway of "the natural and kind affections": this is why the thief and murderer strive so constantly, in their own little world of thieves and murderers, to gain the respect and good opinion of their fellows. The only real sin in this context is the unnatural passion of selfishness or egoism—as these are admitted as passions, warns Shaftesbury solemnly, "a separate end and interest must be every day more strongly formed in us, generous views and motives laid aside" (1.330)—and the punishment of such sin is not, as in Augustine or Law, alienation or estrangement from God, but estrangement from one's fellow beings. This is the vision of Hell as a fall out of human society, as it would survive in Godwin or Dickens:

> Wherever such a creature turns himself, whichever way he casts his eye; every thing around must appear ghastly and horrid; every thing hostile, and, as it were, bent against a private and single being, who is thus divided from every thing.... what must it be to feel this inward banishment, this real estrange-

ment from human commerce; and to be after this manner in a desert, and in the horridest of solitudes, even when in the midst of society? (1.335)

This is as powerful an attack on Hobbesian or Mandevillian egoism as any mounted by Augustan satire, and it brings vividly to light the special problem that Shaftesburian ethical theory posed for such writers as Pope and Swift. For while Augustanism possessed superb literary and intellectual resources for warfare against ideologies of avowed self-interest, it had far fewer for deployment against theories of innate virtue and natural sociability and moral sympathy, and none at all against Shaftesbury's notion, so uncannily and problematically close to its own Augustinian vision, of sin as a form of moral solipsism. For Shaftesbury was clearly in some sense as opposed as any Augustan writer to what Byrom calls a "selfish, separating pride," and it demanded a great deal of thought to see where and how a radical divergence from established assumptions was being introduced here. It was thus during a long moment of Augustan bemusement that, virtually unchallenged by any major writer, a moral universe previously undreamt of in ancient or modern ethics took shape in the early eighteenth century. For it was Shaftesbury who taught mankind, as John Gilbert Cooper was to say in *The Power of Harmony*, "to feel an instantaneous glow of joy / When Beauty from her native seat of Heav'n, / Cloth'd in ethereal mildness, on our plains / Descends . . . / . . . and thro' the world / The heav'nly boon to ev'ry being flows."

So far as it represents a temporal world infinitely more mild or benevolent than any imaginable within the limits of Augustinian orthodoxy, the moral universe glimpsed at any such moment is merely the universe of the new Pelagianism. Yet the virtue of Cooper's *The Power of Harmony* is that it always keeps in view Shaftesbury's special importance within that larger movement, and specifically the manner in which his importance derives from a metaphysics absorbed earlier by Shaftesbury himself from Cambridge Platonism. This is the note one catches in Cooper's mention, amid a more general celebration of ethereal mildness, of an abstract Beauty come down to earth from her seat in a platonic heaven, giving us that distinctively Shaftesburian world in which moral and aesthetic considerations are never entirely separable, and in which even moral sympathy is somehow a mode of aesthetic response. "Here thro' the mental eye enamour'd view / The charms of Moral Beauty," invites Cooper, capturing in a few lines the Shaftesburian essence of eighteenth-century literary sentimentalism: "How, to undistemper'd thought, / Does Virtue in mild majesty appear / Delightful, when the sympathetic heart / Feels for another's woes!"

The tracing of Shaftesbury's debt to Cambridge Platonism does not, however, begin to account for the enormous impact that his elision of the moral and the aesthetic was to have on eighteenth-century thought. That is to be explained by the part the idea actually played in Shaftesbury's larger argument, both as the central principle of his metaphysics and as one of the more suggestive analogies in the history of philosophy. For when one has posited an innate moral sense, some faculty of mind that immediately and intuitively knows good from evil, right from wrong, one yet assumes the burden of showing how it operates. Shaftesbury's answer, breathtakingly simple and yet pregnant with implication, was that it works in just the same way as aesthetic response: as one "instinctively" responds to a dissonance in music or an asymmetry in painting, one responds to moral actions: "no sooner are actions viewed . . . than straight an inward eye distinguishes, and sees the fair and shapely, the amiable and admirable, apart from the deformed, the foul, the odious, or the despicable."[5] Thus the famous analogy that, so much more than being central to Shaftesbury's system, might almost be said to *be* his system:

> The case is the same in the mental or moral subjects, as in the . . . common subjects of sense. The shapes, motions, colors and proportions of these latter being presented to our eye; there necessarily results a beauty or deformity, according to the different measure, arrangement, and disposition of their several parts. So in behavior and actions, when presented to our understanding, there must be found, of necessity, an apparent difference, according to the regularity or irregularity of the subjects. (1.251)

As momentous as were the implications of Shaftesbury's elision of moral and aesthetic response for subsequent eighteenth-century thought, however, and then well beyond the eighteenth century due to its influence on Kant, it is a relatively minor development that has crucial consequences for epistolary audience after the Augustan collapse. This is the notion that moral and aesthetic responses involve a mode of connoisseurship that, although it can ultimately be mastered by anyone possessing the requisite powers of taste, is originally an attribute of patrician or aristocratic sensibility. The notion is powerfully sustained in Shaftesbury's own writing by the impression of an aristocratic mind at work investigating the philosophical basis of its own values, supplying the context in which Shaftesburian ethical theory could be taken as being simply a universalization of patrician sensibility. Nor was Shaftesbury in the least unaware of this implication. "To philosophise . . . ," he had written in the *Characteristics*, "is but to carry good-breeding a step higher. For the accomplishment of breeding is, to learn whatever is decent in company or beautiful in arts; and the sum of philosophy is, to learn what is just in society and beautiful in nature and the order of the world" (2.225).

The notion of good breeding as Shaftesbury invokes it at such moments, never more than a collateral postulate within his philosophy as a whole, would prove to be another revolutionary element in his system. For in rejecting the older notion of aristocracy as a status deriving solely from birth or hereditary right in favor of a notion of connoisseurship open to anyone willing to cultivate the finer feelings (see Markley 216–18), he had invented the terms on which, after the death of Pope, Augustan audience would survive within its altered ideological context. In the register of moral connoisseurship, this gives us, as in Hannah More's verse epistle *Sensibility*, the ground of literary sentimentalism: "Sweet SENSIBILITY! thou keen delight! / Unprompted moral! sudden sense of right! / Perception exquisite!"[6] In the more normal register of aesthetic appreciation, as in one of Allan Ramsay's "Augustan" epistles to Sir William Burnet, it gives us connoisseurship as an immediate claim to patrician sensibility: "Most happy he who can those sweets enjoy, / With taste refin'd, which does not easy cloy. / Not so *plebeian* souls.... / The sweetest plants which fairest gardens show, / Are lost to them, for them unheeded grow."

In Ramsay's verses, even as they dwell on a primary level on the otium scene of Augustan poetry as it is being absorbed into a new benevolist universe of ethereal mildness and divine order, one also senses the new division of the moral world brought about by Shaftesburian ethics. For now those plebeian by birth but endowed "with aristocratic soul" by their reading of Augustan poetry are no longer an abstract or disembodied audience left to wander without an ideological home, but a community of sensibility in their own right, defined entirely in opposition to the "plebeian souls" of Ramsay's poem, who are so not by birth or social status but through their own coarseness of feeling and vulgarity of sentiment. This is the ideological moment, in short, in which the *vulgus* of Augustan poetry is redefined entirely in terms of moral and aesthetic sensibility, thus establishing the terms on which a legitimate claim to aristocratic soul would enter into the process out of which Defoe's citizen tradesmen would emerge as an ascendant bourgeoisie.

Within eighteenth-century poetry generally, the most visible sign of this ideological shift is a movement in which the moral severity of Augustan satire silently gives way to a more benevolist strain until, in a moment of abrupt thematic reversal, its own Augustinian vision of the world becomes an object of poetic attack. The beginning of this movement may be felt in a vaguely deistical exercise like *The Friend*, Richard Savage's epistle to Aaron Hill, as it celebrates a Creator whose boundless love, "to no *one*, no *sect*, no *clime* confin'd," transcends all such divisions and "embraces all *mankind*." The tendency to dissolve all distinctions between saint and sinner, regenerate and unregenerate, may then be felt in a poem such as Soame Jenyns's epistolary *Essay on Virtue*, which admonishes its audience not to imagine God as "Inflicting endless pains for transient crimes, / And favoring sects or nations, men or times," or in more extreme terms in John

Gilbert Cooper's impassioned denunciation of "the worse than atheist, the fond fool" who is led

> To seek the cause of universal good,
> And source of beauty in the demon's cave,
> And, shudd'ring, fancies he at distance hears
> The howls of ghosts, created to endure
> Eternal torments. Let this impious wretch
> Look round this fair creation.

This moment in *The Power of Harmony* may be taken as registering the triumph of Shaftesburian benevolism simultaneously over the Augustan satiric impulse and those theories of egoism or self-interest on which the Augustan poets had concentrated their attack. For what emerges at such moments is that curious sense in which social theorists like Hobbes and Mandeville and satirists like Pope and Swift had all along shared at the deep level an identical set of assumptions about human nature, and were to prove equally vulnerable to assault from the unexpected quarter of a new Pelagian or benevolist vision of the universe. Thus, although we might have expected a writer such as Pope to react, once he had seen which way things were tending, with a certain asperity to the growing influence of Shaftesburian doctrine—"Mr. Pope told me," Warburton wrote Bishop Hurd in 1750, "that, to his knowledge, the Characteristics had done more harm to revealed religion in England than all the works of infidelity put together" (27)—it also comes as small surprise to find Mandeville, sounding for all the world like a disgruntled Augustinian theologian, muttering about "a late author . . . now much read by men of sense," who "imagines that men without any trouble or violence upon themselves may be naturally virtuous. He seems to require and expect goodness in his species, as we do a sweet taste in grapes and china oranges" (1.323).

Yet the rising tide of benevolist influence was by midcentury nearly to have swept away the last remnants of Augustinian orthodoxy. The explanation of its triumph no doubt has to do, as Stephen Cox has persuasively argued, with the manner in which the new theories of moral sympathy worked to counter the solipsistic tendencies of eighteenth-century empiricism, abandoning the world of physical objects to be dissolved into mere mental impressions, and bringing to the foreground instead a social and moral world in which the primary objects of perception were not tables and chairs but the rightness and wrongness of human actions.[7] This then is a world so visibly held together by bonds of moral sympathy, and one in which sympathy operates as so obvious a principle of moral intelligibility,[8] that solipsism becomes an empty threat. All this in turn assumes, at a more essential level, the exaltation of the temporal world, of human beings dwelling within a social present, that would lend so powerful an impetus to bourgeois progressivism. Thus, for instance, Akenside as poetic voice of the new benevolism:

> Say, why was man so eminently rais'd
> Amid the vast Creation; . . .
> To chase each partial purpose from his breast;
> And through the mists of passion and of sense,
> And through the tossing tide of chance and pain,
> To hold his course unfaltering, while the voice
> Of truth and virtue, up the steep ascent
> Of nature, calls him to his high reward,
> The applauding smile of Heaven.

This raising of man and the temporal world to a new eminence amid the vast creation registers the deeper ideological transformation through which benevolist ethical theory was even now being translated into an emergent bourgeois progressivism, its most important symptom being a dramatic shift in public attitudes toward trade and commerce. As a general tendency in eighteenth-century thought, there had always existed that benign vision of commerce that Cecil Moore associated many years ago with the literary tradition he called Whig panegyric. This is the tradition represented in prose by Defoe's *Complete English Tradesman* or Addison's celebratory *Spectator* essay on the Royal Exchange and in poetry by Dyer's *Fleece* or Glover's *London* or, somewhat later, Mickle's translation of *The Lusiad* as an "epic of commerce" offered to English readers as a mirror of their own rising greatness as a commercial nation. Yet within this tradition of Whig panegyric the decisive moment of ideological convergence occurs when such notions meet and blend with benevolist ethical theory. For it is the ruling idea of innate human virtue—"O fair benevolence of generous minds!" as Akenside would sing in *The Pleasures of Imagination*, "O man by Nature form'd for all mankind!"—that ultimately transmutes the optimistic mercantilism of Addison or Defoe into a vision of, as Richard Payne Knight will call it in *The Progress of Civil Society*,[9] "the soft intercourse of commerce," an ideology of national expansion assuming the new money or credit society as a wholly natural state of affairs.

The major contribution of benevolist ethical theory to an emergent progressivism was precisely that it permitted a naturalization of those invisible market forces that seemed able, as in the first intoxication of the new joint-stock companies, to conjure an unimaginable prosperity out of thin air, or equally able, as in the South Sea crash, to plunge an entire society into ruin and despair. For the symbolic power of Augustan satire had, as we have seen, derived from its uneasy sense that the energies of a developing market economy were somehow demonic, blind and impersonal and yet moving relentlessly toward some end unfathomable by human minds—capitalism, in short, in just that demonic aspect that would lend such rhetorical potency to Marx's arguments in the nineteenth century, and give substance to the ruminations of such thinkers as Benjamin and Adorno in the twentieth. Nor, as we have seen in Defoe's half-mystified description of credit as "the essential shadow of something that is not"—the same theme occurs in Addison's allegory of "Publick Credit" as a fainting virgin in *The Spectator* no. 3—was this blind or demonic aspect of the new money society lost even on the Whig panegyricists.[10]

At the same time, Augustanism and Country ideology were always paradoxically aware that the credit arrangements demanded by an advanced commercial economy entail, in order to succeed, something very like virtue or innate benevolence, the simple act of social faith involved in believing that a meaningless piece of paper will be honored at some future moment in an exchange for real goods, or in delivering wares today that will be paid for only a week or a month from now, and in a Hobbesian world would never be paid for at all. This is the benign side of commerce glimpsed by Davenant, that otherwise tireless castigator of the new money society, when he sees that "no trading nation ever did subsist, and carry on its business by real stock; that trust and confidence in each other, are as necessary to link and hold a people together, as obedience, love, friendship, or the intercourse of speech."[11] The vision of benign commerce involved in this had long been drawn on by Whig panegyric in its portrayal of trade as a peaceful alternative to war, a theme briefly taken over by Pope at a crucial moment in *Windsor Forest*, but only in a cultural climate transformed by benevolist thought would it emerge as the central vision of bourgeois progressivism.

This is the context in which Shaftesbury, writing about the innate virtue of humankind with an altogether different purpose in mind, may be said to have invented the ideology of a credit society. Within the sphere of the verse epistle, this movement is felt as an alteration in poetic cosmology, the expansion of the new benevolist outlook from a mere theory of the human world to a vision of the universe as a whole. As an interior scene, the benevolist cosmos was already coming into existence during the Augustan period in Thomson's long and intricate revision of *The Seasons*, from which it would emerge as that harmonious universe born in equal measure of Shaftesburian ethical theory and Newtonian celestial mechanics. Yet the deeper ideological transformation involved may be seen in the degree to which, even as Newton would become in this process a sort of moral philosopher, the moral philosophers became Newtons of the moral world. Thus we encounter Cudworth, for instance, in James Cawthorn's ethical epistle *The Vanity of Human Enjoyments* as a philosopher whose spirit flew "through each vast empire of th'ideal world," and Shaftesbury's *Characteristics*, in William Melmoth's *Of Active and Retired Life*, as the

Principia of moral psychology: "Not orbs he weighs, but marks, with happier skill, / The scope of actions and the poise of will, / In fair proportion here describ'd we trace / Each mental beauty, and each moral grace." When that mental beauty is projected back out onto the Newtonian universe we have the benevolist cosmos as such, the celestial scene gazed upon by watchers of the night sky in *Studley Park*, John Langhorne's epistle to his reverend friend Mr. Farrar,

> Who nobly dare with philosophic eye,
> Through full creation's bounded orbs to fly:
> Pleased, in their well-form'd systems still to find
> The matchless wisdom of th' immortal mind.
> Still charm'd, in Nature's various plan, to trace
> His boundless love and all-supporting grace.

The benevolist universe visible throughout *The Seasons* or *The Pleasures of Imagination* or *The Power of Harmony* provides the generalized poetic setting into which will be gradually absorbed the Augustan landscape left vacant at the death of Pope, yielding an interior scene in which the controlling opposition between country and city is dissolved and Twickenham and the memory of Pope himself linger merely as figments of an emergent bourgeois mythology. The process had begun during Pope's own lifetime, during which the creation by Augustan poetry of an abstract audience excluded by Augustan premises had been felt mainly as a power of unwanted attraction, a flocking to the Augustan standard of the very readers who were supposed to have been targets of the satire. The anomalous success of Pope among such readers occasions one of the more unkind moments in Welsted's *One Epistle to Mr. Pope*: "Blest coupleteer! ... / See, lisping toilets grace thy *Dunciad*'s cause, / ... While powder'd wits, and lac'd cabals rehearse / Thy bawdy cento, and thy bead-roll verse." Yet this is merely an annoyance in comparison to the growing swarm of lesser poets who, all during the last period of Pope's career, set up as Augustan satirists themselves, blasting Dulness and dunces and singing endless paeans to Pope in his Twickenham bower. Thus, for instance, the tailor's son Paul Whitehead, offering in *The State Dunces* his own aid in the battle against the corruption of the times:

> Yet vain, O Pope! is all thy sharpest rage,
> Still starv'ling Dunces persecute the age;
> Faithful to folly, or enrag'd with spite,
> Still tasteless Timons build, and Tibbalds write;
> Still Welsted tunes his beer-inspired lays,
> And Ralph, in meter, howls forth Stanhope's praise;
> Ah! hapless victim to the poet's flame,
> While his eulogiums crucify thy fame.

Such moments mark the precise instant at which the cultural myth created by Pope around Twickenham and his circle of friends begins to pass out of his own control, becoming the public property of an audience clamorously eager to separate itself from the mere vulgar populace through an embrace of Augustan values. Though few of the lesser poets who arose to address this audience were as accomplished as Whitehead—he appears in *Candour*, one of those antisatire satires of the Walpole era that belabor Pope with his unwanted imitators, as "that ape of thy inimitable wit"— they were numerous enough by the last years of Pope's life almost to create the illusion of having overwhelmed Augustanism as such, drowning the voice of genuine moral opposition to Walpole in a merely modish Oppositional din. The crowning episode, perhaps, is James Miller's imaginary dialogue between Pope and Walpole, appearing in 1740 with the title *Are These Things So? The Previous Question, from an Englishman in his Grotto, to a Great Man at Court.*[12] In Miller's poem, printed and widely discussed at a time when Pope had yet four years to live, the cultural myth of Pope-at-Twickenham asserts something very like a complete autonomy.

Miller's poem marks as well the moment at which the audience created by Augustan satire assumes its own autonomy, so secure now in its claim to a properly "Augustan" sensibility that in *The Great Man's Answer*, another poem published by Miller in the same year, an imaginary Walpole is allowed to say the unsayable, denouncing the literary Opposition—the "Patriot tribe," as he calls them—as merely the old mob or *vulgus* under a new name: "Whom minister, nor kings, nor gods can please, / Whose rage my ruin only can appease; / That motley crew, the scum of every sect, / Who'd fain destroy, because they can't direct." This is then the audience that, with Walpole's actual fall from power and the death of Pope a few short years later, will by midcentury have relocated itself within the benevolist universe of the Shaftesburian poets of nature and nature's God, having discovered an alternative claim to aristocratic sensibility in a new world of moral sympathy and ethical sentiment. It is the new voice of benevolist sensibility looking back on a vanished Augustanism that one hears in William Thompson's elegiac *On Mr. Pope's Works*: "Man not alone hath end: in measur'd time, / (So Heav'n has will'd) together with their snows / The everlasting hills shall melt away / . . . Peace then, my soul, nor grieve that Pope is dead."

Within the midcentury poetic landscape, the last lingering memory of Augustanism will be preserved in Twickenham as it survives into a new age, the symbol now not of that heroic resistance to a bleak modernity mounted by Pope and Swift and Gay and Bolingbroke but rather of the "Augustan" attitudes absorbed by an audience conjured into being by their writing. The true end of Augustan satire is not Pope's disillusioned withdrawal from public controversy at the end of the *Epilogue to the Satires*, but an otherwise unremarkable episode that occurs ten years after his death when Paul Whitehead, having now come into a modest fortune, is able to purchase a small estate at Twickenham. The meaning of the episode lies precisely in Whitehead's sense, as he complacently gazes out over a scene in which "Thames, made immortal by her Denham's strains, / Mean'dring glides through Twick'nam's flow'ry plains," that he has purchased not simply a piece of ground but a place inside a literary or poetic landscape, a belated membership in the otium circle once surrounding Pope in his garden and his grotto.

Yet this might be merely innocent presumption, a well-intentioned act of homage to a poet and a literary moment whose passing has left the world a diminished place. The inglorious epitaph of Augustan satire thus comes to be written when Whitehead, in a moment of sublime self-assurance donning the mantle of Pope, proceeds to proclaim himself the new satirist of Twickenham: "Safe, in the harbor of my Twick'nam bower, / From all the wrecks of state, or storms of power; / . . . Whilst here with vice a bloodless war I wage, / Or lash the follies of a trifling age." The tableau of Whitehead strutting about in the role of satirist-physician "whose practice," as he says, "is the mind's disease," is the poignant last emblem of the world that has come into being after the Augustan collapse, a world in which Twickenham is doomed in the end to dwindle to this, the spectacle of Augustan satire persisting for a time as an empty shadow show in a society in which modernity has triumphed, and in which epistolary audience has become an ascendant bourgeoisie honoring the memory of Augustanism only by way of maintaining, now as a matter of mere blind cultural reflex, its own claims to patrician sensibility.

FOUR

THE COMMONWEALTH OF LETTERS

EPISTOLARY VERSE after the death of Pope is a body of poetry sustained by the memory of an Augustanism it knows to have collapsed, a commonwealth of letters in the sense that epistolarity has become in verse the last sanctuary of those scattered souls who persist in gazing backward toward an otherwise vanished world of Augustan values. The verse epistle in this way survives the implosion of Augustan satire, which by the later eighteenth century is already understood to have fallen victim to an internal paradox, the impossibility of the claim that satire exists to reform society. At the beginning of the century, as Stuart Tave and Peter Elkin have shown, this claim gained a special prominence as the Augustan satirist's main line of defense against contemporary charges of malevolence or ill nature, but the same movement toward an inevitable implosion haunts any satiric mode that begins by distinguishing itself from mere raillery. For satire that succeeded in reforming its society would on its own terms have brought about a world in which, men and women being virtuous now, hypocrisy and venality having been banished, satire would no longer be necessary. Satire that expends its energies on trying to bring about such a change and yet leaves the world untouched, on the other hand, will have done nothing more than demonstrate its own powerlessness—Auden's "poetry makes nothing happen"—and at the same time its own superfluousness.

The possibility of a world so redeemed from vice and folly that satire would no longer serve any honorable purpose constitutes a subordinate theme in Augustan satire, where, however, it usually appears merely as an ironic measure of the actual corruption of the times. This is the possibility at which Dryden glances, for instance, at a jocular moment in his epistle to Henry Higden, a lawyer who has translated Juvenal; "if all your tribe," proclaims Dryden, were "led by the rare example you begun, / Clients would fail, and lawyers be undone." In a more broadly parodic key, the same point lies behind the announcement of Swift's Grub Street narrator in *A Tale of a Tub* that, "entirely satisfied" as he is "with the whole present procedure of human things," he is presently "preparing materials toward *A Panegyrick upon the World*" (53), and Swift's rage at what he took to be an actual example of a similarly vacuous optimism was no doubt what motivated his attack on Edward Young's *The Universal Passion*: "If there be truth in what you sing, / Such godlike virtues in the king, / A minister so filled with zeal, / . . . If this be truth, as you attest, / What land was ever half so blest?"

The bleaker possibility that satire is wholly powerless to change the world, on the other hand, arises only in that climactic moment when the Augustan collapse has begun to seem imminent. "To curb the time, can poets hope?" muses Isaac Hawkins Browne: "Peter but sneers, though lash'd by Pope."[1] The same specter of satiric impotence was to be gleefully summoned, during the years of Pope's last satires, by Court writers aiming to discomfit the literary opposition to Walpole; "if solemn songs could exorcise the times," intones the anonymous author of an antisatiric attack *On the Abuse of Wit and Eloquence*, "And crush the growth of pestilential crimes, / 'Twere godlike then to chasten." But solemn songs can do no such thing, leaving inescapable the conclusion that, as Joseph Warton will put it when developing the same theme in his *Essay on Pope*, satires such as Pope's Horatian imitations proceeded merely from "petulance, party-spirit, and self-importance." For Pope, "if he had possessed a thousand times more genius and ability than he actually enjoyed, could not alter or amend the manners of a rich and commercial and, consequently of a luxurious and dissipated nation" (2.426).

At the same time, an uneasy awareness that satire might very well be powerless to alter the world haunted the Augustan enterprise from the outset: Horace had written, after all, and yet Caligula and Nero and Domitian had followed nonetheless, and a consciousness of this is, among other things, what Pope means to announce in calling the satires of his last period imitations of Horace. Despite Dryden's influential direct comparison of Horatian and Juvenalian satire, the two were always understood in the eighteenth century as belonging to wholly different stages of the historical cycle that had carried Rome upward to greatness and then plunged her, in the usual downward spiral of luxury and corruption, toward an inevitable decline. Thus, for instance, Addison on Horace and Juvenal in his youthful dissertation on Roman poetry: "The one was conversant in the most perfectly polite court of Augustus; the other lived in the dregs of Domitian's time; and therefore both these poets accommodated their writings to the manners of the different ages they lived in: for Horace is entirely upon the ludicrous . . . but Juvenal lashes the grossest crimes prevalent in his time, and complains of enormities which one would be ashamed to mention" (39–41).

The Horatian mode of satire belongs, on this view, precisely to that middle state in which the poet gazes backward to the vanished virtue of a lost Republic and forward to some dark imagined moment of tyranny and total corruption. This is satire whose aim of reforming the world derives from its own acute sense of being precariously poised between opposing moral dispensations, which in the Augustan satire of the eighteenth century is always taken to correspond to the theological categories of an Augustinian vision that sees human existence as a middle state between virtue and corruption, between a lost innocence and the perennial danger of a plunge into total depravity and despair.[2] The Juvenalian mode, on the other hand, is satire that has utterly abandoned the project of reforming the world, the last angry voice of a virtue nearly drowned by the rising tide of public corruption. This is the Juvenalian strain as heard in Brown's *Essay on Satire*:

> When rank Adultery on the genial bed
> Hot from Cocytus rears her baleful head:
> When private faith and public trust are sold,
> And traitors barter liberty for gold: . . .
> Then flash her lightnings, and her thunders fly;
> Wide and more wide her flaming bolts are hurl'd,
> Till all her wrath involves a guilty world.

The crucial importance of the Juvenalian prelude to the Augustan implosion is precisely that it signaled to the English society addressed by satire its fatal slippage from the Augustan middle state and into a stage of irreversible decline. The world ushered in by the Augustan collapse will thus be one in which the hope of a redemptive *ricorso* is forever at an end. The post-Augustan landscape will be from one perspective what we glimpse in that strain of elegiac Augustanism in Cowper and Goldsmith—what makes Auburn, as Roger Lonsdale has said in an exemplary analysis of *The Deserted Village*, represent "not merely the rural virtues which avarice destroys, but the kind of poetry which is rooted in them and which is similarly vulnerable in a commercial society"[3]—and from an opposing but complementary perspective the "Hobbesian world" that Ronald Hatch isolates (288) in Crabbe's descriptions of later-eighteenth-century English village life:

> So shall the man of power and pleasure see
> In his own slave as vile a wretch as he;
> In his luxurious lord the servant find
> His own low pleasures and degenerate mind:
> And each in all the kindred vices trace
> Of a poor, blind, bewildered, erring race;
> Who, a short time in varied fortune past,
> Die, and are equal in the dust at last.

Quite as much as the elegiac Augustanism of Goldsmith, that is to say, the social realism of Crabbe draws in direct terms on Augustanism's own last despairing vision of an England sinking rapidly into irreversible decline. Two major categories of post-Augustan poetry are determined by whether such poetry does or does not accept the verdict of an inexorable decline, giving us poems that, like *The Deserted Village* or *The Village* or *The Task*, assume as their moral background an England sinking ever further into luxury and corruption, and poems that on the contrary assume that, there having survived the death of Pope and the fall of Walpole a large body of souls redemptively possessed of Augustan taste and sensibility, the world has after all escaped falling into moral decline.

The poetry of Churchill, which belongs to the first of these categories, has a special status there as an outraged assault on what it represents as the spurious Augustanism of the opposing category, a furious attempt to strip away and expose as mere bourgeois complacency the pretensions of a new social class to Augustan moral sensibility. Churchill's satire may be read as the belated rage of Augustanism at its own powerlessness to alter the world, and then as a redoubled rage that in the wake of the Augustan collapse there has arisen a false society whose crowning hypocrisy is that it cloaks its vulgarity and avarice in a morality it imagines to be Augustan. The Juvenalian strain in Churchill's poetry is in this context especially important as signaling his own unreserved acceptance of the Augustan verdict of irreversible decline. The satirist now really is someone raising a last lonely voice of protest while, as Churchill says in the *Epistle to Hogarth*, "nobles act, without one touch of shame, / What men of humble rank would blush to name; / . . . Whilst Bubbles of Distinction waste in play / The hours of rest, and blunder through the day, / . . . Whilst peers are agents made, and agents peers."

This is the background against which Churchill seemed, to those who admired him, to have discovered a mysterious source of satiric energy, to have somehow recovered the voice of Augustan probity in the midst of the diminishment that had followed the Augustan collapse: "these leaden times," as his friend Robert Lloyd puts it, "this idle age" (*Epistle to C. Churchill*). "Is there a man," asks Lloyd rhetorically in another epistle that is at once to Churchill and about him, "whose genius strong, / Rolls like a rapid stream along? / Whose Muse, long hid in cheerless night, / Pours on us like a flood of light?" (*The Poet*). To those perturbed by Churchill's meteoric rise, of course, this was merely a bankrupt language of mutual admiration, the transparent attempt of the Churchill-Lloyd-Colman coterie to set themselves up as the Scriblerians of a shrunken age. Yet during the brief moment of his ascendancy, Churchill really did seem to contemporaries an unlooked-for genius pouring forth a torrent of powerful satire, and what gave him a magic immunity from moral censure was the brilliant inversion of Augustan satiric values through which he preemptively exposed would-be detractors as hypocritical pretenders to Augustan sensibility.

The great early example of this satiric inversion is *Night*, an epistle to Lloyd throughout which Churchill flirts daringly with an open admission of his own Cyrenaic hedonism, that ethic of wenching and bibbing and nocturnal rampaging that makes him more nearly the brother of the Restoration rake-poets than of anyone in Pope's circle at Twickenham. Yet Churchill's triumph in the poem is to make the daylight world, the ordinary noonday scene of sober enterprise and orthodox morality, a metaphor in its entirety for sham and hypocrisy.[4] This is the reversal through which the hours of night or darkness, laying bare as they do the truth about the world of business and ambition, provide the privileged vantage point of a fierce satiric honesty, allowing Churchill to speak even from among his cups and cards and idle friends in the thunderous tones of the Augustan satirist:

> Stript of her gaudy plumes and vain disguise,
> See where Ambition mean and loathsome lies; . . .
> Through a false medium things are shown by day,
> Pomp, wealth, and titles, judgment lead astray.
> How many from appearance borrow state,
> Whom Night disdains to number with the great!

This is in itself a daring enough inversion, extending to any show of virtue whatsoever the normal Augustan penetration of appearances—"The griping wretch, whose av'rice robs the town, / To gain his point a holy look puts on," Samuel Boyse had said, uttering what in his time and Pope's was a satiric commonplace—and then leaving by default to such scapegrace figures as Lloyd and Churchill any claim to genuine honesty. Yet what earned Churchill his season of poetic freedom was that he had, as though in a moment of inspired penetration, known to aim his satire directly at a target that really did exist, an emergent bourgeoisie busily doing everything in its power to deny the real source of its new dominance in that money or credit society so despised by the Augustan satirists. The target of such poems as *Night* thus becomes the bourgeoisie with its pretensions to gentility stripped away—"Your man of habit, who's wound up / To eat and drink, and dine and sup," as Lloyd puts his own version of the theme, ". . . Who lives by rule, and ne'er outgoes it; / Moves like a clock, and hardly knows it" (*The Poet*)—and this in turn is what locates such poetry, for all its blithe reversal of ethical orthodoxy, within the legitimate tradition of literary Augustanism.

If Churchill's satire may be taken to complete the Augustan critique of emergent capitalism, it is precisely because he has lived to see the upstart class so detested by Bolingbroke and Pope move to the center of the historical stage, and has an even more acute sense than the Augustan writers—as in his scathing description of the new bourgeoisie as "slaves to business, bodies without soul" (*Night*)—of a mankind being turned into the mere puppets of an underlying system of economic arrangements. Yet the great consequence of the Augustan collapse is that there no longer exists any moral alternative to this state of affairs, no counterpart to the otium ideal of Twickenham or the lingering of traditional values in the country houses of Pope's noble friends, which is why Churchill is doomed to write satire in a world providing no center of satiric values. This is the context in which, as so many modern readers have remarked, the dominant note of Churchill's poetry becomes an anxious moral egoism:

> Let the World talk, my friend; that World we know
> Which calls us guilty, cannot make us so. . . .
> In spite of dullness, and in spite of wit,
> If to thyself thou canst thyself acquit,
> Rather stand up assur'd with conscious pride
> Alone, than err with millions on thy side.[5]
>
> (*Night*)

Churchill's satiric solipsism consists in just this note of beleaguered egoism, the rage of a soul Augustan in its temper and yet condemned to dwell in a world utterly bereft of Augustan values. This is the context in which Churchill's frequent assertions of superior sensibility amount only to an unconscious admission that he is living in the dream-world of a remembered Augustanism, permitted a genuine and limited contact with his own actual society only when he attacks an emergent bourgeoisie in its name.[6] The void or ideological vacuum in which Churchill hears nothing but the resonating echo of his own satiric voice becomes, as Eric Rothstein has said (125), the setting in which he is drawn toward a self-destructive hedonism that, like that of the Restoration rakes who were in this his true poetic forebears, is only the outward expression of an inward sense of meaninglessness. At its most innocent, this is the note of Cyrenaic heedlessness that one hears in such poems as *The Ghost*—"Be my employment here on earth / To give a lib'ral scope to mirth, / Life's barren vale with flow'rs t'adorn, / And pluck a rose from ev'ry thorn"—but in the background one always senses the thinly veiled nihilism at which Churchill hints even in an early poem like *Night*, the rage and bafflement of a soul of Augustan sensitivities doomed to linger on in leaden times: "Then in Oblivion's grateful cup I drown / . . . the proud affected state / Of upstart knaves grown rich, and fools grown great."

Within Churchill's own world only his friend Lloyd understood the desperation underlying such moments of utterance—"A rake!" cries Lloyd. "Alas! how many wear / The brow of mirth, with heart of care! / The desperate wretch reflection flies, / . . . And runs to Folly for relief" (*The Poet*)—and Lloyd, by his own choice, was heard merely as a lesser echo of Churchill. In the end, it was the note of hedonistic amorality in his poetry that was to bring Churchill to ruin, for the same Augustanism that he had managed for a triumphant instant to turn against the emergent bourgeoisie would in the longer run conclusively undermine his every pretension to speak in an Augustan voice. "Parts but expose those men who virtue quit," Edward Young had said in an epistle written to Pope at the moment of high Augustanism, looking back on the Restoration but seeming too uncannily to anticipate Churchill's later rise, "A fallen angel is a fallen wit." This is the same judgment one sees taking shape even during the short years of Churchill's ascendancy—"These men the sons of ribaldry and shame," snorted Thomas Vaughn in *The Retort*, pronouncing summarily on the Churchill-Lloyd coterie—and it would, after his premature death, become the settled wisdom of a bourgeois world no longer compelled to deal with his unsettling voice.

Like the elegiac ruminations of Goldsmith, Churchill's poetry in one sense represents a terminal point within literary Augustanism, particularly as his mode of satire gave ghostly voice to the solipsism banished earlier by Dryden and Pope and Swift in the name of a return to organic or traditional society. Yet in another sense, one signaled by Churchill's angry mutterings about "upstart knaves grown rich" as these echo the earlier detestation of such writers as Davenant and Bolingbroke of the "monied upstarts" arisen within a new money or credit society, the satirist of *Night* and the *Epistle to Hogarth* shows himself to be at the center of the most profound ideological shift to emerge from the Augustan collapse, a symbolic movement through which the idealized aristocracy of Dryden and Pope was seen to have given way permanently to a body of upstart plutocrats having bought their way into the peerage during the wholesale corruption of the Walpole years. This is specifically the usurping aristocracy Churchill has in mind whenever he is moved to sound a note of patriot alarm: "Let not a mob of tyrants seize the helm / Nor titled upstarts league to rob the realm, / Let not, whatever other ills assail, / A damned ARISTOCRACY prevail" (*The Farewell*).

The reason that such sentiments on Churchill's part have never seemed puzzling is that his association with Wilkes has always been so readily presumed to explain them. This is the Churchill, in short, of the *North Briton* and *The Prophecy of Famine* and the torchlight parades for Wilkes and Liberty. And the antiaristocratical sentiment of that tumultuous midcentury moment, it was similarly supposed until comparatively recently, was an episode in a story in which a rising tide of bourgeois progressivism sweeps away the last remnants of both feudal social arrangements and their hegemonic ideology. Within the sphere of eighteenth-century poetry, this would then be a movement that becomes visible about the time Defoe writes *The True-Born Englishman* to challenge, as he says, the "vanity of those who talk of their antiquity, and value themselves upon their pedigree, their ancient families" (52), and then culminates at the end of the century in something like Helen Maria Williams's lyrical celebration, in an epistle to her friend Dr. Moore, of the abolition of aristocratic privilege by revolutionary France: "Thy happy peasant, now no more a slave, / Forbad to taste one good that nature gave, . . . / Oppression's cruel hand shall dare no more / To seize its tribute from his scanty store."

The puzzle arises, then, only when we have seen that Churchill's poetry lies within the tradition of literary Augustanism, which with its idealized nobility and gentry was supposed to belong precisely to that feudal ideology now so wholly swept away. And the solution, without which much else in midcentury and later-eighteenth-century poetry remains incoherent or inexplicable as well, is that violent antiaristocratic sentiments like those of Churchill are not a reaction against Country ideology and literary Augustanism but their logical conclusion, an altogether predictable consequence of the verdict that England has entered into an irreversible decline, that English politics have been irredeemably permeated by cynicism and corruption, and that the class of speculators and stockjobbers conjured up by William of Orange and then nurtured by the bribery and venality of the Walpole years has now materialized as the "titled upstarts" whom Churchill curses under the name of a "damned ARISTOCRACY,"[7] a "mob of Tyrants," a tremendous final insult to English probity even in this shrunken age of avarice and lies.

As a polemical tradition within Country ideology, however, this neo-Harringtonian anguish that power is passing into the hands of the new Whig class so savagely satirized by Davenant had always been balanced by an Augustan sense of the genuine or hereditary aristocracy as a class whose highest interests were identical with those of the nation as a whole, giving us the context in which the demand for a return to traditional society was always simultaneously a plea for an England once again dwelling safely within an ideology of aristocratic selflessness. Thus, for instance, the "great disturbers" of Granville's verses to Elizabeth Higgons—seekers of power "who in endless noise, / In blood and rapine seek unnatural joys"— though they are the immediate ancestors of Churchill's "mob of tyrants," are always seen in inglorious contrast to Granville's own genuine nobility, and thus the complaint of a Country tract like Granville's *A Letter from a Noble-Man Abroad, to his Friend in England* (1722) that "we have lived to see the first honors of the peerage bestowed to dignify prostitution" (qtd. in Erskine-Hill, "The Political Poet" 144) is really a plea for England to return to the ancient sources of her civic virtue while there is yet time and moral will sufficient to stem the rising tide of corruption and venality.

In the same way, Bolingbroke's cry in the *Letters on the Study and Use of History* that "the state is become, under ancient and known forms, a new and undefinable monster," chief among these monstrosities being "a senate of nobles without aristocratic independency" (*Works* 2.333), lies at the heart of that sense of oppositional dismay that saw in Walpole only the local representative of an even more monstrous modern corruption. The real enemy is modernity itself, the invisible forces of a new money society eating away at the foundations of English civic virtue, and of these the "titled upstarts" of a new plutocracy are as ominous an emanation as Walpole. For all Fielding's complicated political allegiances, for instance, it is just this same note of generalized oppositional alarm that one hears in his *Essay on Conversation*: "Men are superior to each other in this our country by title, by birth, by rank in profession, and by age; very little, if any, being to be allowed to fortune. . . . Mankind never appear to me in a more despicable light than when I see them, by a simple as well as a mean servility, voluntarily concurring in the adoration of riches" (1.133).

After the Augustan collapse, a major ideological shift occurs precisely because an older ideal of aristocratic honor has vanished along with Augustanism, leaving no moral counterweight to a usurping plutocracy whose gold has brought into its unholy power the very forms and institutions of England's ancient polity. This is the context in which Goldsmith's elegiac Augustanism always turns on a hatred of what he called "vile aristocracy,"[8] which is, for all the otherwise enormous differences between the two poets, identical with Churchill's "damned ARISTOCRACY." Even the anti-aristocratic radicalism of such poems as Peter Pindar's end-of-century epistle to the Earl of Lonsdale must be seen ultimately to originate in the midcentury ideological shift through which the demonic energies of an emergent capitalism are increasingly projected onto a plutocracy that has survived Walpole as the visible emblem of a new social and economic order. Swift's image of Walpole as a nightmarish beast with "all-devouring maw" attains something like its logical culmination in Pindar's bitter portrayal of Lonsdale as oppressor of the Cumberland mineworkers who have had the temerity to ask a redress of their grievances:

> O wake thy plagues, and break the shameful truce!
> Unmuzzle Vengeance: let the blood-hound loose,
> To bid Humanity, pale Fool, adieu,
> And flesh his hunger on the coal-black crew.—
> *Thus* shall the Lowther name again be great,
> Men tremble at the sound, and children sweat.

The notion that Wolcot is at such moments sustaining the tradition of Augustan satire by writing in couplet verse contains an important truth. For the teeming world of stockjobbers and corrupt politicians symbolized by Walpole could be described in various satiric registers, as Gay showed in *The Beggar's Opera* and Swift in doggerel tetrameter verse, but only in the couplet verse of a poet like Pope, enacting an ideal of decorum associated with patrician speech, could the satire simultaneously enunciate an otherwise unspoken moral demand for return to the vanished society associated with aristocratic virtue. This is the situation in which the values of aristocratic honor pass over into the satiric couplet itself: as Dryden's kinsman John Driden or the Bolingbroke of Pope's *Essay on Man* had been symbolic presences within Augustan satire, the representatives of an imperiled ideal of organic community surviving into the modern age, so does the couplet verse of Augustan satire subsequently become for poets such as Churchill and Wolcot a last means of invoking the memory of that same vanished world.

The precise moment at which there begins to dawn on post-Augustan consciousness an awareness that the Walpole-world has not ended with Walpole is memorialized in Mark Akenside's splendidly angry *Epistle to Curio*, written after the fall of Walpole's government as an attack on Pulteney for having deserted the Country party in exchange, as was bitterly said at the time, for power and a peerage.[9] In Akenside's *Epistle*, Curio-Pulteney is imagined as joining a train of "mighty foes of liberty" who throughout history have tyrannized over those aspiring to be free:

> There, black with frowns, relentless Time awaits,
> And goads their footsteps to the guilty gates: . . .
> And still his hands despoil them on the road
> Of each vain wreath, by lying bards bestow'd,
> Break their proud marbles, crush their festal cars,
> And rend the lawless trophies of their wars.

As with Churchill's *Epistle to Hogarth* or Pindar's epistle to Lonsdale, this is epistolarity as an invocation of Augustan values, a last angry summoning against the venal oligarchy of a degraded age the memory of that idealized nobility and gentry so visible in the verse of Dryden and Pope. Yet the symbolic value of the *Epistle to Curio* lies as well in its having been written by Akenside, elsewhere the very voice of the midcentury poetic revival in his renunciation of Augustan couplet verse for the alternative forms—"blank verse, and Pindaric odes, choruses . . . alliterative care, and happy negligence," as Goldsmith would impatiently say in his introduction to *The Traveller* (4.246–47)—in the name of which the Wartons and their school would undertake the revival of a "pure poetry" of personal inspiration. The Akenside in whose career *The Epistle to Curio* stands as a lonely anomaly is the poet for whom, in the patriotic odes, the mere thought of liberty provides inspiration: "Nor Theban voice nor Lesbian lyre / From thee, O Muse! do I require; / While my presaging mind, / Conscious of powers she never knew, / Astonish'd grasps at things beyond her view" (*To Liberty*).

In the midcentury moment, with the rise of this poetry of immediate personal inspiration, the couplet verse of Augustan satire comes to be associated more and more with aristocracy as understood not by Dryden and

Pope but by Milton, not as the living symbol of an imperiled organic society but as an oppressive weight on individual liberty. The normal association of blank verse with a radical Miltonic republicanism may be heard even during the Augustan period as the voice of a dissenting poetics—"Tyrannic rhyme," cries Edmund Smith in an elegiac epistle on the death of John Philips—and by the later eighteenth century has become a commonplace, as in William Hayward Roberts's abrupt dismissal of the heroic couplet as an "iron chain" that "cramps reluctant genius." This gives us the logic of the curious episode in which Akenside, as though renouncing a momentary and unthinking allegiance to Augustan values, recomposes the *Epistle to Curio* as an ode:

> In sight old Time, imperious judge, awaits:
>   Above revenge, or fear, or pity, just. . . .
> And still he asks them of the hidden plan
>   Whence every treaty, every war began,
> Evolves their secrets, and their guilt proclaims:
> And still his hands despoil them on the road
> Of each vain wreath by lying bards bestow'd,
>   And crush their trophies huge, and raze their sculptur'd names.

   In the background of Akenside's rewriting of the *Epistle to Curio* may be glimpsed an entire set of assumptions about the situation of poetry at midcentury. Whatever the virtues of the heroic couplet at the moment Pope was composing his Horatian poems, there is no longer any point to invoking the vision of organic society associated with a virtuous nobility and gentry. The England of Jonson's Penshurst and Garth's Claremont is now forever gone—it is, in Laslett's memorable phrase, the world we have lost—and in place of the Bolingbrokes and Bathursts of Pope's poetry there is only the vile aristocracy of titled upstarts we encounter in the bitter lines of Goldsmith and Churchill. Registering an adequate sense of outrage and despair at this situation thus demands abandoning the couplet, with its now-irrelevant associations of ricorso and civic regeneration, and turning instead to that more radical Miltonic strain that had induced Thomson to compose *Liberty* in blank verse even as Pope was writing his Horatian poems in couplets, a tradition associating blank verse and the rhapsodic irregularities of the ode at once with poetic and political freedom.

   To have seen that something very like this logic must have lain behind Akenside's decision to recompose the *Epistle to Curio* as an ode, however, is to uncover an unexpected problem, which is that generations of readers were to agree in seeing in the *Ode to Curio* a false or weakened version of the earlier poem. For Dr. Johnson, this was simply a matter of authorial self-deception. Akenside had no real talent for lyric expression, but he thought he did: "such was his love of lyrics, that having written with great vigor and poignancy his Epistle to Curio, he transformed it afterwards into an ode disgraceful only to its author." Then, a literary generation later, Macaulay, explaining to a friend that the Curio poem he meant to praise is not the ode: "You are confounding the 'Ode to Curio' with the 'Epistle to Curio.' The latter is generally printed at the end of A's works, and is, I think, the best thing that he ever wrote. The 'Ode' is worthless. It is merely an abridgement of the 'Epistle,' executed in the most unskillful way." Or, nearly a hundred years later, Saintsbury, omitting mention of the *Ode* and remarking that the *Epistle* is filled with a "windy, theoretical republicanism," but echoing Johnson and Macaulay in the judgment that "one must go to Juvenal at one end or Victor Hugo at the other to surpass it for what may be called pulse and rhythm of satiric verse, the cool and stiff heroic couplet being for once red-heated and almost molten."[10]

In such responses to the *Ode to Curio* we may begin to glimpse the deeper truth about ideology of form that would to the end escape not only Akenside but all the poets who saw in such alternative forms as blank verse and the ode the possibility of a freedom more suited to paeans to political liberty. For the Augustan couplet, "tyrannic rhyme" as it might have appeared to be from the perspective of a more radical Miltonic tradition, had in its association with patrician speech and aristocratic values always situated both poetry and the poet inside history, always measured the degeneration of present society against an ideal of a nobler past still living in cultural memory. The vigor that Johnson hears in the *Epistle to Curio*, the molten heat that Saintsbury senses in its angry couplets, is an anger ultimately conceivable only in social terms, one always associated, even if only at one remove, with a notion of civic regeneration and of poetry itself as possessing moral agency within society. This is the sense in which Akenside's *Epistle to Curio* had managed to look at once backward to Dryden and Pope and forward to Churchill and Wolcot.

In the notion of Longinian inspiration, on the other hand, including that rhapsodic ideal of liberty invoked in the *Ode to Curio* and Akenside's patriotic odes, eighteenth-century poetry was to discover the paradoxical idea of a politics outside history, the Greco-Roman myth of republican freedom as a private source of poetic inspiration ceasing to have any necessary reference to a moral and ideological struggle actually taking place in English society. The vanished Republic thus becomes a major source of sublimity in the midcentury revival only as it is insensibly transmuted into a disembodied idea of the irrecoverable past, leading both to experimentation with such alternative forms as the Pindaric ode and Spenserian stanza and to the dream of a past outside history, a realm operating not as a moral alternative to but as an escape from an otherwise inescapable modernity. The movement toward dissociation implied when Akenside rewrites the

Epistle as the *Ode to Curio* looks forward not simply to the medievalism of the Wartons and Gray, the endless fascination with ruined cloisters and heroic legends, but to Macpherson's Ossian poems and Chatterton's invention of Rowley.

For all its evanescent political fervor, the *Ode to Curio* is thus ultimately about the absorption of history into the solitary imagination, the movement toward poetic solipsism that will culminate in Collins's obsession with the phantasms of his own isolated consciousness. This is the moment at which the outward or public scene of Augustan poetry begins to give way to another sort of poetic landscape—

> Temples!—and towns!—and towers!—and woods!—
> And hills!—and vales!—and fields!—and floods!—
> Crowding before me, edg'd around
> With naked wilds and barren ground.
>
> (Dyer, *A Country Walk*)

—and in which poets like the Wartons and Gray will begin, even as they redirect their gaze from the present to a remote and solitary past, to haunt secluded groves at twilight, allowing us to glimpse at midcentury the emergence of a world in which poetry will imagine itself to be dwelling in a landscape outside politics.

With the midcentury retreat to a legendary past, the idealized nobility and gentry of Augustan poetry become themselves legendary, the chivalric race memorialized in such works as Hurd's *Letters on Chivalry and Romance*. This is a moment of the highest importance for a sociopoetics of audience in eighteenth-century poetry, for in the symbolic vacuum created by this vanishing of the aristocratic ideal there suddenly emerges the virtuous middle class of post-Augustan cultural mythology, made sensitive by the Augustan poets to the dangers of corruption and guarded by its own modest social station against the temptations of great power or enormous wealth. This is the class that begins increasingly to be addressed by poets and novelists after midcentury, the "middle order of mankind," as Goldsmith would famously put it in Chapter Nineteen of *The Vicar of Wakefield*, in which is "generally to be found all the art, wisdom, and virtues of a society," a sentiment Cowper then treats simply as an established truth in addressing the imaginary audience of his *Tirocinium: or, a Review of Schools*:

> To you, then, tenants of life's middle state,
> Securely plac'd between the small and great,
> Whose character, yet undebauch'd, retains
> Two thirds of all the virtue that remains,
> Who, wise yourselves, desire your sons should learn

Your wisdom and your ways—to you I turn.
Look round you on a world perversely blind.

(lines 807–13)

The virtuous middle order of post-Augustan writing is precisely the anomalous imaginary audience conjured into being by the Augustan verse epistle from Dryden to Pope, a nonaristocratic class nonetheless thoroughly sympathetic to the values of an older society in which the nobility and gentry had been the natural leaders, thoroughly antipathetic to the new social and economic order ushered in by Walpole. Yet as Churchill had so unerringly seen, this is an antipathy very easily read as empty posturing, the attempt of an emergent bourgeoisie to repress its own origins in Walpole's world of credit and speculation. The symbolic gesture through which Goldsmith's middle order of mankind establishes itself as an imaginary audience is thus a repudiation of trade or commerce in its Whig guise and allegiance instead to an opposing tradition of Tory mercantilism in which commerce is a consequence of, rather than an enemy to, civic virtue. So powerfully does this new mythology of commerce develop in the years immediately after Pope's death that, fifteen or twenty years later, it has brought about the virtual extinction of both civic humanism and the cyclical theory of history.

The notion of Whig commerce, as we have long understood, developed as part of an attempt to provide the society of Walpole and the Hanoverian succession with a civic mythology granting honorable status to the mercantile class with which its fortunes were so closely involved. In *The Spectator*, this gives us Addison's paean to the Royal Exchange or the idealized portrait of Sir Andrew Freeport; in Defoe, it gives us innumerable passages in praise of commerce and the merchant class, as in *A Plan of the English Commerce*: "Trade is the wealth of the world; trade makes the difference as to rich or poor, between one nation and another; trade nourishes industry, and industry begets trade; trade disperses the national wealth of the world, and trade raises a new species of wealth, which nature knew nothing of" (68). In poetry, the same strain gives us what Cecil Moore long ago identified as Whig panegyric, as in Ambrose Philips's description of the Thames, in an epistle to James Craggs, as a "commercial stream": "The boast of merchants, and the sailor's theme! / Whose spreading floods unnumber'd ships sustain, / And pour whole towns afloat into the main."

Yet this is just the development of a sustaining ideology that, as Pocock has shown, gets frustrated and ultimately blocked by Augustanism and Country ideology, the classical republican vision identifying the virtue of the nation with its landed class, corruption with the forces of credit and investment and, in the last analysis, commerce itself. This is the situation in which, in the society projected by post-Augustan poetry, we see an emergent bourgeoisie turning to an alternative tradition of Tory mercantilism in which the commercial greatness of England had always been seen as a consequence of her virtue as a nation. This is a tradition the origins of which may already be glimpsed in the seventeenth century in *Coopers Hill* as Denham pauses to praise the Thames personified as a Spirit of Commerce who,

> to boast or to disperse his stores,
> Full of the tributes of his grateful shores,
> Visits the world, and in his flying towers
> Brings home to us, and makes both Indies ours;
> Finds wealth where 'tis, bestows it where it wants,
> Cities in deserts, woods in cities plants;
> So that to us no thing, no place is strange,
> While his fair bosom is the world's exchange.

In *Coopers Hill*, especially in its association with the phenomenon sometimes called parliamentary royalism,[11] we have the origins of both Country ideology and a poetic tradition in which the celebration of commerce will always be made contingent upon some notion of a restored constitutional balance in English society. The balance envisioned by Denham is of course the Restoration itself, the return of the rightful monarch commemorated in such poems as Waller's *To the King*: "Faith, law, and piety (that banished train!) / Justice and truth, with you return again. / The city's trade, the country's easy life, / Once more shall flourish without fraud or strife." This then becomes the immediate background of the most famous example of Tory mercantilism in Augustan poetry, Pope's vision of English commerce in *Windsor Forest*, in which the idea of restored constitutional balance is the return to Stuart rule, after the aberration of William and his Dutch compatriots, in the person of Queen Anne: "Unbounded Thames shall flow for all mankind, / Whole nations enter with each swelling tide, / And seas but join the regions they divide."

This is, as Earl Wasserman pointed out years ago, a vision of trade as well-accorded strife or *concordia discors* (163), but it is concordia discors as it corresponds to the metaphysics of Polybian constitutional balance, the "well-mix'd state" whose myth, in an age of perceived corruption and decline, lay at the center of the ricorso always envisioned in literary Augustanism and Country ideology. This is why, after the death of Anne and the rise of Walpole under the Hanoverian monarchs, praise of commerce in this tradition is always put in the conditional mood: what will happen *if* England arrests her decline and returns to the ancient sources of her civic virtue. Thus Bolingbroke, for instance, picturing England under the rule of his imaginary Patriot King: "concord will appear, . . . peace and prosperity on the happy land; joy sitting in every face, content in every heart: a people unoppressed, undisturbed, unalarmed; ... fleets covering the ocean, bringing home wealth by the returns of industry, carrying assistance or terror abroad by the direction of wisdom" (*Works* 2.429). In the same way, even those paeans to commerce that we have been taught to consider straightforward Whig panegyric are very often drawn into this tradition by an almost subliminal note of moral contingency, as with Thomson's well-known lines in *Summer*:

> Full are thy cities with the sons of art;
> And trade and joy, in every busy street,
> Mingling are heard: even Drudgery himself,
> As at the oar he sweats, or, dusty, hews
> The palace stone, looks gay. Thy crowded ports,
> Where rising masts an endless prospect yield,
> With labor burn, and echo to the shouts
> Of hurried sailor, as he hearty waves
> His last adieu, and loosening every sheet,
> Resigns the spreading vessel to the wind.
>
> (lines 1457–66)

The importance of such sentiments in Thomson is that they carry us toward that moment when, in *Liberty*—"the last stretched blaze of our expiring genius," as Aaron Hill would call it[12]—Thomson would add his voice to that of writers like Bolingbroke and Pope in an urgent plea for a return to the moral origins of English society. This is the moment of *The Craftsman* and the Leicester House opposition gathered around the Prince of Wales, and of Country ideology as that purely political synthesis McKillop has in mind when he observes that Thomson is seeking in *Liberty* "to evade revolution and extremism in terms of some vaguely conceived ideal of inclusion and harmony" (104–5). Yet it is also the moment, of far greater significance to students of eighteenth-century poetry, at which Country ideology, always before having a merely implicit status in literary Augustanism, is brought under a tremendous pressure of contemporary controversy to explicit expression as a myth of civic origins. This is the context in which, as John Chalker remarks in his discussion of Somerville's *The Chase*, an "emphasis upon freedom of trade and the maintenance of Britain's commercial rights blends rather unexpectedly with nostalgic recreation of the past—Whig principles and Tory sentiment" (182).

This is the background against which, after midcentury, a bourgeoisie newly secure in its post-Augustan status as that "middle order of mankind" in which the virtue of the nation reposes will be able to construe England's growing commercial prosperity simply as an unproblematic token of her national greatness. The Augustan memory will linger in ritual admonitions that such greatness may always be endangered by luxury, as when Mickle undertakes his great translation of *The Lusiad* as an "epic of commerce" for English readers and then immediately writes *Almada Hill* to moralize the tale by warning against the perils of overrefinement and dissipation, but this is a poetry for which the last crescendo of literary opposition to Walpole has nonetheless begun to look like a distempered dream. Thus, for instance, Warton's impatient comment on Pope's last satires in the *Essay on Pope*:

> Our country is represented as totally ruined, and overwhelmed with dissipation, depravity, and corruption. Yet this very country, so emasculated and debased by every species of folly and wickedness, in about twenty years afterwards, carried its triumphs over all its enemies, through all the quarters of the world, and astonished the most distant nations with a display of uncommon efforts, abilities, and virtues. So vain and groundless are the prognostications of poets, as well as politicians. (2.426)

The voice is that of the bourgeois ascendancy, not simply of a modern Britain glorying in her bustling commercial energy and growing imperial ambition, but also of a class at long last arrived, after long delay, at the ideological center of its own society. Warton's remarks may be taken to signal the end of a process whose beginnings had been visible nearly half a century before in Steele's plenary vision of the readership of *The Spectator*, which he had envisioned even then as including "all manner of persons, whether scholars, citizens, courtiers, gentlemen of the town or country . . . and under what fortune or circumstance soever . . . and of what trade, occupation, profession, station, country, faction, party, persuasion, quality, age or condition soever, who have ever made thinking a part of their business or diversion" (4.53–54). At the same time, Warton's barely concealed impatience with Pope and his poetry reminds us of the manner in which Augustan values had worked all during this same period to block the development of bourgeois ideology as such, alerting us to the sense in which the *Essay on the Genius and Writings of Pope* is a declaration as much of ideological as of poetic independence.

This is the situation, as we have seen, in which Shaftesburian ethical theory was to provide an alternative claim to aristocratic sensibility, through which patrician status would come to be perceived less in terms of hereditary right than of moral connoisseurship and a cultivated sociability. "True politeness," James Miller would declare in a 1738 epistle to Lord Harrington, is "nothing but well-dress'd humanity: / That fairest offspring of the social mind, / Nurs'd by good nature, by good sense refin'd: . . . / This forms, guides, checks, inspires, does all it can / To make man mild and sociable to man." This is pure Shaftesbury, and as such the mere versification of doctrines long since established in moral philosophy. Their fascination for poetry thus lies in the process of ideological transformation in which they remain vitally at work, making aristocrats not of those nobly born but of those who feel nobly. "There are, 'tis true," concedes James Cawthorn in *The Vanity of Human Enjoyments*, "plebeian souls array'd / In one thick crust of apathy and shade," but in the world of the bourgeois ascendancy this will always be a matter of moral sensibility rather than social destiny.

Yet there remains the problem of how souls patrician in sensibility but not by birth are to express their claims to superior status, giving us the situation in which the Addisonian voice within *The Spectator* becomes the great model of bourgeois demeanor both during the Augustan period and subsequently. For during the Augustan period itself, Addison's great contribution had been to suggest the possibility of an Augustanism available to those excluded from the world of Pope and his noble friends, a poetic voice as elegantly classical as that of a Dryden or a Pope—"an early acquaintance with the classics is what may be called the good-breeding of poetry," Thomas Tickell had remarked approvingly in his preface to Addison's poems, "as it gives a certain gracefulness which never forsakes a mind" (qtd. in J. W. Johnson 23)—and in the prose of *The Spectator* a voice as genial and assured as that of the most accomplished Roman writers. "Where genius is united with correct taste," Vicesimus Knox will say toward the end of the century, "the judgment, the heart, and the imagination are at once fully satisfied. Such a combination existed in the minds of Pliny and Addison" (2.258).

To think of *The Spectator* as the conduct-book of an emergent middle class, as we have always done, is thus implicitly to recognize bourgeois culture as one of Augustan aspiration—what Samuel Johnson has in mind when he observes that *The Spectator* and *The Tatler* not only had a perceptible influence on their own age, but have retained that influence into the later eighteenth century, and will do so "while they continue to be among the first books by which both sexes are initiated in the elegancies of knowledge" (2.95). The same model of Addisonian politeness, an Augustanism made a matter of sensibility and brought within the reach of anyone willing to cultivate it assiduously, governs as well a body of poetry usually thought to be anomalous or eccentric in relation to Augustan literary standards: working-class or proletarian poetry of the sort written by Stephen Duck or James Woodhouse, women's poetry as given voice by Mary Collier or Mary Leapor, even, later in the century, the dialect poetry of Burns as it represents an interplay of native Scots and classical or "Augustan" idioms. For these too, as much as any verse epistle written by Samuel Boyse or satire written by Paul Whitehead, must ultimately be read as a poetry of Augustan aspiration.

The poetry of Stephen Duck, and the whole phenomenon of the thresher-poet as nine days' cultural wonder, makes clearest the issues involved. The older way of saying that Duck was anomalous in relation to a ruling Augustan norm was to claim him as a harbinger of Romantic primitivism, a figure in whom, once he had been thrown up by a freak of literary fashion, the essential features of Wordsworth's Romantic peasantry were already recognizable. The newer fashion is to see in Duck a sort of proto-Marxist voice of working class dissent, of permanent value because he was so insistently and unexpectedly to demonstrate to an Augustan high culture its unacknowledged material basis in a system of relentless economic exploitation. This is the line taken by Raymond Williams in *The Country and the City*, in which *The Thresher's Labour*, the poem that made Duck an instant celebrity, has nearly heroic status as the work that told the tea-table culture of Pope and Swift where, in effect, its sustenance came from. And there is a great deal in the poem to support such a notion: "Let those who feast at ease on dainty fare / Pity the reapers, who their feasts prepare: . . . / Each morning early rise, go late to bed; / Nor, when asleep, are we secure from pain; / We then perform our labors o'er again."

In the later poetry, the same theme is sustained by Duck's wholly unembarrassed acceptance of his proletarian status, as when in *A Description of a Journey to Marlborough*, the verse epistle to Viscount Palmerston that is in many ways his most remarkable poem, Duck dismounts from his horse to join his former companions the threshers at their work, or when in a later visit to a naval shipyard his eye is constantly drawn to scenes of manual labor: "See! busy smiths around their anvils sweat; / Their brawny arms the glowing anchor beat." For Williams and those who share his admiration of Duck as a voice of demystification stripping the ideological veil away from Augustan high culture, the embarrassment thus comes in Duck's attempts to "classicize" his poetic utterance, which from their perspective amount to little more than a weak attempt to imitate Dryden and Pope, and thus a postponed capitulation to the very Augustanism whose roots in exploitation Duck has otherwise been so uncompromisingly exposing. The tendency they deplore is already visible in *The Thresher's Labour*—

> From the strong planks our crab-tree staves rebound,
> And echoing barns return the rattling sound.
> Now in the air our knotty weapons fly,
> And now with equal force descend from high;
> Down one, one up, so well they keep the time,
> The Cyclops' hammers could not truer chime;
> Nor with more heavy strokes could Aetna groan,
> When Vulcan forg'd the arms for Thetis' son.

—and has become pronounced by the time Duck composes the *Journey to Marlborough*:

> Here curling vines their luscious sweets disclose,
> There fair POMONA loads the blushing boughs:
> See, fruitful CERES crowns the vales with corn,
> And fleecy flocks the verdant hills adorn!

Yet such moments of classical allusion in Duck's poetry are not marginal, or mechanical, or imitative in the weak sense; they are at the very heart of Duck's significance as a cultural phenomenon, and of the thresher-poet as an emblem of an entire literature of Augustan aspiration. For the essential injustice that a large audience in early eighteenth-century England perceived in Duck's poetry was not that some men labor in fields and barns so that others may sit languidly at tea-tables, but that a mind conversant in classical mythology, able to perceive its surroundings in terms of Ceres and Pomona and Vulcan forging arms for Thetis' son, should yet be doomed to inhabit a body unreleased from the lowest forms of agricultural labor.[13] *The Thresher's Labour* had an extraordinary contemporary impact not because it told a reluctant high culture about its basis in economic exploitation but because it held up to an emergent bourgeoisie the mirror of its own exclusion from a patrician-centered world of Augustan values, gave back to an audience that had read its Dryden and Pope and dutifully gone to the school of Addisonian politeness an image of itself as banished nonetheless from those scenes of elegance and ease revealed to them in Augustan poetry.

The weakness of Williams's analysis, in short, is that he momentarily loses touch in the course of it with what is elsewhere his greatest strength, a steady sense of ideology as repression or denial. If *The Thresher's Labour* had in any uncomplicated way undertaken simply to expose to Augustan high culture the unpalatable truth that its roots lay in the relentless exploitation of man by man, there would on Williams's own assumptions have been no widespread literary success for Duck, no lionizing of the thresher-poet at Court gatherings and fashionable soirees, no pension from the government or patronage by Queen Caroline. These are not the rewards of a poet who has just told his society something it desperately wishes not to hear. Thus it is precisely Duck's self-taught classicism that gives us the key to his extraordinary moment of celebrity: an acquaintance with the classics, as Tickell had said, is the good-breeding of poetry, and what Addison and Pope had learned from their early immersion in the classics Duck had now absorbed from Addison and Pope,[14] becoming in the process an extreme and emblematic instance of the mind formed to Augustan taste and Augustan values and yet somehow unaccountably excluded from the Augustan social world.

The significant body of working-class or proletarian poetry written in the wake of Duck's initial celebrity demands to be read in similar terms as a literature of Augustan aspiration, the mirror in which an emergent bourgeoisie would recognize, in the folkloristic or "romantic" predicament of the thresher-poet or the cobbler-poet or the weaver-poet, the story of its own dilemma of exclusion. Thus, for instance, Dodsley in his *Epistle to Stephen Duck* should be heard as giving voice not so much to proletarian sentiment as to bourgeois aspiration—"Nor is't impossible a time might be, / When Pope and Prior wrote like you and me. / 'Tis true, more learning might their works adorn, / They wrote not in a pantry or a barn"—and thus the shoemaker-poet James Woodhouse, imagining an aristocratic dinner party as a "magic circle," an "enchanted round," should be seen as gazing inward at that imaginary center from which not simply a few poetical threshers and cobblers but a large class of "polite citizens" feel themselves to have been excluded:[15] "Where plenty crowns the board with pleasing wealth, / And gen'rous bounty weds with sprightly health; ... / In streams of eloquence the periods glide, / While taste and virtue over speech preside."

The great virtue of proletarian poetry in its more distant relation to this magical or enchanted center of Augustan elegance is thus that it reveals the otherwise unspoken fantasy of class membership that had all along mesmerized its bourgeois readers, which is upper-class or aristocratic existence imagined as a form of romance. This is what we are seeing in Woodhouse's imaginary dinner party, or at similar moments in Dodsley's poetry—"I hear and mark the courtly phrases, / And all the elegance that passes"— and it is something that becomes yet clearer in eighteenth-century women's poetry written in the plebeian voice, in which the double subordination of gender and class, as it increases distance from the enchanted center, brings out even more strongly the romance element. Thus, for instance, Mary Masters in an epistle to the Earl of Burlington: "While you in gilded palaces reside, / The Muses' patron, and a monarch's pride; ... / Far far remote I live, a lowly maid, / In humble solitude and rural shade, / A stranger to the splendors of a court, / Where noble lords and princely dames resort."

Yet so far as the thresher-poets and milkmaid-poets of the eighteenth century enjoyed a brief moment of celebrity precisely because they expressed an otherwise unspoken bourgeois fantasy, their demise as a literary phenomenon was spelled by the bourgeois ascendancy itself, that midcentury assumption of a long-delayed ideological hegemony after which the bourgeoisie would have no more need to fantasize about magical social scenes of elegance and ease. The cry of bitter defeat that is to be heard throughout this poetry, as when Mary Leapor sees that no amount of reading is going to change her social status—"tho' these eyes the learned page explore, / And turn the pond'rous volumes o'er and o'er, / I find no comfort from their systems flow, / But am dejected more, as more I know"—or the weaver-poet John Bancks that poetry will leave his life unaltered—"I found 'twas all a dream, a fable, . . . / Still in the loom I must remain, / All higher thoughts, I doubt, are vain"—is, no doubt, on the individual level just what it poignantly seems, but collectively it is the cry of extinction of proletarian poetry itself, recognition that a time is approaching when, the bourgeoisie no longer needing a mirror of its own social exclusion, the plebeian voice will be left to lapse back into silence.

During the same period that made celebrities of Stephen Duck and Mary Collier,[16] however, there was to emerge a body of women's poetry whose echoes would not die out in the moment of bourgeois ascendancy, not least because of its role in bringing that moment about. For the dominant Augustan discourse that saw in polite male citizens only the importunistic stirrings of an upstart class was patriarchal, a system of assumptions arising from an untroubled acceptance of male power relations, and so unthreatened by mere "female" aspiration. This is the situation in which women, released by their more marginal status from the stoic silence imposed by Augustanism on their husbands and brothers, become in poetry the pure voice of bourgeois aspiration.[17] Thus Eliza Ryves lamenting in an epistle to a nobleman her inability to do justice to the heroic virtue of his ancestors—"But from a woman's voice in vain / Still feebly falters the majestic strain"—represents the more general lament of an emergent bourgoisie excluded by the aristocratic values of literary Augustanism, and thus Mary Barber, poking gleeful fun at one typical male response to her poetry—"I pity poor Barber, his wife's so romantic: / A letter in rhyme!— Why, the woman is frantic!"—is celebrating as well the paradoxical freedom bestowed by her greater marginality as a middle-class woman.

The sense in which women like Ryves and Barber speak in their poetry for the entire bourgeoisie as an emergent class is made clear by the emphasis on Addisonian politeness heard throughout the eighteenth century in what is otherwise a literature of specifically female aspiration. Thus, for instance, an anonymous midcentury epistle *Upon the Cultivation of Taste*, though it displays the normal anger of eighteenth-century feminism at women's exclusion from the sphere of serious learning—"Though tyrant Custom, with decisive air, / From learning's calm recess preclude the fair; / Though pedantry, with self-enamour'd sneer, / Pronounce domestic toils their only sphere"—and though it proposes to women a reading program (Homer, Virgil, Pope, Greek and Roman history, Shaftesbury) designed to overcome this exclusion, culminates in an invocation of the Addisonian model that may be taken as the very voice of a generalized bourgeois aspiration. Read *The Spectator*, the anonymous epistoler urges the young woman addressed by the poem,

> in whose easy page,
> At once is seen the gentleman and sage.
> Here knowledge shines, in fairest colors dress'd,
> The noblest truths in justest words express'd.
> Here cultivate your taste, and form your style; . . .
> Here view with Fancy's eyes the moral dream,
> Or with new relish pass from theme to theme.
> Hence may you learn in every light to please,
> To think with elegance, and write with ease.

As a strain within an emergent bourgeois ideology, in short, eighteenth-century feminism belongs to that larger movement in which the Augustan universal, the belief of writers such as Dryden and Pope and Johnson in a general human nature separate from social condition or circumstance, would be turned in a radical way against the patrician-centered values of Augustanism itself. This was the context in which, there being no fixed essence making some men shopkeepers and others peers of the realm, a merchant could retire to the country and, having gone to school to Dryden's Virgil and Pope's Homer and *The Spectator*, emerge a gentleman, and it is the context in which *The Athenian Oracle* could declare the difference between the sexes to be "only accidental, men and women being in essence the same."[18] The more radical implication that the same model of Addisonian politeness that is to make merchants into gentlemen may also make women the intellectual and social equals of men was thus, as we hear in the epistle *Upon the Cultivation of Taste*, something written into bourgeois ideology from the outset, and in the event would only be recontained by the even more powerful middle-class ideal of companionate marriage.

This is companionate marriage as portrayed by Lawrence Stone and others as both a motive impulse within and central feature of the bourgeois ascendancy,[19] an ideal already to be glimpsed in the figure of Aurelia in *The Spectator* no. 15, raising her family in a state of rural retirement in which her husband appears as "her bosom friend, and companion in her solitudes" (1.68). Yet what matters to the eighteenth-century verse epistle is the sense in which, as Addisonian politeness represents the embourgeoisement of an Augustan social ideal, this notion of marriage represents the ideal of otium friendship adjusted to the demands of an emergent middle-class social reality. Thus it is, for instance, that William Melmoth's epistle *To a Young Lady of Thirteen* will urge young Miss to improve her mind that she may prove in marriage "the lovely mistress, and instructive friend," and thus Peter Pinnel's *To a Lady, on Asking my Opinion of Friendship* can declare the highest bliss of friendship to arrive "When Hymen crowns what Love began, / And two fond hearts unite in one." And thus it is that Francis Fawkes in an epistle to a friend in Yorkshire, registering in the waning moments of Augustanism the influence of a newer ideology, will locate a wife within the otium scene: "Thus to the woodland shades my friend repairs / With the lov'd partner of his joys and cares; . . . / With cheerful converse sweetly form'd to please, / With wit good-natur'd, and polite with ease."[20]

The central role played by companionate marriage in bourgeois social mythology has to do precisely with its appeal to classical otium as a hidden source of ideological prestige. For marriage as a domestic version of the otium ideal not only answers the ethical demands of Aristotelian friendship but surrounds the miniature society of the family with the aura of that organic or traditional society always envisioned as the ideal of literary Augustanism. The bourgeois family as it becomes visible in *The Spectator* no. 15 comes to appear in post-Augustan poetry, and subsequently in the novel from Fanny Burney and Jane Austen onward, as the unexpected outcome on the private level of that ricorso or return to moral origins previously demanded by Augustan poetry for the society as a whole. This is the context in which middle-class marriage, offering the woman of an ascendant bourgeoisie a mode of hegemony at one remove, is able to recontain those intimations of more radical feminist aspiration earlier associated with a developing bourgeois ideology.

The one strain of genuinely radical feminism that would manage to survive the bourgeois ascendancy would thus consist of a female critique, in the Augustan manner of Bolingbroke or Pope or Gay, of the power of a new money or market society to turn women into mere puppets of underlying economic forces. Thus, for instance, Lady Mary Wortley Montagu, whose own aristocratic assumptions left her altogether untouched by bourgeois attitudes, contemptuously describing women who marry for money into the new class of titled upstarts:

> Who legal prostitutes for interest's sake,
> Clodios and Timons to their bosom take. . . .
> Those, titles, deeds, and rent-rolls only wed,
> Whilst the best bidder mounts their venal bed;
> And the grave aunt and formal sire approve
> This nuptial sale, this auction of their love.
>
> (*Answer to a Love Letter*)

At the beginning of the eighteenth century, Defoe had celebrated this new world of rising merchants, "where by marrying the daughter of some person meaner in dignity, but superior in money," many a declining nobleman had managed to restore the fortunes of his family.[21] This is that same world seen from the woman's point of view, the retrospective radicalism of the Augustan writers transmuted into an authentic mode of feminist anger.

By the same token, the strain of feminist thought that leads to Wollstonecraft at century's end is almost entirely that which preserves the radical impulse of the original Augustan critique of modernity, speaking the same language that Pope and Swift had employed against Walpole and the Robinocracy. Thus, for instance, Thomas Seward in *On the Female Right to Literature* will find it wholly natural to use the inferior status of women in a degraded modern Italy as his first lesson to contemporary Englishmen—"Where censors, consuls, and dictators plough'd . . . / Domestic Tyranny has fix'd his throne"—and then to use the language of Country ideology and Patriot opposition in denouncing the oppression of women generally; "let us scan," says Seward, "The coward insults of that tyrant, man. / Self-prais'd, and grasping at despotic pow'r, / He looks on slavery as the female dow'r; / To Nature's boon ascribes what force has giv'n, / And usurpation deems the gift of Heav'n." Like that nineteenth-century parliamentary radicalism having its roots in Bolingbroke and Country ideology, this is a feminism that was to remain radical precisely as it resisted absorption by a newly dominant bourgeois ideology, prolonging into a new age the Augustan critique of a world moving increasingly to the blind rhythms of an impersonal market economy.[22]

Yet the voice of eighteenth-century feminism as it culminates in Wollstonecraft's *Vindication of the Rights of Women* would eventually be made to appear eccentric in relation to bourgeois ideology, which is doubtless why the full force of Augustan radicalism comes to be preserved not in English poetry at all but in the poetry of Burns, in which Scots dialect could create an illusion of otherness keeping from an English middle-class readership the tremendous secret that it was itself the target of a bitter meditation on economic exploitation. As with the working-class poetry of Duck or Collier or Woodhouse, the name of this otherness in the older literary histories is "primitivism," the difference in the case of Burns being that this actually was the category imposed on his poetry by contemporary English readers in a repression or denial of its potential ideological disruptiveness. The real genius of Burns's celebrated pose as heaven-taught ploughman lay in the way it allowed him, very often half contemptuously, to exploit this tendency to denial, as, famously, in the epistle to Lapraik: "I am nae poet, in a sense, / But just a rhymer, like by chance, / An' hae to learning nae pretence, / Yet, what the matter? / Whene'er my Muse does on me glance, / I jingle at her."

The subterfuge that allowed Burns to be read in England as the poet of a guileless primitivism serves to explain the popularity of his poetry among middle-class readers, who were thus permitted to gaze upon a pleasing allegory of their own earlier rise from obscurity and their own present claims to an "Augustan" sensibility compounded of Addisonian politeness and Shaftesburian ethical sympathies. The Shaftesburian strain in Burns's poetry, evident especially in his intimate relation with literary sentimentalism, has been increasingly documented in recent years (see McGuirk). Yet it is Burns's equally intimate relation to literary Augustanism that accounts for the manner in which his poems were to hold up a mirror to a newly hegemonic middle class, for like Stephen Duck and the imaginary young lady of *Upon the Cultivation of Taste* and a thousand polite citizens of London and Norwich and Bristol and Bath, Burns the ploughman has taken his lessons not from heaven but from Addison and Pope. "My knowledge of modern manners," he says in the well-known letter to Dr. John Moore, "and of literature and criticism, I got from the Spectator," mentioning as well, in a virtual syllabus of Augustan aspiration, "Pope's works, some plays of Shakespear" and "Locke's essay on the human understanding" (1.109).

When Burns undertakes to write in an Augustan poetic form like the verse epistle he is simply drawing in a subliminal way on a background common to himself and English middle-class readers, perpetuating an "Augustan" tradition that had begun in Scots poetry a generation earlier with Allan Ramsay's epistles to William Hamilton of Gilbertfield, which so wonderfully give the impression of having magically transposed the congenial discourse of Bolingbroke and Pope into an unfamiliar landscape.[23] Even in Ramsay's epistles, however, there is an occasional hint that this is not merely or altogether a literature of Augustan aspiration, that the radical Augustan critique of a society of speculators and stockjobbers has here been unexpectedly given a voice in Scots dialect, as when, in an epistle to Duncan Forbes, Ramsay is moved to denounce those upstarts who, "proud as the thief in Hell," "Pretend, forsooth, they're gentle fowk. / 'Cause chance gi'es them of gear the yowk, / And better chiels the shell." This then becomes a note so often sounded in Burns's poetry that one sometimes seems to be hearing Augustan satire living out a delayed life in the lowlands of eighteenth-century Scotland, as in the second epistle to Lapraik: "Do ye envy the city-gent / Behint a kist to lie an' sklent, / Or purse-proud, big wi' cent per cent, / An' muckle wame, / In some bit Brugh to represent / A Baillie's name?"

Yet the strain of Augustan radicalism was to survive in Burns only because his English readers, taking such raillery to be Scots and wholly local, never recognized themselves as its ultimate target. For Burns always wrote with a brilliant intuitive awareness of the ideological shift that had transmogrified the monied upstarts so despised by Davenant and Bolingbroke into that "middle order of mankind" in which the virtue of the English nation was now presumed to repose, and that after Walpole's fall had instead come to project the demonic energies of the economic order so feared by Pope and Swift and Gay onto a usurping aristocracy of titled upstarts. This is the situation in which Burns, the genuine radicalism of his sentiments still masked by the otherness of his poetic idiom, would repeatedly slip into an open language of class antagonism that in English poetry would be countenanced only during the first heady days of sympathy for the French Revolution:

> Think ye, that sic as you and I,
> Wha' drudge and drive thro' wet and dry,
>   Wi' never-ceasing toil;
> Think ye, are we less blest than they,
> Wha scarcely tent us in their way,
>   As hardly worth their while?
> Alas! how aft, in haughty mood,
>   GOD's creatures they oppress!
> Or else, neglecting a' that's guid,
>   They riot in excess.
>
> (*Epistle to David Sillar*)

The sad and early end of Burns's poetic career is implicit in such moments of angry radicalism, for the same pose as heaven-taught plowman that gave Burns the freedom to speak this way simultaneously allowed him to be heard only as a voice from a remote and primitive world, his fate thus becoming that of a poet permitted to hold a mirror up to a society grounded in inequality and exploitation only so long as it never recognized its own reflection in the glass. The social or political rage that simmers beneath the carefree surface of Burns's lyric utterance thus involves, quite as much as the labile anger of Churchill's poetry, the dilemma of satiric solipsism, Augustan outrage having outlived its moment to find itself, as Rothstein says of Churchill, roaring in the void. And it is then the context in which the defiant hedonism of Burns's poetry, that heedless language of drink and song and sexual pleasure, was lived out in his life as a kind of nihilistic doom, a wandering on in tentless heed, as he says in the epistle to James Smith, "How never-halting moments speed, / Till fate shall snap the brittle thread." Yet the new world of polite citizens that gave Burns his short moment of celebrity had been cajoled into looking into the mirror nonetheless, and in the social anger running as a dark counterpoint to Burns's lyric genius Augustan satire was to take a belated and unlikely revenge.

The bourgeoisie as attacked by Burns or Churchill would remain sublimely oblivious to such outrage, however, busy in its doings and cheerful in its sense that the plunge into corruption and decline predicted by Pope—and accepted as the central fact of English life by Churchill and Cowper and Crabbe, by Goldsmith in some of his moods, and by Burns beneath his sentimentalism and lyric unconcern—had never come about, having been averted by the unexpected rise of a virtuous middle order of mankind incorporating Augustan attitudes into its own system of values. The voice of this bourgeoisie as it appears not from the glowering vantage point of Churchill's *Night* or Burns's epistle to David Sillar but from within the more innocent precincts of its own ideology is Anstey's *New Bath Guide*, that collection of verse letters from Simon Blunderhead and company that was to enjoy such enormous popularity with later-eighteenth-century readers before fading to become a curiosity of literary history. It was in *The New Bath Guide* that the polite citizens of a newly ascendant bourgeoisie were at last permitted to see, to their infinite delight, their own reflection in the glass.

The epistolary audience of *The New Bath Guide* is preeminently the imaginary audience conjured into being by the Augustan verse epistle and then shut out by the fixed retrospective gaze of Augustanism toward a vanished traditional past. In Bath as a locale recreated in Anstey's verse this audience was at last to discover, for however short-lived a literary moment, its own poetic landscape and its own social world, due not least to the sense Anstey conveys of Bath as an "artificial" setting, a locale situated at the intersection of poetry and history because the new social codes being invented there are so obviously a response to shifting property relations in the larger society. This is the Bath of Beau Nash and the eighteenth-century novel, the marriage market and social mecca that has, in Mary Chandler's 1734 poem about the city and its medicinal waters, already forsaken any pretense of being simply a refuge for the sick and convalescent. The Bath of her poem is already a scene "where music warbles, and the dancers bound, / While the high roof re-echoes to the sound," a transient society settling into a new system of distinctions even as it sports: "There blooming virgins kindle am'rous fires; / And there the god of wit and verse inspires. . . . / Th'important bus'ness of the fair, quadrille, / Employs those hours which dancing cannot kill."

Yet the medicinal role of the waters is nonetheless solemnly emphasized by Chandler—"Blest source of health . . . / The min'ral steams which from the baths arise, / From noxious vapors clear the neighb'ring skies"— for it is always the physical reality of illness that sustains the notion of Bath as ideologically neutral ground, enforcing the idea that in certain extraordinary situations class distinctions within a society are irrelevant. This was a notion already implicit in the institution of the public baths in Rome, that democracy of the unclothed body in which patrician and plebeian saw each other simply as fellow citizens, and the symbolic implications of that institution are still visibly present in the Roman arches and conduits of Chandler's or Anstey's Bath. It is then the deeper notion that social distinctions cease even more to matter in pain or illness, that in the misery of sickness the laborer and the Earl are one, that gives Bath its symbolic status as an eighteenth-century locale.

By the time Mary Chandler comes to portray Bath as a cheerful round of dancing and quadrille, however, there has been a decisive ideological shift in favor of that emergent middle-class that has been exploiting the medicinal pretext to mix with its social superiors. For, the freedom to drink the waters being in practice restricted to those with the money to travel and take up residence away from home, the spa had been from the first a scene not of genuine social equality but of bourgeois aspiration. Thus, for instance, the social melange of Bourbon l'Archambault as the object of satire in Scarron's seventeenth-century verse epistle *La Légende de Bourbon* may already be seen to lie behind Rochester's mocking description of a visit to Tunbridge Wells: "I trotted to the waters, / The rendevous of fools, buffoons, and praters, / Cuckholds, whores, citizens, their wives and daughters."[24] This note of aristocratic disdain will have all but vanished by the turn of the eighteenth century. "Prithee," asks a character named Loveworth in the anonymous 1704 play *Tunbridge Walks*, "what company does the place afford?" The response: "Like most public assemblies, a medly of all sorts, fops, majestic and diminutive, from the long flaxen wig with a splendid equipage, to the merchant's spruce 'prentice. . . . In short, 'tis a place wholly dedicated to freedom, no distinction, either of quality or estate, but ev'ry man that appears well converses with the best" (qtd. in Ashton 332–33).

There is a strong element of satire in this, for like Davenant's Tom Double, Reynard is speaking for that upstart class of modern Whigs at which Augustan satire would direct its ridicule over the next forty years. Yet there is also a revolutionary element in this notion of the spa as a place where, removed from the settled and ancient distinctions of neighborhood and region, people are compelled to take one another's measure through an elaborate decoding of external appearances. This, the same world of coaches and silk waistcoats and outward politeness celebrated in *The Spectator*,[25] is the very image of a new bourgeois order struggling to emerge from the remains of that traditional society mourned by the Augustan poets, and by the time Anstey writes *The New Bath Guide* sixty years later it has done so. "What place, my dear mother, with Bath can compare?" asks Simkin delightedly in one of his first epistles home: "Of all the gay places the world can afford, / By gentle and simple for pastime ador'd, / Fine balls, and fine concerts, fine buildings, and springs, / Fine walks, and fine views, and a thousand fine things."

This is Bath, in short, not simply as a place where a democracy of medicinal purpose has permitted the early emergence of the bourgeoisie onto the social scene, but a setting that has played an active role in bringing about its ascendancy. The crucial figure in the background here is Beau Nash, that tireless inventor of the codes of speech and dress and behavior that were to govern class distinctions in the new society, codes radical in social implication precisely because they posited outward appearance rather than birth or ancestry as the mark of status in a world just coming into view. One of the clearest signs that *The New Bath Guide* regards the revolution in social attitudes over which Nash symbolically presided as being complete is precisely its fond retrospective glance at his role as preceptor to an emergent bourgeoisie. "If the spirit's immortal," says Anstey,

> as poets allow,
> If life's occupations are follow'd below:
> In reward of his labors, his virtue and pains,
> He is footing it now in th' Elysian plains,
> Indulg'd, as a token of Proserpine's favor,
> To preside at her balls in a cream-color'd beaver.

Yet if *The New Bath Guide* represents a newly ascendant bourgeoisie celebrating its own arrival at the ideological center of its society, it also reveals a middle-class acutely aware that it is insulated from a more demotic or openly bourgeois status only by its "Augustan" values. Thus there is, for instance, the ritual castigation of an upstart class, not, as in Pope or Swift or Bolingbroke, to try actually to stem the noisome modern tide, but rather to show that the speaker has read and absorbed Pope and Swift and Bolingbroke: "And is it not right they should all be caressed, / When they're all so polite, and so very well drest, / When they circulate freely the money they've won, / And wear a lac'd coat, tho' their fathers wore none?" In the same way, *The New Bath Guide* itself, even as the story told by its verse letters registers the pull toward narrative that has already produced the epistolary novel as a bourgeois form, continuously insists on its own status as "Augustan" utterance by being poetry.[26] This is something Anstey goes out of his way to joke about by having Simkin defend his own verse—"Don't wonder, dear mother, in verse I have writ, / For Jenny declares I've a pretty good wit; . . . / Declares 'tis the fashion, and all the world knows / There's nothing so filthy, so vulgar as prose"—but the point is wholly serious, the very rationale of the *Bath Guide* as celebration of a society inherited by genuinely polite citizens.

The ultimate guarantee of "Augustan" sensibility in *The New Bath Guide* is Anstey's own posture as a member of the lesser gentry, someone living in a midcentury version of otium retirement and writing for the amusement of himself and a few friends. It is the voice of Goldsmith's middle order of mankind in its small-gentry guise that we hear, for instance, as Anstey half-jokingly defends himself against the charge that his muse has been "indecently droll"; should that slanderous charge be true, says the author of *The New Bath Guide*, "may this drowsy current (as oft he is wont) / O'erflow all my hay, may my dogs never hunt, / May those ills to torment me, those curses conspire, / Which so oft plague and crush an unfortunate Squire." The same picture of Anstey as the cheerful poetical squire in his landscape emerges in unmistakable form in the memoir written by his son for his collected poems: "Habituated to the charms of literary ease and retirement, passionately fond of the sports of the field . . . in the enjoyment of a competent and independent fortune [he] found leisure for the study of the Greek and Roman authors, and the poetry and polite literature of his own country" (*Poetical Works* xiii).

The overtones of Dryden's kinsman John Driden on his country estate, of Granville in rural retirement or Pope at Twickenham, are conscious and insistent here, as they are meant to be, and yet the roots of Anstey's posture as poetic voice of the small gentry are not in Dryden and Pope but in that embourgeoisement of the otium ideal that begins at the turn of the eighteenth century with Pomfret's *The Choice* and then emerges at midcentury at the center of the ideology giving an ascendant bourgeoisie its claims to moral privilege as a virtuous middle order of mankind. As with otium retirement in the genuine Horatian tradition, all the emblematic details are present—the moderate independent fortune, the small but self-contained country estate, the use of leisure for reading classical and modern authors—except, as Eric Rothstein has noted in connection with *The Choice*,[27] the one element giving meaning to the whole: an overwhelming moral and symbolic tension between country and city that is simultaneously, within the Augustan tradition, also a tension between traditional and modern society, simplicity and corruption, and a vanishing world of republican virtue as opposed to a new world dominated by money and economic relations.

To remove the ideal of otium retirement from this moral and symbolic context, in which otium always appears as a last besieged sanctuary of traditional values, is thus precisely to transform it into a legitimizing bourgeois fantasy of landed status, the ideological entitlement that Defoe's well-to-do citizens had imagined themselves to be purchasing along with their estates in the countryside. The fantasy as given early expression by Pomfret is echoed with a hundred variations in eighteenth-century minor poetry, as when Matthew Green imagines himself in a rural setting in *The Spleen*—"A farm some twenty miles from town, / Small, tight, salubrious, and my own; . . . / Where decent cupboard, little plate, / Display benevolence, not state"—or Thomas Lisle dreams about a country estate for himself and his sisters—"The apartments not small, nor monstrously great, / But chiefly for use, and a little for state"—and in the figure of Anstey as he presides over the epistolary exchanges of *The New Bath Guide* it takes on a habitation and a name. In the poetical squire gazing benevolently on the amusements of a new bourgeoisie we are given the ideological essence of post-Augustan poetry.

Yet the post-Augustan mode was to prove self-exhausting, a poetry of more or less remarkable single attempts that, like *The New Bath Guide*, would then suggest nothing further in their own vein. This too is a matter of poetic audience, for the drama of moral choice that had made epistolary audience a continuously generative principle in Dryden or Pope had ended with the Augustan collapse and the fall of Walpole, leaving a world in which poetry wishing to honor that vanished tradition could do so only by exploiting the memory of Augustanism, congratulating its imaginary audience on having incorporated into its own readerly sensibility something of its wit and patrician elegance. It is the act of congratulation, properly speaking, that is self-terminating here, allowing epistolary audience a glimpse of itself in the glass of post-Augustan verse but having nothing to offer beyond that. This is the fate lamented by William Mason, whose *Heroic Epistle to Sir William Chambers* had been as great a success in its season as *The New Bath Guide*. "I, like Anstey," he confesses sadly to a nation awaiting his next effort, "feel myself unfit / To run, with hollow speed, two heats of wit."[28]

The moment of post-Augustan poetry and its audience was itself to prove brief and precarious, reminding us at the last that this world of polite readers and lingering Augustan values has all along been something having its being more within poetry than in the realm of the actual. Already *The New Bath Guide* is glancing uneasily at a new social order in which a bourgeoisie altogether innocent of Augustan aspiration will take as its mirror not verse epistles tracing their literary lineage back to Horace's *Epistulae* but letters written in prose by a newly literate class attempting to find its way in a world of unstable social distinctions. The voice of this class is the "lady" in the Appendix to *The New Bath Guide*, advising Anstey how to write if he wants to be a popular author in the new age—

> Why, if thou must write, thou hadst better compose
> Some novels, or elegant letters in prose,
> Take a subject that's grave, with a moral that's good,
> Throw in all the temptations that virtue withstood,
> In epistles like PAMELA's chaste and devout—
> A book that my family's never without.

—and, though there remain to be written a few poems such as Mason's epistle to Chambers, the end of the post-Augustan mode may be heard in the dying echoes of her monitory speech. With the disappearance of that imaginary audience conjured into being by Augustanism and surviving its demise by a few short years, the commonwealth of letters will be given over wholly to epistolary novels, and to what readers like this lady imagine, in their innocent vulgarity, to be elegant letters in prose.

FIVE

THE EMPIRE OF CHAOS

AS IT CONCERNS the poetics of the eighteenth-century verse epistle, the empire of chaos is not simply the cultural apocalypse imagined in the last thunderous and gloomy lines of the 1743 *Dunciad* but a fall into solipsism as Pope and the Augustan poets had always feared it, a world of solitary souls operating in isolation from one another and cut off from any ground of transcendent reality. This is Augustine's humanity-in-God when God has disappeared, the universal darkness of an age when, metaphysics having called for aid on sense, as Pope puts it, the mind is left to decipher its surroundings in wholly empirical or "natural" terms. In literary terms, the fall into solipsism involves a dispersal or atomization of audience such that the collective vision of Augustan poetry, that remembered ideal of organic society that had always previously sustained the verse epistle as a drama of moral choice, eventually ceases to exert any control over poetic form. This is the context in which the vanishing of epistolary audience was to clear the space for that midcentury revival of "pure poetry" that would seek a new source of poetic utterance in solipsism itself.

A more immediate consequence of the return of solipsism, however, was to bring about the end of that diminished poetic world I have called the commonwealth of letters, in which the memory of Augustanism would sustain a fitful epistolarity in English poetry through to the end of the century. As we have seen, a lingering metaphysics of community had been able to bestow on the satire of Charles Churchill a curious vitality even in this diminished context, making him seem, especially in his attacks on the spurious Augustanism of an emergent bourgeoisie, the very voice of Dryden or Pope suddenly come alive in an alien world. Thus it is that one must turn to Churchill's friend and literary companion Robert Lloyd, composing incidental poetry in a world he knows to be diminished, writing a steady stream of burlesque epistles in mockery not of Augustan forms but of his own pretensions, for the true measure of an age now never free from the specter of poetic solipsism. This is a world in which one writes not out of high moral purpose, but simply because one cannot cease from writing: "Howe'er the river rolls its tides, / The cork upon the surface rides. / And in ink's ocean, lightly buoy'd, / The cork of vanity is Lloyd."

The great example in the immediate background of Lloyd's doggerel rhyme is the poetry of Swift, particularly as its odd or unexpected power has been accounted for by Edward Said. For the literary interest of Swift's verse paradoxically persists, argues Said, precisely because Swift was more than anyone else "able to exploit the negative aspects of the medium: its airiness, its impermanence, its potential for solipsistic debasement" (62). Said isolates in *Poetry: A Rapsody* the essence of Swift's own mode of poetic inconsequentiality, the mixture of burlesque and uneasy self-mockery that then engenders the diminished world of writers like Lloyd and Bonnell Thornton and later the efforts of T. J. Mathias or the *Rolliad* authors or Wolcot's Peter Pindar. The reason that Swift appears as the originator of this mode lies in the bitter dilemma out of which his utterance may be seen to have arisen, an acute consciousness of having lived to a time when poetry has been exiled to the margins of history, remote from any determination of the actual. For Swift's poetry "derives its strength not only from the vehemence of its attack on debased poetry, but also from a despair that this debasement, after all, is what poetry now really is" (60).

Up to the Tory demise of 1714, maintains Said, when Bolingbroke and his friends were sent by the death of Queen Anne into permanent political exile, Swift thought of himself as an *écrivain* in Barthes' sense, a writer dwelling within a living historical order who views his own writings as events within that order. After the Tory demise, however, the order of "real history" would come to be identified in Swift's mind with Walpole and emergent capitalism, locating him as a writer in an unreal shadow world outside living history; the self-chosen inconsequentiality of Swift's doggerel mode, then, as well as its labile anger and self-mockery, express in direct terms his rage at the inconsequentiality of poetry in the age of Walpole and modernity. The great importance of this analysis is that it so immediately suggests a similar perspective on poets like Lloyd: as the age seemed to Swift in the wake of the Tory demise that sent him and Bolingbroke and Pope into perpetual opposition, so did the world seem to Lloyd and Richard Tickell and John Wolcot after the Augustan collapse, the failure of the Augustan writers to stem the tide of modernity through poetry and satire and polemic.

This is why Lloyd is at such pains to construct for himself a poetic patrimony out of the tradition of Augustan light verse in which Swift is a central figure—"A vein, which though it must offend / You lofty sirs who can't descend, / To fame has often made its way / From Butler, Prior, Swift, and Gay"—and it is why the claim, on the face of it, possesses a certain plausibility. For Butler had made a poetic career of, as Lloyd says, "spinning unlaborious rhyme," and Prior had often enough chosen as his favored mode the "paultry burlesque stile" whose lineage Dona Munker has traced back to Archilochus and Theocritus—"the world agrees," Prior had joked in his epistle to Fleetwood Shepherd, "that he writes well, who writes with ease: / Then he, by sequel logical, / Writes best, who never thinks at all"—and even Pope, as he once admits in an epistle to Henry Cromwell, had not been above "a little fooling, / Just while your coffee stands a cooling":

> The season of green peas is fled,
> And artichokes reign in their stead.
> Th'Allies to bomb Toulon prepare;
> G—d save the pretty ladies there!
> One of our dogs is dead and gone,
> And I, unhappy, left alone.

Yet the crucial distinction is that such foolery always occurs in the Augustan tradition against a background of serious moral purpose, as when Butler spins his unlaborious rhymes in insouciant contempt of the excesses of Puritan sobriety, or Prior and Gay glance even in their lightest verse at the same world of knaves and fools that occupies Pope in his Horatian satires. The illusion that Lloyd legitimately belongs to this tradition, in turn, is sustained to a degree by those poems within the larger body of his verse that attack the bad poetry of his own age, particularly what he saw as the false sublimity produced in the name of "pure poetry" by the Wartons and their school. Thus, for instance, the *Two Odes* published by Lloyd and his friend Colman in 1760 parody the odes of Gray and Mason, and thus Lloyd in a subsequent epistle to a friend "about to publish a volume of miscellanies" makes delighted fun of the new vogue for blank verse—"'tis by those / Milton's the model mostly chose, / Who can't write verse, and won't write prose"—and imitations of Spenser, particularly the midcentury poet who "thinks his strong Muse takes wond'rous flights, /Whene'er she sings of peerless wights, / Of dens, of palfreys, spells and knights."

Lloyd's verse at such moments is participating in the post-Augustan reaction against midcentury sublimity that, for the relatively brief moment of its duration, seemed in a minor way to have summoned the spirit of *Macflecknoe* and the *Dunciad* back to English poetry. In the register of serious discontent, this gives us Goldsmith as we have heard him in the dedication to *The Traveller*, muttering unhappily that every absurdity now has a champion to defend it: "What criticisms have we not heard of late in favor of blank verse, and Pindaric odes, choruses, anapests and iambics, alliterative care, and happy negligence" (4.246–47). In a nonserious register, it gives us the wonderful burlesque ode by Soame Jenyns recently recovered by Eric Rothstein, a parody not simply of such midcentury effusions as Akenside's patriotic odes but of the whole notion of liberty as a source of Longinian inspiration:

> Hail Liberty, fair goddess of this isle!
> Deign on my verses and on me to smile!

> Like them unfettered by the bonds of sense,
>   Permit us to enjoy life's transient dream,
> To live and write without the least pretense
>   To method, order, meaning, plan, or scheme;
> And shield us safe beneath thy guardian wings,
> From law, religion, ministers, and kings.

This is the strain of post-Augustan parody that comes to its proper end in Alexander Shomberg's *Bagley* (1777), famously addressed to "the authors of elegies, visions, legendary tales, and allegorical poems, the great assertors of true poetry in the present age" (qtd. in Chapin 88).

Yet there may be heard in such post-Augustan burlesque, even at its most exuberant, a submerged note of anxiety that any sense of community being sustained by this late satiric reaction is a mirage, that the new midcentury poetry of twilight groves and visionary musings is, for all its occasional bathos and overwrought sublimity, the true poetry of an age of solipsism. Lloyd's verse, in particular, is haunted by a sense that its own energetic defense of the mere outward forms of Augustan poetry is somehow an empty enterprise, a last futile attempt to assert community in negative terms, through attack on a common satiric object, when all positive visions of community have failed. When this illusion of community dissolves in its turn, we thus have the Lloyd who has appointed himself laureate of the diminished world, his plight that of the poet without an audience and without a community, washed up on the shores of history with nothing to express except a plaintive sense that times were once nobler than these: "Who, but a madman, would engage / A poet, in the present age? / Write what we will, our works bespeak us / Imitatores, servum pecus."

Lloyd's poetry thus becomes within the self-imposed limits of its own inconsequentiality an exploration of poetic solipsism, an enterprise beginning in Lloyd's rejection, as epistolary audience, of those same polite citizens whose spurious Augustanism had so enraged his friend Churchill—that "public taste," as Lloyd himself once puts it, "Which thinks no wit or judgment greater / Than Addison and his Spectator" (*Epistle to Mr. Colman*)—and his reaching out to an audience, however fugitive or vestigial, that shares his own nostalgia for the world before the death of Pope. Unlike the moral nostalgia of Goldsmith or Cowper,[1] however, Lloyd's is a poetic nostalgia, and in this lies the crucial distinction between his own diminished world and the world of Swift's poetry. For Swift's sense of dwelling in a poetic shadow world outside living history would to the end call forth a mighty indignation, while Lloyd's poetry at the last plaintively expresses his awareness that his audience has dwindled to a few companions, literary outcasts like himself, and that its interior setting has shrunk to the scene of sad revelry on which Churchill had attempted to put so brave a face in *Night*, an epistle addressed, fittingly and emblematically, to his friend Robert Lloyd.

At the same time, another possibility of epistolary audience is to be glimpsed in Lloyd's verse that, though exploited only irregularly by Lloyd himself, was to generate the last significant mode of epistolarity in eighteenth-century poetry. This is the possibility that arises when the poet assumes the posture of jester or buffoon, offering the poem itself as a last fleeting occasion of community in the moment of shared laughter it creates around itself, what Lloyd has in mind in declaring that if sometimes his "easy vein" of pleasantry, "form'd into verse, hath pleas'd a while, / And caught the reader's transient smile, / My Muse hath answered all her ends" (*A Familiar Epistle to *******). The vein of easy ludicrousness that permits a last conjuration of community through laughter is what gives Lloyd's verse its kinship with such productions as Churchill's *Gotham*, and both with the antic posture of Sterne in *Tristram Shandy* or *A Sentimental Journey*, themselves attempts to defeat solipsism through the indirect means of writing, as Tristram once puts it, against the spleen. This is then the antic vein from which would emerge, at century's end, John Wolcot's poetic alter ego Peter Pindar.

Yet the comic odes and epistles of Peter Pindar, though they similarly offer themselves as occasions of community-in-laughter, mark as well a significant innovation: where Lloyd had in a general sense assumed the role of public clown or jester, Peter Pindar speaks specifically as a Dunce, one of the bad poets or petty scribblers or heavy pedants of Augustan satire come improbably to life in the waning years of the eighteenth century as proof that the world predicted in the last lines of *The Dunciad* has come true. This is why Pindar's verse so often goes out of its way to signal its own affiliations with the Grub Street world of the Augustans, as when, for instance, the sort of solemnly nonsensical footnotes provided by the pedant Scriblerus in the *Dunciad Variorum*—"The poet . . . beginneth by showing (what is ever agreeable to Dulness) his high respect for antiquity and a great family, how dull, or dark soever: next declareth his love for mystery and obscurity; and lastly his impatience to be reunited to her" (5.339)—are transformed into the "arguments" prefixed by Peter Pindar to his poems: "The poet . . . maketh a fine comparison between himself and purling streams; also between curs, cats, and courtiers—the poet declaimeth virtuously and politically against swearing in a passion—. . . the poet exhibiteth more instances of grandeur of soul—still more nobleness—still more . . ." (*Works* 2.255).

By the time Peter Pindar is composing such arguments to his poems, the huge irony that the dunces have survived to go on mindlessly scribbling while the great Augustan satirists lie silent in their graves is already a long-established literary joke, the premise underlying Bonnell Thornton's occasional forays as "Martin Scribbler, Jun." and such productions as *The Pursuits of Literature*, the *Rolliad*, *The Baeviad* and *The Maeviad*. Similarly, the dunce's-eye view that dissolves Augustan satiric universality into mere topicality is already implicit in much post-Augustan verse, as in Richard Tickell's *The Project*, an epistle to the Reverend Dean Tucker: "From bench to bench, in spite of gout, / The soften'd Chatham moves about: . . . / 'Good-day, my lord! I could say more; / but I must talk to dear Lord Gower.' / Chas'd is the cloud from Shelburn's brows; / How graciously to Bute he bows!" The entire mode of comic topicality out of which Peter Pindar will make a poetic career is already implied in such lines, and part of the joke is precisely their satiric particularity: the sense of cosmic warfare that in Augustan satire surrounds such figures as Walpole and Cibber with an aura of universal implication has altogether dissipated, and all that remains is to watch the poets and politicians of a pygmy age blunder through their parts in a history that has become farce.

The great significance of Wolcot's verse is that it was to draw these various motifs into a single focus in the imaginary personality of Peter Pindar, a poetic dunce who cheerfully gibes at the foibles of his pygmy age while showing, with an equal cheerfulness, that he knows his own productions to be little more than Grub Street rhyming. The role of audience in this situation is equivocal to the last degree, for those who enter into the spirit of so dunciacal a project presumably have something of the dunce about themselves, and yet Peter Pindar managed, doubtless because of the sheer innocuousness of his early verse, to establish himself almost from the beginning as a public favorite. The venturing onto dangerous ground thus occurs only with Pindar's gradual discovery of his greatest comic subject, the portrayal of George III as "Farmer George," the slightly dimwitted monarch of Great Britain. The figure of Farmer George may be glimpsed as early as Pindar's *Congratulatory Epistle* to James Boswell: "He everybody knows, and every thing; . . . / Which gardener hath most cabbages and peas, / And which old woman hath most hives of bees; / Which farmer boasts the most prolific sows, / Cocks, hens, geese, turkeys, goats, sheep, bulls, and cows."

Even at such moments, however, Wolcot is to a large extent drawing on an established tradition, for Farmer George had some time since come to exist as a comic figure in the popular imagination, and had already appeared in such satiric poetry as the *Probationary Odes* written by the *Rolliad* authors: "Oh! Europe's pride! Britannia's hope! / To view his turnips and potatoes, / Down his fair kitchen-garden's slope / The victor monarch walks like Cincinnatus." When Peter Pindar begins to concentrate more and more on the figure of Farmer George, then, until it becomes clear that this monarch of turnips and potatoes is going to emerge as the comic protagonist of his poetry, he is so far simply elaborating a largely indulgent public perception of the king as a haplessly unregal soul. There is something very nearly affectionate in the way Peter, the self-appointed Pindar of a shrunken world, reports the slightest doings of its monarch, as when in *The Royal Tour*, an epistle to the present Laureate, George III's eyes light upon a drover and his cattle:

> A batch of bullocks! See great Caesar run:
> He stops the drover; *bargain* is begun.
> He feels their ribs and rumps; he shakes his head:
> "Poor, Drover, poor; poor, very poor, indeed."
> Caesar and Drover haggle; difference split:
> How much? a shilling? what a *royal* hit!

This is meant merely as topical humor, a royal outing by George III and the Queen providing the same sort of innocent merriment that Peter Pindar finds elsewhere in Boswell's Highland tour with Samuel Johnson or Lord Macartney's voyage to China, and yet there now arises an inevitable paradox: the monarch, no matter how limited or flawed in his personal character, is yet the universal symbol of the nation, a figure existing not only in ordinary life but in the larger civic mythology sustaining England as a community with a shared historical destiny. This is the monarchy as celebrated in the tradition of seventeenth-century English panegyric studied by James Garrison, and as idealized in the eighteenth century with even greater urgency in the Whig panegyric intended to provide ideological support for the Hanoverian succession. In the background of Peter Pindar's comic depictions of Farmer George lie a hundred poems like the verse epistle in which Ambrose Philips had once called upon Englishmen to imagine to themselves the scene in which an earlier George "serene in majesty appears / And plans the wonders of succeeding years! / There, as he walks, his comprehensive mind / Surveys the globe, and takes in all mankind: / While, Britain, for thy sake he wears the crown."

The tradition of Whig panegyric that celebrated the monarchy in such terms, however, had always existed in ideological counterpoint to an Augustan critique portraying the Hanoverians as lumpish pretenders to a throne vacated by Anne as the last genuine monarch of the English people, as the tawdry symbols, like Walpole and his Robinocracy, of a new age of money and speculation and parvenu importunity, the erosion of traditional values in a world driven by the market and the stock exchange. This is the shrunken and deformed monarchy mirrored in the bitter satire of Pope's epistle *To Augustus*, and it is what Pope has in mind when he remarks that "Kings now . . . [are] the worst things on earth, they are turned mere tradesman" (Spence 1.246), or Bolingbroke in the *Letters on the Study and Use of History* when he describes England as a nation ruled over by "a king without monarchical splendor" (*Works* 2.333). A work such as *The Idea of a Patriot King*, Bolingbroke's vision of the monarchy as the symbolic center of a restored organic society, must thus be taken as the bleakest of judgments on the Hanoverians, the pygmy rulers of a world of stockjobbers and tradesmen and citizens grown polite.

Even at their most innocent Peter Pindar's comic portrayals of Farmer George thus awaken powerful memories of the Augustan resistance to modernity, moving his verse almost in spite of itself in the direction of a more radical critique of the social and economic order that has emerged in the years after the Augustan collapse. The full force of Augustan retrospective radicalism may be felt in Wolcot's growing sense that, with the dissolution of those bonds of mutual responsibility that had linked wealthy and poor together in an earlier traditional community, the new money society has created a floating mass of urban and agricultural poor for whom, quite literally, no one cares. These are the poor as they are left to fend for themselves in a world in which, one's worth being determined now solely by one's value on the labor market, unemployment means actual starvation. This is the dark shadow of social unrest that now begins to cast itself over the otherwise sunlit world of Pindar's Farmer George, as when we see him reacting to his estate manager's hesitant suggestion that the dearness of provisions may drive the poor to desperation:

> "Frost, Frost, no politics; no, no, Frost, no:
> You, you talk politics! oho, oho!
> Windsor come down about our ears! what, what? . . .
> Pull Windsor down? Hae, what? a pretty job!
> Windsor be pulled to pieces by the mob?
> Talk, talk of farming; that's your *forte*, d'ye see:
> And mind, mind, politics belong to *me*.

In Peter Pindar's verse, in short, we begin to glimpse the strain of radicalism, long ago remarked by Isaac Kramnick, that runs in an underground channel from Bolingbroke and the Augustan poets to writers like Cobbett and the parliamentary radicals of the nineteenth century. This is the dark vision of a world in which implacable market forces are at work to condemn a growing population of the dependent poor to hunger and hopelessness, that world of a suffering urban and agricultural proletariat that would then call forth the revolutionary urgency of Marx and Engels fifty or sixty years later. For in the new world of the cash nexus, to be without money is not simply to be subject to the blind fluctuations of invisible market forces lying outside human control, but in extreme cases literally to starve. This is the reality with which Peter Pindar begins increasingly to confront his readers, as in a bitter footnote to *Hair Powder*, a superficially innocuous epistle to Pitt protesting various new taxes: "the inhabitants of Brentford, during the late unexampled frost, when they should have thought of nothing but *dying*, . . . those very people, not worth a groat, starving, shivering, and in rags, dared to proceed in a body, . . . with their unhallowed feet, into the *sacred* gardens of Richmond and Kew: where they wickedly, *inhumanly*, and feloniously, cut down and maimed a number of trees . . . to warm their own vile bones."

In this situation, however, Peter Pindar is no more able than had been Goldsmith or Akenside or Churchill before him to imagine as the source of such misery the hidden workings of impersonal historical forces, and so like them he is moved to attack, as the visible cause of all that disturbs him, that same race of "titled upstarts" who are the villains of *The Deserted Village* and Akenside's Curio poems and Churchill's "patriot" poetry in support of Wilkes. This, once again, is a theme going back to the beginnings of Augustan poetry and Country ideology—"More than the wealthiest lord, who helps to drain / The famish'd land, and rolls in impious gain: / What can I hope in courts?" Granville had asked in his verses to Elizabeth Higgons—and in Wolcot it emerges as Peter Pindar's ironic paean to a nobleman in his *Commiserating Epistle to the Earl of Lonsdale*: "Yet, yet I see the feudal times return, / When tyrants bid in chains the million mourn; / When slaves to grandeur crouch amid the dust, / And havoc roams to please the ruling lust." This is then the strain of native radicalism that, in the first heady months after the storming of the Bastille, was to prompt English sympathy for the French Revolution; "hang the French dogs," cries Pindar with a bitterness that goes beyond irony, "a mangy mongrel cry, / That, running riot, on their huntsman fly!"

In conventional terms, such utterance takes us to the outer limits of Peter Pindar's increasingly angry radicalism, and yet the more genuinely radical moment in his poetry occurs elsewhere in this same *Epistle to Lonsdale*, where he sees in a clairvoyant instant a truth that no other post-Augustan poet had been permitted to glimpse, that the same money society that had earlier produced Walpole and the Robinocracy and has now produced aristocratic tyrants like Lonsdale must in the longer run lead to a more general social equality. For the same impersonal laws of equivalency that reduce all human values to interchangeable market value, that very feature of the new social and economic order so hated and feared by the Augustans, must then with equal inevitability produce individuals as political units who state their own equality as a demand:

> Grant wealth, no more the humble cobbler cow'rs;
> And boldly deems *his* blood as rich as *ours*,
> And *blasphemously* thinks th'Almighty's plan
> Ordain'd *no difference* between man and man.
> Such is the *sad* effect of wealth, rank pride:
> Thus, mount a beggar, how the rogue will ride!

Yet even as he glimpses the possibility of a new age of vastly increased social and political equality, Peter Pindar remains for the most part blind to the implications of what he has seen, which is why the radical turn in his poetry has more to do with its ratio of address than with its political content as such. For in such poems as the *Epistle to Lonsdale* Peter Pindar has begun to imagine an audience never before posited in eighteenth-century poetry, an emergent class of readers whose existence *as* a class would on the political or historical level be recognized only decades later in the Great Reform Bill. The cataclysmic effect of events in France has been to raise up in the verse epistle a possibility of audience that is simultaneously a vision of community, and with it the intoxicating hope that the specter of solipsism haunting the post-Augustan world had been, after all, no more than an illusory imprisonment within the false categories of a dying ideology. This is the possibility that is then extinguished, along with so much else, by the turn of the French Revolution to bloody terror.

Though Wolcot's early and fervent sympathy for the French Revolution would leave him in an increasingly exposed position all during the last decade of the eighteenth century, the end of his experiment in satiric radicalism does not come until 1800, when it is dealt a blow by William Gifford's *Epistle to Peter Pindar* from which neither Wolcot nor English verse satire would ever recover. For Gifford's epistle, which has in our own time been consistently misread as a mere exercise in uncontrolled vituperation, brings Peter Pindar's career to an end by seeming to show that the world is so improved that satire no longer has a place in it, a move that then allows him to separate Peter Pindar out from his own imaginary audience and isolate him as a target of satiric contempt. This is where Gifford, who as editor of the *Anti-Jacobin* might have been expected to follow the usual line of denouncing Pindar's audience as a mob, the insolent creatures of an aimless *ressentiment*, instead wins a conclusive victory by turning the verse epistle as a drama of moral choice to one last triumphant use of his own choosing.

Gifford's attack on Wolcot derives from his having understood that satire depends for its forward impetus on that tension between the real and ideal that David Miller, in the case of narrative, calls "discontent," a purely structural striving toward some ideal state, always projected as such by the work itself, in which its own premise as a discourse would be abolished. Gifford's move is simply and grandly to declare that England, even as Peter Pindar mocks George III and fulminates against the ministry, has attained such a state. The nobility is virtuous, the prelates of the land walk "in the path their SAVIOUR trod,"

> While, with a radiance yet to courts unknown,
> Calm, steady dignity surrounds the throne
> And the tried worth, the virtues of thy King,

> Deep in thy soul infix the mortal sting.
> Why, Peter, leave the hated object free,
> And vent, poor driveller, all thy spite on me?

Yet Gifford's strategy at this moment is not original, for an antisatiric tradition going back to the beginning of the Augustan period had consisted of little more than variations on this theme. Thus, for instance, we may hear Jonathan Smedley attacking Swift over half a century earlier, on the occasion of the Drapier controversy, in nearly the same terms: "The grand dispute! you've made an end on't: / Our State and Church are independent. / The weather's good, and Phoebus smiles, / On this, as on other isles." A slight adjustment of the same idea then yields the terms on which Walpole's *Gazetteer* was accustomed to mock the moral pretensions of the Augustan satirists—"If their representation of things is true, there never was a people so degenerated and sunk so low in vileness and infamy as we"[2]—or of a nobleman like Bolingbroke as he exemplified an Augustan moral ideal: "Far, far from courts, hence, wisely trust for fame. . . . / By gentle Bard be sunk in gentle stream, / And the calm hero of a couplet reign" (qtd. in Goldgar 167). After the Augustan collapse, the same notion will most often assume the same form it has in Gifford—"Sedition and tumult and discord are fled," announces Edward Moore in an epistle to Henry Pelham[3]—but the underlying theme will have been the same throughout: when the realm is blessed, satire can only be explained as an expression of the twisted nature of the satirist.

The originality of the *Epistle to Peter Pindar* lies in Gifford's having seen that the moment of triumph for this antisatiric strategy had at last arrived, and that in the symbolic demise of Peter Pindar the alliance between satire and a new radicalism, doubly dangerous because it was so legitimately rooted in the older radicalism of Augustanism and Country ideology, could be extinguished at the moment of its birth. For as the millenarian promise of the French Revolution gave way to Robespierre and the Reign of Terror, as Napoleon rose out of blood and anarchy to autocratic authority, and as Britain moved into a long and bitter war with a France yet clamorously proclaiming revolutionary principles, an England that had always before seemed a mere idealized figment of Whig panegyric could be made to seem a nation existing in historical fact. *The Epistle to Peter Pindar* removes from the conditional mood that shining vision of England always held up by the Opposition poets of Walpole's last years and claims for it, in contrast with France in the terrible grip of its Jacobinical fervor, an existence in simple fact. This is the England previously described in Thomson's *Summer* seen, now, as having been there all along:

> Rich is thy soil, and merciful thy skies;
> Thy streams unfailing in the summer's drought;
> Unmatched thy guardian-oaks; thy vallies float

> With golden waves, and on thy mountains flocks
> Bleat numberless; while, roving round their sides,
> Bellow the blackening herds in lusty droves.
> Beneath, thy meadows flame, and rise unquelled
> Against the mower's scythe. On every hand
> Thy villas shine. Thy country teems with wealth;
> And Property assures it to the swain,
> Pleased and unwearied in his certain toil.
>
> (lines 1445–56)

In the ideological moment of the *Epistle to Peter Pindar*, to deny this peaceful vision of bounty and order would be to deny the contrast between England and revolutionary France. This is the essence of the strategy through which Gifford, the moving spirit of the *Anti-Jacobin*, daringly conjures out of disparate and unregarded materials a "tradition" that had in reality had no previous existence. The logic of the move, and its relation to literary Augustanism, is identical to that of Burke's writings on the French Revolution: while such writers as Dryden and Pope and Swift had looked for their ideal England to a vanishing traditional past, invoking its nobler memory as a witness against the depredations of modernity and the new money society, writers such as Burke and Gifford have been driven by the historical shock of events in France to see that, underneath the superficial dislocations of material progress, the England prematurely mourned by the Augustans had never disappeared. The England of Magna Carta and common law and the "ancient constitution" so elegiacally memorialized by Bolingbroke and Country ideology, the England praised only on conditional terms by patriot poets like Thomson and Glover, is England as she really after all exists.

The devastating power of the *Epistle to Peter Pindar* lies not in the way Gifford managed to triumph over Wolcot on some contested ideological ground, but in the way he takes away from Wolcot the very premise of his satiric utterance. This is the moment at which Wolcot stands isolated both from his imaginary audience and from the vision of community that had sustained his radical anger, a moment in which he is wholly vulnerable to Gifford's overwhelming scorn. The terms of the attack as it now comes have been called Juvenalian, doubtless by scholars aware of Gifford's later career as a translator of Juvenal and his association with the "Juvenalian revival" of this period, but really it is something else, the return of satire to its ancient origins in a magic of curse and ritual. The aim, quite literally, is to kill off the imaginary persona called Peter Pindar and all he has come to symbolize: "Come then, all filth, all venom as thou art, / Rage in thy eye, and rancor in thy heart, / Come with thy boasted arms, spite, malice, lies, / Smut, scandal, execration, blasphemies; / I brave them all."

Even at so seemingly uncontrolled a moment as this, however, Gifford is engineering a last ideological reversal that will take away from Wolcot any remaining possibility of response. For the language Gifford is using here, an imagery of insect and reptilian repulsiveness, had always been used in the Augustan tradition for those outside the limits of its own ethical order. This is the imagery that gives us Pope's Sporus as a "familiar toad" or Churchill as described by Beattie, who raises the rhetorical ante as though in anticipation of Gifford's attack on Pindar: "Driveling and dull . . . crawls the reptile Muse, / Swoln from the sty, and ranking from the stews, / With envy, spleen, and pestilence replete, / And gorg'd with dust she lick'd from Treason's feet." To mobilize this imagery against Wolcot is thus in a single stroke to sever the connection between Peter Pindar and the radical Augustan critique of modernity in which his satire has its legitimate roots, leaving him naked and exposed.

Gifford now makes a last decisive move against Wolcot, turning away from Peter Pindar toward that imaginary audience his poetry has been summoning into being, offering it, in just the manner that Augustan satire had earlier offered epistolary audience a choice between its own world and a corrupt modernity, a last opportunity to save its own moral nature. This is a move Goldsmith had anticipated with his glance at an anonymous body of "readers" duped by Churchill—"Him they dignify with the name of poet; his tawdry lampoons are called satires" (4.247)—but the choice is posed by Gifford in starker terms:

> Lo, HERE THE REPTILE! who . . . spews
> The crude abortions of his loathsome muse,
> On all that genius, all that worth holds dear,
> Unsullied rank, and piety sincere;
> While idiot mirth the base defilement lauds,
> And malice, with averted face, applauds!

This is a choice neither Peter Pindar nor English verse satire can survive, for if the imaginary audience chooses Pindar, it is exiled forthwith to the outer darkness of its own debasement, while if it chooses Gifford, idiot mirth and malice will have been banished from the world and satire will have lost its last remaining reason for being. In the stroke through which epistolary audience is abolished as the locus of any possible further discourse, the *Epistle to Peter Pindar* marks the end of the epistolary moment in English poetry.

Yet the emblematic significance of Gifford's attack on Peter Pindar lies, finally, in what it tells about the situation of English poetry in the halfcentury after the death of Pope. For the *Epistle to Peter Pindar* signals no victory of one ideological dispensation over another. The vision of organic or traditional English society summoned by such writers as Gifford and

Burke against the terrors of French radicalism was soon enough to prove itself a mirage, an illusion of community engendered by tremendous historical pressures and doomed to vanish when the sense of crisis was past. The ultimate importance of that vision is that it was to provide a moment of briefly recovered ideological security in which it became possible to see, if only for an instant, the degree to which the English verse epistle had long since already been fatally subverted by a larger movement toward poetic solipsism. This is the subversion the *Anti-Jacobin* has in mind in declaring the typical poet of its own age to be an escapist, someone who has given up on the regenerative power of poetry in a tawdry age—"Of taste, of learning, morals all bereft, / No hope, no prospect to redeem it left"—and whose own solitary retirement is a gesture of cultural despair: "As, from the loop-holes of retreat, he views / Our stage, verse, pamphlets, politics, and news, / He loathes the world—or with reflection sad, / Concludes it irrecoverably mad."

The immediate glance of the *Anti-Jacobin* here is at the Cowper of *The Task*, but more generally the pronouncement is upon elegiac Augustanism as such, which we have always been inclined to view as part of the broader phenomenon that John Sitter has called the post-Augustan flight from history—not simply Cowper in rural retirement, but the Wartons in their new poetry of melancholy musing, Gray in his turning away to a mythic or primitive past, Collins in his rhapsodic preoccupation with an interior world of private sensations and emotions. Yet the the *Anti-Jacobin*'s treatment of Cowper makes it clear not simply that elegiac Augustanism and the midcentury poetic revival were movements in opposition to each other, but that elegiac Augustanism must in fact be taken as an implied critique of the midcentury revival. This was not a critique at the obvious or parodic level at which Robert Lloyd pokes fun at the medieval preciosities of the midcentury poets, or Soame Jenyns pours out his ecstatic mock-ode to poetic and political liberty, but a critique at the deeper level of unspoken ideological assumptions, and particularly of the midcentury revival as the poetic expression of an emergent bourgeois ideology.

The central figure in this critique is John Gilbert Cooper, in whose Aristippus epistles the Augustan otium ideal is transmuted into an extraordinary pre-Paterian aestheticism that implicitly repudiates the bustling, vital, progressive world celebrated in Whig panegyric, and more particularly the phenomenon of the "polite citizen" as encouraged by Addison's popularizations of Shaftesburian ethical doctrine—in Lloyd's phrase, once again, that public that "thinks no wit or judgment greater / Than Addison and his Spectator." Yet Cooper himself figures only marginally in the tradition of elegiac Augustanism, as a poet whose epistles define one of the limits or boundaries of the post-Augustan mode. In his best-known work, *The Power of Harmony*, Cooper is the most Shaftesburian of eighteenth-century ethical poets, and it is against the Addisonian or bourgeois perversion of Shaftesbury that he poses his own vision of aesthetic retirement from the world: "Secure of living while I live, / Each momentary bliss I seize, / Ere these warm faculties decay, / The fleeting moments to deceive / Of life's allotted day."

The role of Shaftesburian doctrine in the development of bourgeois ideology as such, we have seen, had to do with the way it resolved the dilemma of an epistolary audience at once created by and excluded from the inner world of Augustan poetry, offering an alternative means to that "aristocratic" sensibility symbolized by Pope in his otium circle. "The taste of beauty and the relish of what is decent, just, and aimiable perfects the character of the gentleman and the philosopher" (2.256), Shaftesbury had said, inventing the formula according to which the successful citizens so admired by Defoe would, having made their money and bought their country estates, set out to become polite. Yet there is evident even in Shaftesbury's formulation of the idea a radical tension between two opposing tendencies, one toward solitary aesthetic contemplation—"the taste of beauty" for its own sake—and the other toward the active involvement in the world more obviously demanded by benevolism. Thus it is that we begin to hear Shaftesburian benevolism being defended in eighteenth-century poetry against the subversive claims of an equally Shaftesburian aestheticism, as in Dyer's epistle *To Mr. Wray*:

> I wonder at their turn of mind who seek
> Lone shades and melancholy cells, remote
> From each occasion of performing good,
> While all the busy world around them rolls:
> While vice contends with virtues . . .
> . . . they lend no helping hand,
> Yet dream, by contemplation, best to serve
> Omnipotence and Wisdom.

The great threat posed by aestheticism is precisely that it represents a recognizable version of the Augustan otium theme, and therefore of an ideal by now indissolubly associated with an aristocratic ethical and literary tradition. The lone shades and melancholy cells decried by Dyer do belong, ultimately, to the interior landscape of midcentury poets like Gray and the Wartons, but before that they are the Augustan otium scene when it has lost any power to provide moral leverage against a corrupt or fallen society, an embrace of otium as a solipsistic dream in which one's only hope, as Cooper puts it, is to seize each momentary bliss, deceive through the exquisite sensations of an aestheticized perception the fleeting moments of life's allotted day. This is an implication absorbed into bourgeois ideology along with Shaftesburian connoisseurship: if the taste of beauty is what perfects the character of a gentleman, then a gentleman is perhaps most perfectly one who devotes himself solely to the taste of beauty.

Yet bourgeois ideology had earlier found a way to immunize itself against the solipsistic implications of Shaftesburian aestheticism by turning the otium ideal of Augustan poetry into a psychological state, a realm of private repose that could be carried about inwardly in the new world of commercial bustle and changing property relations. This, more than anything else, had been Addison's great contribution to bourgeois ideology in *The Spectator*. So far as Addison in his famous series on the imagination simply stresses aesthetic response as a means to "aristocratic" sensibility, he is speaking as a popularizer, raising to explicit formulation in *The Spectator* something a thousand readers of Shaftesbury would in any event have seen for themselves. The truly revolutionary moment thus occurs when Addison gives central importance to another idea only glanced at in passing in Shaftesbury's writings,[4] the notion that aesthetic appreciation is actually a form of ownership in disguise, a way of looking at the world that makes it the property of the beholder in a sense superior to mere mundane legal arrangements. The man of polite imagination, Addison goes on to say, "often feels a greater satisfaction in the prospect of fields and meadows, than another does in the possession. It gives him, indeed, a kind of property in everything he sees" (3.538).

The revolutionary element in Addison's reworking of Shaftesburian aesthetic theory lies in this, a barely metaphorical idea of dispossession that at the abstract or ideological level may be taken as the equivalent of a peasant army storming the great house of a lord. The impact of the idea, with its implications of a wholesale transfer of property from a dying aristocracy to an emergent bourgeoisie, was almost immediately to alter the complexion of eighteenth-century aesthetics. "Tho' only few possess / Patrician pleasures or imperial state," proclaims Akenside in *The Pleasures of Imagination*, the man of polite imagination, capable of a Shaftesburian aesthetic response to all he beholds, is their true owner: "Whate'er adorns / The princely dome, the column and the arch, . . . / Beyond the proud possessor's narrow claim, / His tuneful breast enjoys." The most important consequence of this idea would be a translation of the otium ideal into a purely psychological state into which the man of polite imagination may retreat in the midst of an active life. "A man should endeavor," says Addison, ". . . to make the sphere of his innocent pleasures as wide as possible, that he may retire into them with safety" (3.539). This is the heart of the Spectatorial posture itself, the great contribution of Addison and Steele to the new bourgeois epistemology that, granting the busy world of commercial bustle and urban vitality its own self-sufficient existence, moves through the streets at once observant and unseen, taking in everything and altering nothing as it goes. The point of Mr. Spectator's famous visit to the Royal

Exchange is precisely that the Exchange, the very symbol of the speculative or money society so loathed by the Augustans, does not know it is being visited. This is Shaftesburian connoisseurship reconstituted as a version of the otium or contemplative ideal wholly in harmony with, rather than antagonistic to, the new eighteenth-century social and economic order.

Yet the transmutation of otium into the separate psyche of bourgeois social existence, a floating spectatorial consciousness carrying its own world within itself wherever it goes, attests at the same time to the ideological moorings of Addisonian politeness in the new money society. Addison's "man of polite imagination" is from this perspective no different in kind from the grasping puppets of Walpole's Robinocracy or the "titled upstarts" who rule the country after Walpole's fall, both belonging to a bourgeois dispensation in which, as Churchill so angrily saw, the ascendant middle class attempting to cloak itself in a borrowed Augustan sensibility is no more than the "monied upstarts" of Davenant and Bolingbroke in polite disguise. This is the situation in which John Gilbert Cooper's celebration of otium as aesthetic contemplation emerges as an uncompromising rejection not simply of the new money society and its creatures, but of Addisonian politeness as a false ideal. Cooper's declaration of personal independence employs a conventional otium vocabulary of court-as-corruption and retirement-as-virtue, but a new note of social fastidiousness suggests its special burden of post-Augustan implication:

> In courts, my lord, let others lead . . .
> The crowd of tinsel'd slaves, who tread
> The miry ministerial road
> To modern Honor's dark abode,
> Where dwell th' *high* vulgar of the town,
> Which England's common courtesy,
> To make bad fellowship go down,
> Politely calls good company.

At the same time, Cooper's rejection of Addisonian politeness as a vulgarization of Shaftesbury is undertaken in the spirit of a more "pure" Shaftesburian doctrine, a theory of moral and aesthetic response that itself begins in a repudiation of money and power and ambition. The Shaftesbury of the Aristippus epistles is he who had sung, in *The Moralists*, the joys of solitude: "Ye fields and woods, my refuge from the toilsome world of business, receive me in your quiet sanctuaries, and favor my retreat and thoughtful solitude. . . . Blessed be ye chaste abodes of happiest mortals, who here in peaceful innocence enjoy a life unenvied, though divine; whilst with its blessed tranquility it affords a happy leisure and retreat for man, who, made for contemplation, . . . may here best meditate the cause of things" (2.97–98). This is the note of pure Shaftesburian contemplativeness, infinitely closer to the Epicurean origins of the otium ideal and to its aristocratic literary tradition, that one then hears not simply in Aristippus but elsewhere in the verse epistle after midcentury. "But Innocence is there," says Sneyd Davies, musing on rural retirement in an epistle to Frederick Cornwallis, "And simple Quiet with her downy couch, / Meads lowing, tune of birds, and lapse of streams."

This last pursuit of the otium theme in eighteenth-century poetry is thus a powerful counterstatement to the Addisonian notion of aesthetic response as a mode of property. For otium as celebrated by Aristippus becomes in this context a principle of disinterestedness almost in the sense that Kant, himself more distantly under Shaftesbury's influence, would place it at the center of both art and morality. "O arts divine!," exclaims Langhorne in Epistle II of *The Enlargement of the Mind*, a poem always insistent upon the Shaftesburian inseparability of the moral and the aesthetic, "Lost in their charms each mean attachment ends, / And taste and beauty thus are virtue's friends." The threat posed by the Aristippus mode of otium to a bourgeois order driven by economic self-interest would be allegorized by Thomson in *The Castle of Indolence*, and indeed the voice of bourgeois urgency is occasionally heard even within this last body of otium poetry—"Life's whole business this!" Sneyd Davies hears it say in the epistle to Cornwallis. "Is it to bask i' the sun? if so, a snail / Were happy crawling on a southern wall"—and yet in *The Epistles of Aristippus in Retirement* may nonetheless be heard a last quietly defiant utterance of the doctrine that, in a world propelled by interest, the mere disinterested enjoyment of life is virtue:

> An osier on the stream of time,
> This philosophic wanderer
> Floating thro' ev'ry place and clime,
> Finds some peculiar blessing there.
> Where e'er the winding current strays
> By prosp'rous mount or adverse plain,
> He'll sport, till all his jocund days
> Are lost in life's eternal main.

The Aristippus epistles represent a controlled and deliberate farewell to the epistolary audience earlier summoned into existence by Augustan poetry, a permanent valediction to the possibility of regenerating a fallen society through satire or ethical verse, and an embrace of something very like Pater's notion of the world as a dream of the solitary mind. For with the shrinking of the Augustan otium scene to a landscape identical with the limits of individual consciousness, and with the hedonistic desperation of Churchill and Burns refined into a Shaftesburian aestheticism that makes seizing each momentary bliss a matter not of nocturnal carousing but of exquisite perception, the Augustan verse epistle has imploded on the secret center of solipsism—the blankness of the page, the aloneness of the epistoler in his scene—that had from the beginning lurked at the heart of epistolarity in poetry. This allows us suddenly to grasp the sense in which Churchill in his solipsistic rage, Lloyd in his haunted sense of a diminished world, or Goldsmith and Cowper in their moral nostalgia had all along been addressing not Augustan audience but the mere fading memory of Augustan audience, and of a time when its very reality as a literary possibility bespoke a fuller and more hopeful world.

Yet the shrinking of the world to the limits of solipsistic consciousness, so equally embraced in the Aristippus epistles, was more generally felt as a spiritual and literary crisis, which in the elegiac Augustanism of Cowper gives us the moments of personal anxiety in *The Task* or the near-desperation of *The Castaway*, and in Goldsmith those times when, as in *The Traveller*, the author of *She Stoops to Conquer* and *The Vicar of Wakefield* can sound so hauntingly like an eighteenth-century Byron: "My prime of life in wandr'ing spent and care: / Impell'd, with steps unceasing, to pursue / Some fleeting good, that mocks me with the view; / . . . My fortune leads to traverse realms alone, / And find no spot of all the world my own." At its furthest extreme, this same sense of crisis will then produce that poetry of assumed personality and poetic insanity that runs in submerged and always somewhat mysterious counterpoint to the more conventional verse of the later eighteenth century: the incantatory rhythms of Smart or Collins, Macpherson in the Ossian poems, Chatterton in the imaginary voice of the medieval monk Rowley.

The poetry of Chatterton, in which the motifs of assumed personality and poetic insanity converge, demonstrates in exemplary fashion the way the Augustan verse epistle would disintegrate under the pressures of an encroaching solipsism, grasping frantically after an audience already becoming spectral as it wavers uncertainly in the register of its simultaneous address to lector and epistolary audience. In, for instance, the *Epistle to the Reverend Mr. Catcott*, a divine whose work on geology and Creation had made him a luminary in Chatterton's little world at Bristol, the crisis of solipsism may be urgently felt as a pathology of audience, a contradictory attempt both to satirize Catcott and his admirers and to awaken their admiration. What is needed to reconcile the contradiction, appeal over the head of both Catcott and his Bristol readers to the wider English audience that poetry in the days of Pope could simply assume to exist, is no longer available. "What man of sense would value vulgar praise?" demands Chatterton, himself obviously longing in the most fervent way for nothing else:

> Tho' pointed fingers mark the man of fame,
> And literary grocers chaunt your name;

> Tho' in each tailor's bookcase Catcott shines,
> With ornamental flow'rs and gilded lines;
> Tho' youthful ladies, who by instinct scan
> The natural philosophy of man,
> Can ev'ry reason of your work repeat,
> As sands in Africa retain the heat:
> Yet check your flowing pride: will all allow
> To wreathe the labor'd laurel round your brow?

The tendency to fantasy or delusion involved in this breakdown of epistolary address emerges in *The Defense*, in which Chatterton describes to a friend the reaction he expects to the Catcott epistle: "why must Chatterton selected sit, / The butt of ev'ry critic's little wit?" For Chatterton is the butt of no one's wit. He is an obscure hack writer living in an out-of-the-way corner of England and entertaining fantasies about being the same sort of commanding public figure as Dryden or Pope. This is the dilemma to which the Rowley world was a solution. "The poetry that lay deep within the Bristol apprentice gained utterance," observed R. D. Havens many years ago, "through his abandoning the drab present for a remote, legendary past. When Chatterton locked himself in his attic room with his bits of parchment, . . . he locked out the eighteenth century, his friends, his enemies, his family, and most of all himself. . . . As Wordsworth said of his own college days: 'I had a world about me—'twas my own, / I made it, for it only lived to me'" (30).[5] This is the context in which insanity or assumed personality becomes the means of dissolving the claims of the Augustan legacy on the poet, allowing escape from a world of fragmentation and decline at the terrible cost of leaving behind as well one's right mind or ordinary self.

This poetry demands to be seen as a direct response to the crisis of solipsism precisely because it so obviously accepts the Augustan verdict on eighteenth-century England as a corrupt and declining society, an empire of chaos resulting not simply from an actual disintegration of community but from the vanishing of community as a moral and literary ideal. Here lies the radical distinction between the poetry of insanity and assumed personality, and another body of poetry it sometimes superficially resembles—that produced by the midcentury revival as a phenomenon of what John Sitter, thinking of the soliloquies and lyrics of midcentury poetry, has called literary loneliness. Yet the lyrics of midcentury bear an extremely complex relation to the verse epistles they displace, for they represent, in effect, a momentous countermovement, the verse epistle boldly retracing in reverse the story of its own development, returning in a spirit of new-found optimism to its origins in epistolary solipsism. The ground of this optimism is, as we have seen, ideological, a buoyant sense that the dark

Augustan vision of modern corruption had been no more than a distempered dream, and a first dim stirring of the notion that history might after all be, contrary to ancient schemes of cycle and decline, a story of progress. In Pope's last satires, we recall Joseph Warton saying, England "is represented as totally ruined, and overwhelmed with dissipation, depravity, and corruption." Yet in the twenty years since Pope's death this very country has "carried its triumphs . . . through all the quarters of the world, and astonished the most distant nations with a display of uncommon efforts, abilities, and virtues" (2.426).

This is the basis for Warton's impatient dismissal of the notion that the Augustan collapse involved the demise of genuine poetry in England: "I am not persuaded that all true genius died with Pope: and presume that the Seasons of Thomson, the Pleasures of Imagination, and Odes, of Akenside, the Night-Thoughts of Young, the Leonidas of Glover, the Elegy of Gray . . . were not published when Dr. Warburton delivered this insinuation of a failure of poetic abilities" (1.141). The rejection of Augustanism through which the midcentury poetic revival establishes its own alternative claims is made possible precisely by the new Addisonian or Spectatorial notion of individual consciousness as a secure private world floating along amid the outward bustle of contemporary society. To be sure, there remains a hint of insecurity or precariousness in all this. Yet the significant thing is that the threat now does not come from solipsism, that dissolution of community and terrifying isolation of the individual mind that had so haunted the Augustan enterprise. It arises, rather, from the power of a teeming bourgeois actuality to absorb into itself all merely inward experience, and the defense against it is simply to assert the claims of mind or consciousness as a world of equal interest and integrity.

The primary means through which midcentury poetry manages this enterprise is the retroactive construction of an alternative poetic tradition, which is the point of Joseph Warton's mention of Akenside's *Pleasures of Imagination* and Young's *Night Thoughts*. Their brilliance as propagandists of this alternative tradition makes the Wartons central figures in the midcentury revival, giving such manifestos as the *Essay on Pope* and the *History of English Poetry* a far greater significance in the longer run than any poem written by either Warton. By the same token, the Longinian revival that prepared the way for the inward or "pure" poetry of midcentury is significant not simply as having provided a rationale for the celebration of intense inner experience, but also as providing a directive for constructing an alternative poetic tradition. "Like bold Longinus of immortal fame," Christopher Pitt had cried in an epistle to Joseph Spence, "You read your poet with a poet's flame; / With his your generous raptures still aspire, / The critic kindles when the bard's on fire."

The occasion of this utterance is Spence's essay on Pope's *Odyssey*, and nothing could more clearly intimate the role played by Longinus in the midcentury reorientation of poetic values that then underwrites the poetry of the Wartons and their school. For Pitt's enthusiasm here is itself Longinian, and in catching the poet's flame from Spence as Spence had caught it from Pope and Pope from Homer he exemplifies the revisionary process through which, in a sudden circumvention of Augustan poetics and all that was once meant by neoclassicism—the delivery of Homer as the great poet of universal nature to an English audience steeped in classical attitudes—he constructs in the image of his own eager response a "romantic" Homer, a "romantic" Pope, and a Spence whose virtue as a reader lies in his romantic response to both. At such a moment, when the Pope of the *Essay on Criticism* and neoclassic poetics generally is seen as having been absorbed into the primitive strangeness of a Homer who sings as the bard of a magical past, the energies of Pitt's own address to Spence begin to push against the imposed constraints of its epistolary form, as though in a prelude to the formal rupture through which midcentury poetry may so often be seen to emerge directly out of the Augustan verse epistle.

The great example of this generative bursting of epistolary form is Collins's *Epistle to Sir Thomas Hanmer*, in which a ceremonial address to an editor of Shakespeare's works moves insensibly toward the recovery of a romantic or magical Shakespeare seen as having been suppressed by the dead weight of Augustan assumptions about poetry. The spirit in which Collins approaches Shakespeare is Longinian, that reading of a poet with a poet's flame that then, as torch lights torch in a lengthening procession, brings forth its own poetic rapture. What is consumed in Collins's rapture in the *Epistle to Hanmer* is epistolary form itself, and out of its ashes arises, in Collins's invocation of Shakespeare as tutulary spirit, the apostrophic mode of Collins's own odes and midcentury poetry generally:

> O more than all in pow'rful genius blest,
> Come, take thine empire o'er the willing breast!
> Whate'er the wounds this youthful heart shall feel,
> Thy songs support me, and thy morals heal.

At any such moment, as Martin Price remarked in a seminal essay on the eighteenth-century sublime, the poet moves out of one world and into another: "This is a movement into a sacred precinct, a movement to a realm where the powers of awareness are different. . . . The precinct is sacred because it is inhabited by a power, and to be drawn into its realm is to be made one with that power. The poet has the capacity to imagine such a realm and to seek it; he often calls upon a greater power to descend and take him there. The passivity of the poet is an appeal to otherness" (200).[6] This is the interior world of mind or imagination as it appears in the new security of bourgeois consciousness, the disembodied sphere of Addisonian or Spectatorial awareness as it has been freed to investigate the sources of its own sentience.

The great project of the midcentury revival is the search for a landscape corresponding to this interior realm of sublime or intense experience, the outward setting of solitude or gloom that then becomes its characteristic scene. Yet the profound consequences of this project for later English poetry were to arise precisely because the landscape thus recovered was not an actual but a poetic landscape, a bleak and melancholy setting that had always been previously present and uneasily glanced at in Augustan poetry, the repressed other of that teeming world of men and manners in which Augustanism had waged its losing war against modernity. In the poetry of the Wartons or Thomas Gray, we enter less into a new poetic landscape than into one liberated from its repressed status in Augustan verse, a setting always haunting the dark margins of Augustan consciousness and glimpsed only in rare moments of unguarded perception.

Whenever we do catch a glimpse of this repressed or excluded landscape in Augustan poetry it is likely to be because someone has been sent into exile, banished from a world of moral purpose where everything has meaning in terms of a controlling symbolic tension between country and city, ancient traditional society and modern urban flux, to a world where the barren landscape gives back only an image of the solitary mind in its isolation. Thus, for instance, an epistle written to Pope at home in England from Parnell in Ireland, gazing out on a landscape whose barrenness betokens a kind of poetic sterility as well: "Here moss-grown trees expand the smallest leaf, / Here half an acre's corn is half a sheaf, / Here hills with naked heads the tempest meet, / Rocks at their side, and torrents at their feet." Viewed from within the sphere of Augustan assumptions, this is the very landscape of solipsism, a setting utterly outside the world of human moral concern, and yet it is nonetheless the scene in which midcentury poetry will most often seek the outward image of its own intensity of inner experience.

More often in Augustan poetry, this landscape of barrenness or mental vacuity is glimpsed as lying just beyond the borders of its own interior setting, permitting a momentary glance in the direction of a world gone spiritless in the absence of ethical purpose. Yet even this involves a notion of exile, the world becoming a solipsistic reverie in the moment that the mind is banished from the sphere of social concern. Thus Pope's *Epistle to Miss Blount, on Her Leaving Town, After the Coronation:*

> In some fair evening, on your elbow laid,
> You dream of triumphs in the rural shade; . . .
> Before you pass th' imaginary sights
> Of Lords, and Earls, and Dukes, and garter'd Knights;
> While the spread fan o'ershades your closing eyes;
> Then give one flirt, and all the vision flies.

> Thus vanish sceptres, coronets, and balls,
> And leave you in lone woods, and empty halls.

This is the landscape repressed by Augustan poetry in its normal preoccupation with social and moral conflict, "the realm," as David Morris has said, "where nothing ever happens. It is a world set apart from history, where the most momentous action is escapist dreaming" (25). This will constitute, precisely, its attraction for midcentury poetry.

The dream of a world outside history is not escapist in midcentury terms, however, for in the new light of bourgeois progressivism history is precisely something that can be left to itself, a process of social and material improvement moving steadily toward a general amelioration of the human condition. To see in the immediate background of the midcentury revival the dawning moments of what P. A. Sorokin calls progressive linearism, that theory of history that would achieve its eighteenth-century apotheosis in the writings of Condorcet or the Saint Simonians, is thus to see why for the midcentury poets the inward exploration of mind or consciousness suddenly comes into view as a great overlooked poetic resource. For now the gloom and solitude and melancholy that to the Augustans had spoken so dismayingly of the mind's aloneness in the world instead speak reassuringly of something primal or prerational at the deepest level of human consciousness, something increasingly to be valued in an age moving ever more inevitably away from its origins in the primitive and the magical. The midcentury revival is not in this perspective a flight from but an acquiescence in history, a determination to rescue for the imagination a sense of the magical otherwise dying out in the inevitable advance of social progress.

The midcentury project of liberating a landscape of gloom and solitude from its repressed status in Augustan poetry thus constitutes an implicit rebuke to Augustanism itself, a demonstration that the specter of solipsism haunting Pope's last poetry had been no more than a hobgoblin conjured into being by a false theory of history, a scheme of cycle and decline unthinkingly taken over from ancient Greece and Rome and wholly irrelevant to the modern age. The moment at which midcentury poetry claims this landscape as its own, at once exorcising the specter of solipsism and proclaiming a new and positive fascination with the strange or marvelous, is Joseph Warton's exaltation of *Eloisa to Abelard* as Pope's greatest poem, and of the lines describing the lonely setting of Eloisa's nunnery—Warton calls them "truly sublime"—as the very essence of pure poetry:

> But o'er the twilight groves and dusky caves,
> Long-sounding isles, and intermingled graves,
> Black MELANCHOLY sits, and round her throws
> A death-like silence, and a dread repose;

> Her gloomy presence saddens all the scene,
> Shades every flower, and darkens every green,
> Deepens the murmur of the falling floods,
> And breathes a darker horror on the woods.

Warton is reading *Eloisa to Abelard*, in short, in a world where solipsism, no longer implying the terrible isolation of the mind from man and God, appears instead as a pleasingly mysterious aura glimmering around the physical landscape and answering to mysterious depths in the consciousness of the beholder. This is the ground for the midcentury reordering of eighteenth-century poetry that conjures a "tradition" into existence simply by emphasizing any earlier concern with the primitive, the strange, the sublime, or all these together as they take as their image what Thomson once calls "the wild romantic country."[7] Thus it is, for instance, that John Philips describing an earthquake in *Cyder*—"Horror stalks around / Wild staring, and his sad concomitant / Despair, of abject look"—may be heard from the midcentury perspective as a precursor of Collins, or Thomson himself in his occasional glance toward the primitive—"These are the haunts of meditation, these / The scenes where ancient bards th'inspiring breath, / Exstatic, felt"—as a precursor of Gray or the Wartons, and thus it is that in an obscure locodescriptive poem such as *The Country* there may be glimpsed, along with the "hanging precipice / In air high-nodding, whence hoarse waterfalls / Dashing their waves against the hoary rocks /Tumble down headlong," the essential features of the midcentury poetic landscape as it had even then, in the early eighteenth century, been taking shape on the margins of the Augustan enterprise.

As midcentury poetry comes increasingly to dwell in these haunts of meditation, its soliloquizing takes on more and more the appearance of epistolary verse retracing its steps in search of its solipsistic origins. For as the verse epistle begins in writerly solitude, most often in the scene of otium retirement in which a friend as the "other self" of Aristotelian and Epicurean doctrine is imagined as the absent addressee, and then summons into existence a wider audience and a world, the soliloquy or ode is more likely to revisit the same scene and insist now on the literal absence of audience, the aloneness of the speaker in a world where the otium friend lingers merely as a vestigial presence. The process of reversal may already be glimpsed in a verse epistle such as Langhorne's *Studley Park*, in which the "awful pleasure" impressed on the speaker's soul by something very like the midcentury landscape—"the sacred solitude, the lone recess"—eventually puts him in mind of the absent friend: "wert thou, my Farrar," exclaims Langhorne, but "witness to my joy!" By midcentury, however, as in Thomas Warton's *Ode. Sent to a Friend*, the absence of the friend has more usually become the actual subject of the poem:

> Who now shall indolently stray
> Through the deep forest's tangled way . . . ?
> Who mid thy nooks of hazel sit,
> Lost in some melancholy fit;
> And listening to the raven's croak,
> The distant flail, the falling oak!

This is the world of solitude verging on solipsism, a memory not of otium friendship but of the friend himself as a *poeta ignotus*, a lonely wanderer in twilight groves whose surroundings belong at least as much to his own imagination as to any actual landscape. For what has made the deep forest a haunt of meditation is its sense of primal isolation from historical progress, those forces of social and material improvement whose only great liability is their desacralization of the world. This is Reason as once described in a verse epistle by Richard Bentley—"She wins her way, wherever she advances; / Satyr no more, nor faun, nor dryad dances. / The groves, tho' trembling to a natural breeze, / Dismiss their horrors, and show nought but trees"—and the midcentury poetic revival is in one important aspect nothing other than the project of restoring the satyrs and dryads to their groves, saving through poetry and imagination what is being lost in the advance of a progressive history. Those midcentury soliloquies that seem so hauntingly like the verse epistle revisiting its origins in silence and solitude seem so precisely because of their attempt to recover a state of consciousness existing prior to community or society, that submerged level of mind from which satyrs and dryads may be thought to have once arisen.

The gaze of midcentury poetry toward a primitive or magical past belongs to this project of reconsecrating the world through imagination, the strongest argument for the possibility of seeing enchantment in everyday existence being that whole societies once saw it that way. The "romantic" Shakespeare recovered by Collins in the *Epistle to Hanmer* is the poet of a world where the lowliest peasant sees magic in his surroundings—"Where swains contented own the quiet scene, / And twilight faeries tread the circled green"—and the same theme lies at the center of Collins's *Ode on the Popular Superstitions of the Highlands*, which like Warton's *Ode. Sent to a Friend* is vestigially epistolary in form. The absent friend is in this case John Home, to whom the poem was originally addressed, and its occasion is Home's return to a Highland society in which magic is still real. Yet the point of the poem is Collins's own ability to imagine this as he writes, bringing magic to life in the midst of an eighteenth century increasingly unsympathetic to its intimations:

> 'Tis Fancy's land to which thou set'st thy feet
> Where still, tis said, the fairy people meet

> Beneath each birken shade, on mead or hill. . . .
> Such airy beings awe th'untutor'd swain;
>   Nor thou, tho' learn'd, his homlier thoughts neglect,
> Let thy sweet Muse the rural faith sustain.

In purely literary terms, this same impulse gives us that more total reordering of earlier English poetry that will take as its center of value the magical world of the old romances, as in Thomas Warton's *Observations on the Faerie Queene*: "such are their terrible graces of magic and enchantment . . . that they contribute, in a wonderful degree, to arouse and invigorate all the powers of imagination, to store the fancy with those sublime and alarming images, which true poetry best delights to display" (Elledge 2.785–86). This is not some perfunctory rearrangement of literary values, for in midcentury poetry itself it is the imagination thus invigorated, the fancy thus stored with sublime images, that will then permit the transformation of the Augustan landscape of Pope and Swift into the far different landscape of the midcentury revival. Thus, for instance, the sudden glimpse of another world that occurs in *Newmarket*, a satire written when Thomas Warton was still feeling his way out of the Augustan mode, as the speaker catches sight of the "Gothic towers," rising above the forest of an old English country seat: "Whose rafter'd hall the crowding tenants fed, /And dealt to Age and Want their daily bread: / Where crested knights, and peerless damsels join'd, / At high and solemn festivals have din'd."

At any such moment, however, it is possible to see that the midcentury mode in poetry is already threatened with its own eventual implosion, a collapse into solipsism as, in the Augustan sense, the isolation of the mind in its own dream of the world. For as the emphasis on magic and romance makes clear, the midcentury focus on a twilight scene of solitary musing concerns not the response of mind to landscape but an attempt to project mind or imagination onto landscape, the great unintended consequence of which is a landscape ultimately indistinguishable from mind. This is the danger lurking, for instance, in the movement of Warton's *Ode. Sent to a Friend* from a simple lament that there is no longer anyone with poetic imagination present to appreciate this rural vista—"Who now shall climb its brows to view / The length of landscape, ever new, . . . / Who mark, beneath, each village-charm, / Or grange, or elm-encircled farm?"—to the much more radical claim that the landscape, in the absence of the friend, is now depopulated. For the Bard, as Warton says to the silent scene, "who peopled all thy vocal bowers / With shadowy shapes, and airy powers" is gone, and with him has departed its sense of enchantment: "With hollow shriek the nymphs forsake / The pathless copse and hedge-row brake."

In the immediate background of Warton's *Ode. Sent to a Friend* may be glimpsed the pure solipsism of an imaginative world in which the external landscape has dematerialized and the poet is left alone inside his mind with nothing upon which to focus but its shadowy or dreamlike contents. As the poetic expression of this solipsism may be found in certain of Collins's "allegoric" odes, its theory may be found in a tract like William Duff's *Essay on Original Genius*, in which the original genius is he who, "by the vigorous effort of a creative imagination, . . . calls shadowy substances and unreal objects into existence. They are present to his view and glide, like spectres, in silent, sullen majesty, before his astonished and entranced sight" (177). Duff's *Essay* marks the end of the long road from solipsism as derangement to solipsism as a source of "pure poetry," for this is the midcentury poet as the unwitting successor of Pope's mad versifier in the *Epistle to Arbuthnot*, scribbling with charcoal round the darkened walls of an isolated cell that is ultimately, when its true nature is grasped, the Paterian prison of the solitary mind, the very terror that Augustanism had predicted to be lurking in the dissolution of traditional society.

The lingering memory of epistolarity invoked when an ode such as Warton's is "sent to a friend" permits us to grasp the sense in which so much midcentury poetry, particularly the ode as the emblematic form of the midcentury revival, represents the verse epistle gone back in search of its solipsistic origins. For in the otium ideal of Aristotelian friendship a hint of unresolved solipsism had always remained, a mirroring of minds never entirely dispelled when Augustan poetry turned its gaze outward to a world of bustling urban importunity. In the midcentury setting, as the literal absence of the sympathetic friend enters into the mood of twilight musing, the effect is not simply of a spectralization but an internalization of audience, a locking of the mind into the empty echoes of a dialogue with itself from which there is no escape. For such a dialogue, as Martin Price remarks, is the very essence of this poetry: "The sense of otherness remains, of course. . . . But the otherness has been displaced into a vision of *the other self*, the self at last controlled by powers that have been submerged by culture, the self either mastering the familiar world or annihilating it" (201–2).

This explains one's sense of the midcentury poetic revival as a self-contained and terminal episode, a literary movement looking back to the origins of Augustanism and not, for all the generations of students taught to see in the poetry of Collins and Gray and the Wartons a phenomenon known as pre-Romanticism, any strong anticipation of Wordsworth and Coleridge. For to glimpse the living and urgent relation of the midcentury ode or lyric to the Augustan verse epistle, or the even more profound relation between the entire poetic generation of the Wartons and the earlier generation of Pope and Swift, is to see that the midcentury revival was in an important and genuine sense the last episode of literary Augustanism, the return of poetic solipsism upon a scene from which, in a tremendous mobilization of wit and learning and moral energy, it had been forcibly excluded for over forty years. In the notion of the midcentury ode as epistolarity confessing its failure to conquer solipsism, attempting one last avenue of escape into a pure sublimity of self, we have the curious sense in which the midcentury revival was simply Augustanism coming at the last to rest in that solitude of mind in the denial of which it had begun.

Yet the collapse into poetic solipsism was to have one momentous consequence for the emergence of Romanticism, for in that collapse the "wild romantic country" that midcentury poetry had chosen as its setting was in effect to take on a life of its own, float free to become an object of poetic contemplation in its own right, with no further demand that there be projected onto it any redeeming qualities of mind or imagination. It is the quietest of poetic revolutions, the moment at which the landscape becomes available in this neutral way, not as the object of physicotheological rapture, as in Akenside or John Gilbert Cooper or Thomson in his occasional mood of Shaftesburian transport, and not as the gloomy mirror of midcentury melancholy, but simply as an object of contemplation. This is the landscape visible in Langhorne's *Studley Park* when from the summit of a neighboring rise the speaker pauses to gaze around the "far horizon" "where dales descend, or ridgy mountains rise, / And lose their aspect in the falling skies."

The view from the summit in *Studley Park* brings to a conclusion in an important sense a movement that had begun over a hundred years earlier in *Coopers Hill*, in which the speaker's gaze outward over a landscape saturated in ideology had given rise to the controlling opposition between country and city that would then give shape to Country ideology and literary Augustanism. In *Studley Park* and certain other later-eighteenth-century verse epistles, on the other hand, we may see emerging from the Augustan collapse a landscape innocent of those ideological oppositions, and yet one that recognizably includes, along with the deep forests and solitary groves of midcentury poetry, the ordered countryside of Augustan verse. The verse epistle that more clearly than any other registers this development, perhaps, is John Scott of Amwell's *Winter Amusements in the Country*, in which nothing so clearly testifies to the dissolution of Augustan moral oppositions as Scott's benign view of the city, "Where glittering shops their varied stores display, / And passing thousands crowd the public way: / Where Painting's forms and Music's sounds delight, . . . / And conversation's sober social hours / Engage the mind, and elevate its pow'rs."

Nonetheless, the dissolution of the country-city opposition was not, as we know, in itself brought about by the Augustan collapse, for a strong symbolic tension between country and city persists in the elegiac Augustanism of Goldsmith and Cowper, and is as starkly insisted upon in a poem like *The Task* as anywhere in Dryden or Pope or Gay. This is why Scott's exhilarated sense of urban possibility must be seen, however indirectly, as another important consequence of the midcentury poetic revival, which by shifting the moral center of gravity of English poetry in a certain radical way had for a protracted literary moment made the country-city opposition simply irrelevant to the deeper concerns of the poetic imagination—a memory, merely, of the dead Augustan past. Thus it is that such poets as Scott were able to turn in the later eighteenth century toward a rural landscape that, no longer implicated in an invisible warfare between traditional values and a demonic modernity, may be gazed upon as possessing a value of its own. The city, if not a scene precisely innocent, has taken on the status of a neutral fact of modern life, while the countryside has become, or is on the verge of becoming, nature.

This is the final reordering of poetic values that would produce the phenomenon once known as pre-Romanticism, a revisionary drawing-together of the scattered moments of minute or detailed description in earlier eighteenth-century verse to create a "tradition" that could then be viewed as having been there all along, submerged or hidden but tending irresistibly toward an interest in the landscape as an autonomous object of contemplation. The earliest instance of such description in eighteenth-century poetry is the extraordinary verse epistle written by Ambrose Philips from Denmark in 1709, the epistoler just having awakened to find the world covered with snow: "All pleasing objects which to verse invite . . . / The flowery plains, and silver-streaming floods, / By snow disguised, in bright confusion lie, / And with one dazzling waste fatigue the eye." For what has been effaced is not an actual countryside but a poetic landscape, the Augustan way ("flow'ry plains," "silver-streaming floods") of looking at nature, and the winter scene that then becomes visible is strange or magical precisely as the poet has been compelled to gaze upon it without preconceptions:

> For every shrub, and every blade of grass,
> And every pointed thorn, seem'd wrought in glass;
> In pearls and rubies rich the hawthorns show,
> While through the ice the crimson berries glow.
> The thick-sprung reeds, which watery marshes yield,
> Seem'd polished lances in a hostile field.

The same tendency in *The Seasons*, in which the physicotheological impulse moves Thomson almost inevitably toward isolated moments of minute description, is responsible for the "pre-Romantic" Thomson who figured so largely in the older literary histories.[8] The extraordinary thing about this tendency in Thomson is that it was so immediately perceived as demanding a poetics of its own. The revisionary process through which a pre-Romantic tradition would be constituted even before the eighteenth century had ended may be seen to be already at work in a verse epistle addressed to Thomson in his own lifetime by James Dalacourt, which begins in a vaguely "Augustan" register—"Blest Bard! with what new lustre dost thou rise"—but then transposes into a wondering description of nature as it has suddenly become visible in Thomson's poetry: "O'er the black heath the bittern stalks alone, / And to the naked marshes makes his moan; / Engulf'd in bogs behold his muddy beak, / And the brown partridge feeding on the brake." By the time William Hayward Roberts comes to write his epistle to Anstey some decades later the revisionary process is virtually complete, Thomson having by now been enshrined as the poet who "examin'd every drop / That glistens on the thorn, each leaf survey'd / Which Autumn from the rustling forest shakes, / And mark'd its shape, and trac'd in the rude wind / Its eddying motion."

In *The Seasons* and elsewhere, the tendency of this poetic mode is toward a subdued impersonality of natural description—this is what Roberts means when he says that Nature placed in Thomson's hand "a pencil, dipp'd in her own colors"—an absorption of mind into landscape such that landscape seems for the moment to have become the only reality. When this occurs in the verse epistle, what is absorbed is the entire complex interplay of the epistolary situation itself, a suspension of the drama of direct and indirect address in favor of a single plenary gaze toward the natural setting. Thus, for instance, Samuel Henley in an epistle to a friend "just leaving a favorite retirement" concentrates not on the friend but on the countryside he is forsaking—"the grey church peeping half through trees, / Slopes waving corn as list the breeze, / The podding bean-field strip'd with balks, / The hurdl'd sheep-fold, hoof-trod walks"—and thus John Scott of Amwell's contemplation of a farm in wintertime actually becomes one of the winter amusements that are the subject of his poem: "The barn's long ridge, and doors expanded wide, / The stable's straw-clad eaves and clay-built side; / The cart-shed's roof, of rough-hewn roundwood made, / And loose on heads of sere old pollards laid."

As in those midcentury odes preserving a vestigial memory of epistolary form, the friend of otium tradition is likely to linger in such poems as these as a reminder of an earlier poetic world, but the epistoler's increasing forgetfulness of audience in favor of a greater imaginative concentration on the landscape moves his utterance toward a mode of soliloquy or inward meditation that is the very opposite of the midcentury poet's excursions into his own consciousness. For in verse epistles such as those of Scott or Henley, in which the absorption of the mind in the outward scene serves to guarantee the real existence of a reality external to consciousness, the poem is free at long last to dwell entirely on the relation between mind and world. The notion of being alone with nature in this sense once again goes back ultimately to Shaftesbury, but the mood in these epistles is rather that described by Thomson in his last revision of *Spring*, a "lonely musing," a "dream ... of careless solitude" that amounts to a kind of quietism in which "wandering images" of the natural landscape "Soothe every gust of passion into peace, / All but the swellings of the soften'd heart, / That waken, not disturb the tranquil mind" (lines 461–66).

In the transmutation of Shaftesburian enthusiasm into the almost pietistic tranquility of Thomson's "dream of careless solitude," finally, may be traced the underlying shift in poetic epistemology that at midcentury will inspire the extraordinary blank-verse epistles of Sneyd Davies and later such descriptive epistles as Henley's *To a Friend* and Scott's *Winter Amusements*, all of these together prefiguring that more radical transformation that, beginning with *Lyrical Ballads*, will take shape as the Romantic solution to the problem of solipsism. Yet if the Romantic theme of mind and nature as separate aspects of a single transcendent reality may already be glimpsed in these epistles, and if the Romantic notion of solitude and inward meditation as a means to transcendent vision is already implicit in the epistoler's turn toward soliloquy, it is precisely because the superficialities of Shaftesburian benevolism, that cheerful Pelagian sense that the Creator is wholly benevolent and human evil by and large an unsocial delusion,[9] will have begun to give way to something much more resembling the Augustinian vision that had earlier sustained the verse epistle in its long war against the forces of a corrupt modernity. It is, strangely and unexpectedly, the memory of that more darkly complex Augustinian reality that is honored in these verse epistles of a newer world.

The figure who symbolically presides over this moment of submerged continuity in English poetry is, once again, William Law, not as the theologian of literary Augustanism but now as the Boehme-inspired mystic who had so profound an influence on Coleridge and, through Coleridge, on English Romanticism. This is the Law of *The Way to Divine Knowledge* and *An Appeal to All That Doubt*, and, reading those works, one comes upon the curious sense in which the vision of Pope and Swift and the vision of the first Romantics was, with certain radical readjustments, the same. It may be found summarized, as usual, in the homely rhymes of John Byrom, as in his *Epistle to a Gentleman of the Temple*: "Why look we then with such a longing eye / On what this world can give us, or deny; / Of man and angel fallen, the sad remains? ... / Sons of eternity, tho' born on earth, / There is within us a celestial birth; / A life that waits the efforts of our mind / To raise itself." To look backward from this to Dryden or Pope is to do no more than remind ourselves of the Augustinian grounding of the Augustan verse epistle, its steady insistence on the ultimate reality of the City of God in the deranged and disordered world of contemporary eighteenth-century society. To look forward, however, is to glimpse a

Wordsworthian possibility of "celestial birth" never imagined by the Augustans themselves but nonetheless strangely consonant with their own deepest notions of reality.

In its larger outlines, this gives us the movement we have already traced in the verse epistles of Scott and Henley, an imaginative concentration on landscape so total that audience seems virtually forgotten, to the point that a poem such as *The Naturalist's Evening Walk*, an epistle from Gilbert White to Thomas Pennant—"high in the air and pois'd upon his wings, / Unseen, the soft-enamor'd woodlark sings"—may be seen to be moving toward something very close to the fully universalized audience of so much Romantic poetry. In more specific terms, however, the same movement involves the opening up of a new range of thematic concerns unknown to the Augustans, most having to do with possibilities of celestial birth or shadowed divinity already present in the world of men. Thus, for instance, Helen Maria Williams in an epistle written from France in 1791 will immediately envision the French Revolution—"those scenes, whose birth / Forms a new era in the storied earth"—as a new dawn for humankind, and thus Sneyd Davies in an epistle to Charles Pratt written nearly fifty years before had already been visited by a sense of childhood as "nature's morning": "vital prime! where Thames / Flows by Etona's walls, and cheerful sees her sons wide swarming.... / O never hope again, / (Impossible! untenable!) to grasp / Those joys."

In a very real sense, the story of the eighteenth-century verse epistle ends here, half a century before Gifford's *Epistle to Peter Pindar* and at a time when scores of epistolary poems yet remain to be written. For in the body of blank-verse epistles composed by Sneyd Davies in his midcentury obscurity the hidden moment of transmutation may be discovered in which the verse epistle passes from being the dominant form in English poetry, a mode that in its very dialectic of audience had been able to shadow forth the possibility of a transformed or regenerate society, an object to be collectively sought in the fallen world even as men individually sought their salvation in another, to anticipation of a new mode of lyric expression in which speaker and audience will be subsumed in a larger divinity. The precise moment within Davies' epistolary verse where this occurs, perhaps, is an address to his friend Dr. Thomas Taylor in which Davies turns resolutely away from public affairs—"French pow'r, and weak allies, and war, and want— / No more of that, my friend"—to a scene instantly recognizable to any reader of Wordsworth: "This gentle evening let the sun descend / Untroubled, while it paints your ambient hills / With faded lustre, and a sweet farewell: / Here is our seat." At this moment, though it will live a fitful life in other registers and move toward other exhaustions, the Augustan verse epistle has already begun to give way to the lyric voice that a later age will agree to call Romantic.

NOTES

INTRODUCTION

1. Today most conveniently available as reprinted in Tompkins's *Reader-Response Criticism*, which also contains, along with its collection of essays representing the various major positions in audience and reader-response theory, a useful annotated bibliography of theoretical and practical writings on the subject. See also Suleiman and Crosman, which contains a bibliography annotated from a somewhat different theoretical perspective.

2. The only noteworthy attempt to develop a theory of internal audience outside the boundaries of American formalism during this period was Gerald Prince's work on the "narratee" in fictional narrative. See his "Introduction to the Study of the Narratee" in Tompkins's collection, 7–25.

3. That is, so far as reader-response criticism held to a declared interest in the mental processes of actual readers, its tendency was to put any subsequent inquiry into the question of audience *in* literature out of theoretical reach. This was the underlying issue in a *Critical Inquiry* exchange some years ago between me and Peter Rabinowitz on the subject of internal audience, in which Rabinowitz took occasion to sum up his final position thus:

> Even if Dowling were correct that the actual audience has "no relevance to questions of literary meaning," he could hardly assert that it has no relevance to questions about literary history, sociology, or pedagogy. If we wish to explore, along with Ian Watt, how changes in the reading public influence the development of the novel; if we want to know why *I, the Jury* sold as well as it did; if we want to know why a particular young woman named Margaret, coming to class on a particular Tuesday, has the particular bias she does toward *The Bald Soprano*, then actual audiences surely do come into play. (586)

Though my own views on internal audience have altered somewhat in the period since that exchange, this argument still seems to me deeply confused. My essential point then, which still seems to me valid, was that each of these inquiries involves a different *universe of discourse* positing a different *object of inquiry*. In the Ian Watt case, the object of inquiry is not literary works (*Tom Jones*, *Tristram Shandy*) but the demographics of an actual body of eighteenth-century readers. In the *I, the Jury* case, the object of inquiry is not the novel but the book-buying habits of American readers at a certain point in the twentieth century. In the case of the young woman named Margaret, the object of inquiry is not *The Bald Soprano* but the psychological processes of a certain college student at a certain moment in her undergraduate career—more abstractly, perhaps, the psychological processes of student readers generally. (This would give us something like Holland's *Five Readers Reading*.) But none of these involves a *literary* question, in the sense that "Why does Hamlet delay avenging his father's murder?" or "How old is the *lady* in *To His Coy Mistress*?" are literary questions. Even the contention that such examples involve literary questions because they "have something to do with" literature—e.g., that one is trying to find out why people bought a certain book entitled *I, the Jury*, rather than a certain brand of refrigerator—which is itself so vague as probably to have no theoretical value, seems to me false: in a wholly demonstrable sense, the literary work (as an object of inquiry posited by its universe of discourse) does not exist for such questions.

For accounts of the theoretical incoherence introduced by the focus on reader response, see Seamon and Henkel.

4. The term "unmasking" as used in contemporary literary studies normally bears traces of its long association with an older Marxism. As regards my own use of the term in the following chapters, then, it might be well to point out that it was a key term, long before Marx or Marxist cultural analysis, for the Augustan writers. Thus, for instance, Bolingbroke in the *Remarks on the History of England*:

> But if the spirit of liberty, which begins to revive in this country, becomes prevalent, there will remain nothing to fear from any faction whatever, whether masked, or unmasked. Whilst it is masked, and the instruments or members of it pursue the national interest, though they intend another, the bad principle is however so far productive of good, and the cause of virtue is so far promoted by vice itself. When it comes to be unmasked, and the instruments or members of it are hurried by indiscretion, or forced by the course of events, as they must be, to show their game, faction is that moment disarmed. (2.311)

5. In addition to Willeman and de Lauretis, see Morley, "Texts, readers, subjects." Paul Smith, whose *Discerning the Subject* attempts a summary account of this body of theory, expands as follows on the notion of the subject-in-history:

> The crucial point ... is that there is a distinction to be made between the subject-position prescribed by a text and the actual human agent who engages with that text and thus with the subject position it offers. Clearly, any given text is not empowered to *force* the reader to adhere to the discursive positions it offers—the text is not, in Althusser's terms, a repressive state apparatus. Furthermore, a cinematic or literary text is never addressed at a reader it knows and thus can never articulate itself with its reader in a predictable fashion. It can, of course, offer *preferred* positions, but these are by no means the conditions with which a reader must comply if he/she wishes to read a text. And that is because what always stands between the text's potential or preferred effect and an actualized effect is a reader who has a history of his/her own. (34–35)

For an attempt to show that the critique of Althusserian theory is preempted by a properly complex understanding of Althusser himself, see Sprinker, *Imaginary Relations*.

6. The implications of such a mistake are nicely brought out by Marian Hobson in an essay on "history" as it emerges from Derrida's engagement with Hegelian theory in *Glas*, particularly as Derrida deals in that work with cases in which "the impossibility of conceptual opposition" creates a tension that must then somehow be resolved by a philosophical system:

> This tension creates for Hegel, says *Glas*, an effect of transcendence, of mastery, of standing outside the network. Now such an effect underpins much writing of history or about history. In practice, such writing will not explicate fully its own position in regard to the past (it also cannot, by a necessary impossibility which is not recognised, by a kind of wilfulness); in its theory, it invokes the name of History to make it act as a backstop,

as that which judges and limits other codes, other writing. But such a stance is an "effect," a "leurre," a trap, and will collapse back into the network which it seemed momentarily to transcend. (109)

See also Bennington, "Demanding History," and Culler, "The Call to History."
The groundwork for a philosophically adequate understanding of such concepts as "realism" and "materialism" in literary and cultural studies is provided by Hilary Putnam in two recent books, *Reason, Truth, and History* and *The Many Faces of Realism*.

7. For an account of the critique in contemporary Marxist theory of economic determinism and "teleological" Marxism, see my *Jameson, Althusser, Marx*, especially Chapter Three. For an account of "cultural materialism" as it has emerged from this critique, see Jonathan Dollimore's introduction ("Shakespeare, Cultural Materialism, and the New Historicism") in *Political Shakespeare*.

8. The ultimate source is Kristeva. Ellis is discussing Kristeva's development of Lacanian theory, particularly the problem of how ideology complicates Lacan's theory of the symbolic: "consciousness itself is affected by the movement in which signifiers are altered, disturbed, or put into crisis by the contradictions between the superstructure and/or forces of production, when they become antagonistic. This experience is one of consciousness encountering an external process which it has not yet organized into language, has not yet symbolized" ("Ideology and Subjectivity" 190).

9. As it occurs in Riffaterre's own discussion, the notion simply makes explicit a view always implicit in classical formalism. The particular virtue of Riffaterre's formulation seems to me to lie in the manner in which it gestures toward a domain traditionally seen to lie beyond the reach of any formalism:

> As we readers perceive traces left by history, these are no longer explainable as a result, but as a point of departure, as the starting point of interpretation. Once in the text, for them to be active components of literariness, it is enough that they should be a representation of the past. They stand for it, as a sign stands for something, but you do not need to know the something, or to learn more about it in order to perceive the referentiality. You do not need to explore the referent for referentiality to work; all you need is the presupposition of a referent. Just as the traces are now entirely linguistic, the presupposition is now purely semantic; it is a logical mechanism, a pointing gesture. (174–75)

CHAPTER ONE

1. "For all the unassailable privacy of each man's conceptual and linguistic worlds, language was sufficient for social intercourse—because language is, after all, a matter of consensus, the medium in which all communication might take place, the medium also in each man's mind between himself and the world external to himself" ("Locke and the Publication of the Private" 35).

2. Quoted in Redford, 1. Redford takes the title of his study of the eighteenth-century familiar letter from this passage ("Who then shall decline the converse of the pen? The pen that makes distance, presence," etc.).

3. This is the context within which feminist criticism has recently begun to assert that Ovidian poetry is always the usurpation of female emotional and expressive

space by male authors, with the isolation and powerlessness of women reimagined in ways complicit with a dominant patriarchial ideology. For this argument as it pertains to Pope's *Eloisa to Abelard*, see Pollak, 181–87. See also Joan DeJean, "Fictions of Sappho," *Critical Inquiry* 13 (1987): 806–24.

4. Cf. Eric Rothstein on the "urbane style" in eighteenth-century poetry:

> The style conforms to three senses of the word "urbane" or its Latin root, *urbanus*: courteous, polished, and sophisticated. Because the speaker is a public man, he follows the laws of social courtesy, to be clear, concise, informative, frank within the bounds of taste, entertaining without frivolity. . . . Finally, the urbane style is sophisticated in its wit, its taste, its classical allusions, and its subtlety and balance of feelings because speaker and audience are worldly men, educated in schools and salons; hard-headed men, too, whose shrewdness has displaced any wonder at the works of other men. I emphasize "men" because the style supposes an education and a worldliness quite possible for eighteenth-century women but only if they were willing to adopt male values. (75)

5. The way absence of audience translates into routine rhetorical advice for letter-writers is evident in a work such as Thomas Blount's *Academie of Eloquence* (1654): "For your interest or favor with him, you are to be the shorter or longer, more familiar or submiss, as he will afford you time. For his capacity, you are to be quainter, or fuller of those reaches or glances of wit or learning, according to his comprehension" (qtd. in Irving 143). And a similarly unperturbed quality may be seen in Pope's anecdote about a nobleman composing letters: "Lord Peterborow could dictate letters to nine amanuences together. . . . One perhaps was a letter to the Emperor, another to an old friend, a third to a mistress. . . . And yet he carried so many and so different connections in his head all at the same time" (Spence 112).

6. In contrast to the more typical social situation described by Laslett:

> The plain Richard Hodgsons, Robert Boswells, Humphrey Eltons and John Burtons of the English villages, the laborers and husbandmen, the tailors, millers, drovers, watermen, masons, could become constables, parish clerks, churchwardens, ale-conners, even overseers of the poor. They had something of a public life, even within the tiny boundaries of the village, and this might give them a minor consequence in the surrounding villages. If they happened to be technically qualified, they might even cast a vote at an election. But in none of these capacities did their opinion matter very much, even in the last. . . . As individuals they had no instituted, recognized power over other individuals. . . . Directly they acquired such power, whether by the making or the inheriting of wealth, or by the painful acquisition of a little learning, then they became *worshipful* by that very fact. Then and then only could they know anything substantial of the world, which meant everything that went on outside their own localities, everything rather which was inter-local, affecting more communities and localities than one. (28)

7. A splendid account of epistolarity as a central impulse within humanism is given in Clough.

The importance of the epistle in the career even of minor humanists is made clear in Caro Lynn's wonderful biography of Lucio Marineo, and the survival of a humanist epistolary tradition into the later seventeenth century is well documented by Rosalie Colie in *Light and Enlightenment*.

Part of the humanist tradition is to keep in touch with scholars across national boundaries, and this Limborch certainly did.... In his letterbook, "Epistolae ad Anglos," are his copies of letters to many liberal bishops—Richard Kidder, Bishop of Bath and Wells; Gilbert Burnet, Bishop of Salisbury; William Lloyd, Bishop successively of St Asaph, Lichfield and Coventry.... but all these names are overshadowed by the correspondent to whom Limborch wrote more often than to any of these and whose letters stand by themselves, John Locke. (30)

8. Thus Thomas Mayo in *Epicurus in England*:

The independent cities had been swallowed in the unwieldy post-Alexandrian empires of the eastern Mediterranean. His part of the world was ruled by hybrid emperors never seen by most of their millions of subjects. Great strange armies swept periodically across the land in confused and meaningless struggles.... The ordinary citizen, repelled by a public life grown too vast and complex for him to grasp, was thus driven to work out some philosophy that would give significance to his own tiny separate existence. (xviii–xix)

Mayo's account represents a view of Hellenistic philosophy that has more recently been contested, but it accurately reflects the idea of Epicureanism found in seventeenth-and eighteenth-century English poetry.

For a splendid account of ancient philosophy conceived as a form of life, see Hadot.

9. Donald Livingston has argued in an important recent study that Hume is dramatizing at such moments what he understands to be a false way of doing philosophy. My own argument should be taken to deal with Hume as he was read in the eighteenth century—by, e.g., Beattie or Reid—at the beginning of the tradition of the "false Hume" against which Livingston is concerned to argue.

10. The degree to which empiricist thinking and its skeptical implications were felt as an antagonistic or threatening presence in Augustan poetry is nicely captured in Robert Dodsley's epistle *Modern Reasoning*:

> In fire no heat, no sweetness in the rose;
> The man's imposed on by his very nose;
> Nor light nor color charms his doubting eye,
> The world's a dream, and all his senses lie.
> He thinks, yet doubts if he's possess'd of thought;
> Nay, even doubts his pow'r to doubt.

CHAPTER TWO

1. A good discussion of Cowley's shifts in political viewpoint as complexly representative of the nation as a whole is contained in Jose 124–33.

2. The best analysis of the Court attempt to develop a "Ciceronian vision" as a response to the Opposition myth of Catonic martyrdom is Reed Browning's *Political and Constitutional Ideas of the Court Whigs*. See especially Chapter Eight.

3. Michael Meehan points out that the notion of the Augustan poets as writers whose minds were "still republican" may be found in eighteenth-century poetry as early as Blackmore's *The Nature of Man*:

> 'Tis true the genius and heroic fire,
> The generous thoughts which freedom did inspire
> Some years retained their force, nor greatly fail'd,
> While those who born while liberty prevail'd,
> Applauded worthies, trod the Roman stage,
> Supported and adorn't the great Augustan Age.

Meehan's is the best extended treatment of this idea as it developed in the eighteenth century (see *Liberty and Poetics* 67–69). Of particular interest is his citation of John Upton's *Critical Observations on Shakespeare*: "however half-seeing critics may extol the golden age of Augustus, yet all that blaze of wit was kindled during the struggle for liberty: 'twas then indeed they had leisure to exert their faculties, when their country had a little respite from civil commotions" (69).

4. Cowper beautifully captures a sense of this in Book VI of *The Task*, in the passage describing the rites through which a "blind antiquity" honored its sense of the divine-in-the-natural, creating deities

> Female and male, Pomona, Pales, Pan,
> And Flora, and Vertumnus; peopling earth
> With tutelary goddesses and gods
> That were not; and commending, as they would,
> To each some province, garden, field, or grove.
>
> (6.233–37)

CHAPTER THREE

1. Cf. Dyer in *The Ruins of Rome*:

> And see from every gate those ancient roads,
> With tombs high verg'd, the solemn paths of Fame:
> Deserve they not regard? O'er whose broad flints
> Such crowds have roll'd, so many storms of war;
> So many pomps; so many wondering realms:
> Yet still through mountains pierc'd, o'er valleys rais'd,
> They stretch their pavements.

Likewise Thomson in *Liberty*, Book I, 69–73:

> For ages laid,
> Deep, massy, firm, diverging every way,
> With tombs of heroes sacred, see her roads
> By various nations trod, and suppliant kings;
> With legions flaming, or with triumph gay.

2. For an illuminating discussion of this theme in relation to eighteenth-century fiction, see Beasley, "Portraits of a Monster."

3. Cf. Colin Manlove:

In the destruction of Auburn, Goldsmith is not portraying simply the effects of the Enclosure movement or even inveighing against the luxurious vices of his own day; he is depicting the final departure of the humanist values of grace, proportion and harmony.... For Jonson, Penshurst was still an isolated reality; for Pope, Dulness was a terrifying possibility; but for Goldsmith a whole conceptual landscape has been swept away forever, and ... the painting is not a warning but an account of what he felt to be an event already performed. (177)

See also F. V. Bogel, whose account of the "rhetoric of insubstantiality" (47–73) is fundamental to an understanding of elegiac Augustanism:

While lamenting the loss of Poetry and those other virtues that had fostered England's dignity and worth in the past, and hoping for the future life of those values in another land, Goldsmith also creates an extended present moment—the poem itself, and especially its last thirty-six lines—that is informed by precisely those values. In Collins, as in Goldsmith, the contemplation of absent powers shades at times into a partial recapturing of them, invocation becomes address, and the substantiality of an earlier time informs, for a moment, the sphere of the present. (89)

4. Shaftesbury's name for the principle of innate virtue when freed from the limiting or deforming constraints of misguided social custom: "It is equal, constant, accountable to itself, ever satisfactory, and pleasing.... And to have this entire affection or integrity of mind, is to live according to nature, and the dictates and rules of supreme wisdom. This is morality, justice, piety, and natural religion" (1.301–2).

5. The source is Theocles' speech in *The Moralists*, in which the relation between Shaftesburian ethical theory and Cambridge Platonism is evident:

Is there then ... a natural beauty of figures? and is there not as natural a one of actions? No sooner the eye opens upon figures, the ear to sounds, than straight the beautiful results and grace and harmony are known and acknowledged. No sooner are actions viewed, no sooner the human affections and passions discerned (and they are most of them as soon discerned as felt) than straight an inward eye distinguishes, and sees the fair and shapely, the amiable and admirable, apart from the deformed, the foul, the odious, or the despicable. How is it possible therefore not to own "that as these distinctions have their foundation in Nature, the discernment itself is natural, and from Nature alone." (2.137)

6. Quoted by Wilkinson (227) in making a persuasive connection between More's variety of diluted Shaftesburianism and the decline of verse satire in the eighteenth century.

7. The degree to which the power of benevolist theory to lay solipsistic anxieties to rest was already present in Shaftesbury is captured in one of his remarks in the *Characteristics*:

Let us carry scepticism ever so far, let us doubt, if we can, of everything about us, we cannot doubt of what passes within ourselves. Our passions and affections are known to us. They are certain, whatever the objects may be on which they are employed. Nor is it of any concern to our argument, how these exterior objects stand: whether they are realities or mere illusions; whether we wake or dream. For ill dreams will be equally disturbing. And a good dream, if life be nothing else, will be easily and happily passed. In this dream of life, therefore, our demonstrations have the same force. (1.336–37)

8. Cox, whose argument concerning benevolist ethical theory is admirable throughout, treats Adam Smith's theory of moral sympathy in a way that allows one to glimpse the manner in which it provided an alternative to Augustinian introspection. Cox sees the theory in the form Smith would give it as originating with certain reflections made by Hume, e.g., "'We can form no wish, which has not a reference to society.... Whatever other passions we may be actuated by, ... the soul or animating principle of them all is sympathy, nor wou'd they have any force, were we to abstract entirely from the thoughts and sentiments of others'" (29). This then becomes the basis on which Smith posits a social existence as the indispensable ground of morality: "'Were it possible that a human creature could grow up to manhood in some solitary place, without any communication with his own species, ... [he would be unable to perceive] the propriety or demerit of his own sentiments and conduct'" (30). This is to take the Augustan notion that I know what is occurring in your mind by consulting my own because we are both included in a universal humanity-in-God and, following the move originally made by Shaftesbury and the Latitudinarians, relocate that same principle within the temporal world. This is the context in which Smith's form of the moral sympathy argument no doubt completes the Pelagian enterprise.

9. Quoted in Sekora (107), whose informative discussion of the poem as a rhymed version of *The Wealth of Nations* I assume in quoting it in this context.

10. Pocock quotes in this connection a wonderfully revealing passage from Defoe's *Review*:

> Trade is a mystery, which will never be completely discover'd or understood; ... today it obeys the course of things, and submits to causes and consequences; tomorrow it suffers violence from the storms and vapors of human fancy, operated by exotic projects, and then all runs counter, the motions are eccentric, unnatural, and unaccountable—a sort of lunacy in trade attends all its circumstances, and no man can give a rational account of it. (453–54)

11. Quoted in Pocock (440), who discusses such moments in Davenant as movements toward a Christian ethic of trade, and as reflecting the early emergence of an ideology, already stated in explicit terms by Montaigne and others, that would portray a land-based feudal society as harsh and primitive and see in modern credit arrangements a progress toward a higher stage of civilization.

12. The best discussion of the background of Miller's two poems may be found in Goldgar 210–11.

CHAPTER FOUR

1. Elegiac Augustanism as a mode is defined in part by its acceptance of this state of affairs. Cf., for instance, Cowper in Book II of *The Task*:

> Yet what can satire, grave or gay?
> It may correct a foible, may chastise
> The freaks of fashion, regulate the dress,
> Retrench a sword-blade, or displace a patch;
> But where are its sublimer trophies found?

> What vice has it subdu'd? whose heart reclaim'd
> By rigor, or whom laugh'd into reform?
> Alas! Leviathan is not so tam'd:
> Laugh'd at, he laughs again; and, stricken hard,
> Turns to the stroke his adamantine scales,
> That fear no discipline of human hands.
>
> (2.315–25)

2. The degree to which the notion of satiric modes as corresponding to different stages in the cyclical history of a society had become a commonplace of Augustan poetry itself is evident in a poem such as Boyse's epistle *To the Author of The Polite Philosopher*:

> So is the piece proportion'd to the times,
> For every age diversifies its crimes; ...
> In different shapes pursues the lasting trade,
> And makes the world one changing masquerade.

The notion of a satiric cycle is necessary, by the same token, to explain something like the *Anti-Jacobin*'s short-lived Juvenalian revival at the end of the eighteenth century, which explicitly invokes Pope's earlier satires as poetry of a more innocent middle state:

> Yet, venial vices, in a milder age,
> Could rouse the warmth of Pope's satiric rage:
> The doting miser, and the lavish heir,
> The follies and the foibles of the fair,
> Sir Job, Sir Balaam, and old Euclio's thrift,
> And Sappho's diamonds with her dirty shift.

3. "*The Deserted Village* itself enacts the collapse of the very poetic conventions in which it might have sought refuge: the pastoral and georgic modes are devastated within the poet's own imagination, the traditional celebration of retirement is mocked by the ruined village to which the poet has 'retired,' the only topography worth describing is the landscape of memory, ... and the whole poem negates the familiar 'Whig' panegyric of English commerce and liberty" (26–27).

4. The "Augustan" version of the same idea, which Churchill brilliantly exploits in inverting its underlying assumptions, may be found in a poem like *The Seasons*:

> Now, while the drowsy world lies lost in sleep,
> Let me associate with the serious Night,
> And Contemplation her sedate compeer;
> Let me shake off th'intrusive cares of Day,
> And lay the meddling senses all aside.
>
> Where now, ye lying Vanities of Life!
> Ye ever-tempting ever-cheating train!
> Where are you now? and what is your amount?
> Vexation, disappointment, and remorse.
>
> (*Winter* lines 204–12)

5. Stephen Cox quotes a passage from Chatterton's modern tale *The Unfortunate Fathers* that may be taken to have been produced (as were, I shall argue, Chatterton's medieval forgeries) by something like Churchill's own sense of ideological vacuum:

> There is a principle in man, (a shadow of the divinity) which constitutes him the image of God; you may call it conscience, grace, inspiration, the spirit, or whatever name your education gives it. If a man acts according to this regulator, he is right: if contrary to it, he is wrong. It is an approved truth, that this principle varies in every rational being. As I can reconcile suicide to this principle, with me it is consequently no crime. (Cox 103)

6. Peter Briggs more recently makes the same point in a slightly different way: "where Pope praises moral independence, Churchill wants something more like *epistemological* independence: he is not only free from worldly partiality, but he would also be free to construe his experiences and the world he knows as he himself sees fit" (46). To my mind, the centerlessness of Churchillian satire becomes evident in its full consequences only in *Gotham*, which may be taken as the poetic possibility that remains when Churchill's satiric attack on the Augustan pretensions of the new bourgeoisie has exhausted itself.

7. A scrutiny of the *OED* listing under "aristocracy" suggests that the years immediately following the Augustan collapse and the death of Pope were the precise time that the word shifted from its earlier meaning of "government by the best in a society" to something like "oligarchic domination." This of course assumes the notion of aristocracy-as-plutocracy projected by late Augustanism.

8. "It was not the power . . . of the old noble families of which he wrote so bitterly," explains Howard Bell, whose treatment of this theme in Goldsmith remains fundamental, "but rather the increasing power of the newly rich commercial class. The members of this class, as he conceived of them, were unscrupulous, scheming, and power-mad" (759).

Goldsmith's elegiac Augustanism in turn assumes as its literary background such poems as John Brown's *Honour*, an epistolary meditation on nobility addressed to Viscount Lonsdale:

> In vain, O Studley, thy proud forests spread;
> In vain each gilded turret rears its head;
> In vain thy lord commands the streams to fall,
> Extends the view, and spreads the smooth canal,
> While guilt's black train each conscious walk invade,
> And cries of orphans haunt him in the shade.

The ideological shift through which Wolcot's epistle to the Earl of Lonsdale completes a movement originating in Pope's portrait of Timon is especially evident in such poems as Brown's.

For a parallel discussion of Goldsmith's response to government by plutocracy, see Bender, "Prison Reform and the Sentence of Narration."

9. Thus, for instance, the delight of that cheerful pragmatist Charles Hanbury Williams at finding that the morals of the Opposition were, like the morals of a whore, no better than they ought to be. Williams's *The Country Girl* was inscribed to the Earl of Bath, which is the title to which Pulteney had been raised in 1742:

> So virtuous Pult'ney, who had long
> By speech, by pamphlet, and by song,
> Held patriotism's steerage,
> Yields to ambition mixt with gain,
> A treasure gets for Harry Vane,
> And for himself a peerage.

The special bitterness of the Pulteney episode was, no doubt, that his elevation to the peerage so obviously fit the anxieties raised by the emergent specter of the aristocracy-as-plutocracy.

10. Quotations in this paragraph are taken from Houpt (100–104), who discusses at some length the reception history of the Curio poems.

11. Thus John M. Wallace: "Our present knowledge of the phenomenon is a reconstruction from a thousand sources, the most important of which is Clarendon's *History*, but letters, diaries, county archives, Guildhall records, and diplomatic correspondence have all contributed a little to the received narrative. *Coopers Hill* . . . makes more vivid, as only poetry can, the strength of the feelings to which Denham appealed. At their center lay a patriotic regard for England, for monarchy, and the person of the king; no less formidable was the desire for peace, recently symbolized by the treaty [this is the so-called treaty of Ripon, concluded in October 1640 between the invading Scots Presbyterian party and the forces of Charles I], and a wish for a reformed episcopacy between the alternative extremes. By holding out the hope of greater economic prosperity Denham flattered self-interest and the City, and by suggesting the possibility of a foreign war he encouraged religious unity and sentiments of English grandeur" (535).

Literary students of *Coopers Hill* will automatically correct for Wallace's notion, as a historian, that poetry is simply a way of giving attractive rhetorical dress to political or ideological positions. Beyond that, I think the only thing to be seriously questioned in his otherwise admirable account is the notion that Denham's praise of commerce was little more than a bone of material interest tossed to the City: the notion that mercantile prosperity is both possible and desirable *within the context of a restored constitutional balance* is central to the entire tradition that has its origin in Denham's lines.

12. Quoted in McKillop: "'I look upon this mighty work, as the last stretched blaze of our expiring genius. It is the dying effort of despairing and indignant virtue, and will stand, like one of those immortal pyramids, which carry their magnificence thro' times, that wonder, to see nothing round them, but uncomfortable desart!'" (100).

This occurs in the midst of McKillop's groundbreaking effort to show, in *The Background of Thomson's "Liberty,"* that *Liberty* was not straightforward "Whig panegyric" but, on the contrary, a poem that makes sense only when read against its more complex background in Country ideology.

13. Donna Landry intelligently observes that writers like Duck and Collier "appropriate the classical figures most easily allied with labor" because "they perceived there to be a certain useful congruence between the apprehension of manual and agricultural work as lived experience in the texts of antiquity and their own" (110).

14. Duck's apostrophic address to Addison gives some indication of the role played by *The Spectator* in his self-education:

> Nor less thy soft diurnal essays please,
> That glass, where ev'ry fool his folly sees;
> Where virtue shines with such attractive grace,
> She tempts the vicious to her chaste embrace.
>
> (*A Journey to Marlborough*)

As nearly always in the poetry of Augustan aspiration, the Addisonian voice is taken as the appropriate register of expression for a Shaftesburian moral sensibility ("Where virtue shines with such attractive grace," etc.).

15. I take the phrase "polite citizen" from an anonymous writer in the *Universal Journal* of 1724, who laments that no such figure, though common enough in English society, is ever portrayed on the stage: "I am sure it is not for want of a sufficient number of real examples.... View the assemblies of our citizens, when met on business; attend a general court, and you shall hear 'em debate with the same ease, and the same eloquence as at the bar, or in the senate: in company with the ladies we find 'em complaisant gallants; they can there lay aside all thoughts of business, and enter on a tea table topic with as much humor as the best lady's man about town" (qtd. in Loftis 35).

16. Donna Landry sees the central problem of *The Woman's Labour* as being Mary Collier's unaccountable failure "to invent a suitably oppositional discourse" (106). Collier's unwillingness to portray the situation of writers like herself and Stephen Duck as "an enticement to social revolution" (116) is ultimately to be explained, Landry decides, by the fact that such writers were "exploited by patrons and audiences, whose consciences could be soothed by promoting exceptional ability among the industrious poor" (115).

17. For an account of a somewhat similar dynamic at work in the eighteenth-century novel, see Nancy Armstrong, *Desire and Domestic Fiction*.

18. This occurs in the *Oracle*'s response to the question "Is't probable there will be any sexes in Heaven?" The answer is no: "this difference is only accidental, men and women being in essence the same. But in a state of bliss and perfection, all that's imperfect or accidental shall be removed, and accordingly one would think sexes should" (1.408). The answer is especially valuable at catching the moment in which the notion of an essential human equality emerges out of an older theological context—the *Oracle* is using "accidental" here in its full Aristotelian-Thomistic sense—to become the central tenet of bourgeois liberalism.

19. Ellen Pollak's criticism of what she sees as Stone's too-great sympathy for the ideal of companionate marriage seems to me to entail a dispute about present-day political attitudes rather than eighteenth-century literature in its ideological context, but my own present argument, that the notion of companionate marriage worked to recontain the radical implications of an earlier bourgeois feminism, runs parallel to what I take to be Pollak's assumptions.

20. The first appearance of the rational woman of bourgeois ideology within the otium scene is, so far as I am aware, the problematic female "friend" of Pomfret's *The Choice*, who is an ambiguous figure precisely because Pomfret was writing at just the moment that the older otium ideal of Augustan poetry, revolving around an Aristotelian ideal of male friendship as "rational" not simply because of the

superiority of male intellect but because male friendship is free from the importunities of lust, is giving way to an emergent bourgeois ideal of companionate marriage. For an account of the trouble caused in Pomfret's personal life by this mysterious female "friend," see Johnson's "Life" of him.

21. "To speak truth the ancient families are so reduced or so many of them extinct, that we find abundance of the mansions and parks and estates and inheritances of the most ancient extinct families bought by citizens, merchants, lawyers, etc., and the old race gone and forgotten; and for the decayed families of our gentry, nay, and even of the nobility, we find the heirs fly to the city as a last resort, where by marrying a daughter of some person meaner in dignity, but superior in money, the fortunes of the family are restored" (*The Compleat Gentleman* 259).

22. Thus, for instance, one hears in Bolingbroke's *Craftsman* the voice of a radical feminism very obviously emerging from the Augustan critique of emergent capitalism, as in the letter from "Britannica" in *Craftsman* 38 (17 April 1727): "They [men] allow us at best to be good domestic drudges only, fit to manage the affairs of a family; . . . In short they treat us, as if we were of another species, as well as of another sex; and as if there was as much difference between them and us, as between the rational and irrational part of the creation. . . .

Indeed, too many, even among us, through custom, education, and early impressions given them in their childhood, look upon themselves in the same light. They have been bred up in this opinion; and being contented, either through indolence or want of thought, with the humble station, which is allotted them, jog on in their low sphere, without any ambition, and really imagine themselves an inferior sort of beings to mankind; possessed with meaner capacities and more confined understandings" (1.236–37).

23. Thus Weston: "These epistles produce the constant impression of unwavering friendliness and of total unity of values and interests, an impression of two men of mutual understanding and sympathy, at one with each other and their chosen world, although surrounded by an alien one" (190).

24. Farley-Hills (194) suggests *La Légende de Bourbon* as the source of Rochester's *Tunbridge Wells*.

25. The best discussion of *The Spectator* as both reflecting and helping to create a new social world where distinctions are understood through a constant "Spectatorial" scanning of the social surface—i.e., clothes, manners, equipage, etc.—is Ketcham's *Transparent Designs*.

26. The anapestic meter of *The New Bath Guide* was, in terms of the "ideology of form," itself a small triumph: a way of invoking Augustan claims without laying claim to the Augustan inheritance that satire written in heroic couplets inevitably entailed. This is what William Hayward Roberts is paying tribute to in congratulating Anstey on having invented the metrical scheme of the poem:

> For thee the Muse
> Reserved a secret spot, unknown before, . . .
> . . . Graceful sit
> Thy golden chains, and easy flows the rhyme
> Spontaneous. While old Bladud's sceptre guards
> His medicinal stream, shall Simkin raise
> Loud peals of merriment.

27. "*The Choice* says not a word against city and court, whose exhausting and terrifying rage for power are no longer an issue" (46).

28. For background on this episode see Martin S. Day, "Anstey and Anapestic Satire" and "The Influence of Mason's *Heroic Epistle*."

CHAPTER FIVE

1. I should note, however, that the other side of Cowper's elegiac Augustanism is epistolary verse written, most often, in Lloyd's mode; such epistles as *To the Rev. William Bull*, *To Lady Austen*, and, fittingly and preeminently, *An Epistle to Robert Lloyd, Esq.*, belong to what I am calling the "diminished world."

2. The entire passage is noteworthy in its attempt to turn the otium ideal of Augustan satire against the satirists:

> If their representation of things is true, there never was a people so degenerated and sunk so low in vileness and infamy as we; for I think, according to their account of the matter, there are not above ten or a dozen wise or honest men in the nation, and those all within the circle of their own friends and acquaintance. (qtd. in Goldgar 169)

3. The mock-speakers of Moore's epistle *To the Right Hon. Henry Pelham* are "dealers in rhymes, / And writers of scandal, for mending the times" imagined as presenting a petition to Pitt to let the country descend back into corruption so that they will have employment again, as satirists did before the fall of Walpole:

> But now (and they speak it with sorrow and tears),
> Since your honor has sat at the helm of affairs,
> No party will join 'em, no faction invite
> To heed what they say, or to read what they write;
> Sedition and tumult, and discord are fled,
> And slander scarce ventures to life up her head.

4. And one related in a crucial way to Shaftesbury's principle that aesthetic taste gives us "property in ourselves": "You, Philocles, who are such an admirer of civil liberty, . . . can you imagine no grace or beauty in that original native liberty, which sets us free from so many inborn tyrannies, gives us the privilege of ourselves, and makes us our own, and independent? A sort of property, which, methinks, is as material to us to the full, as that which secures us our lands, or revenues" (2.44).

5. Donald Taylor makes a similar point in emphasizing the imaginative completeness of Chatterton's medievalism in his more recent study of the poetry: "He went about authenticating his Rowley world in three major ways—inventing its special language, imagining the ancient physical city, and writing the Rowleyan documents. All three ways share a common factor—density of imagining, something akin to what literary criticism calls verisimilitude" (49).

6. Cf. Max Byrd, *Visits to Bedlam*: "Where the Renaissance melancholic tends to isolate himself only to bemoan an unrequited love, betraying the Italian origins of Renaissance melancholy, his eighteenth-century counterpart transforms himself into a dreamlike figure, one prepared by time and place to receive visitations; he becomes a solitary creature living at the limits of his sensibility, a prophet, a hermit, an enthusiast" (123).

7. The submerged process through which the classical otium ideal lends its eventual authority to midcentury poetic solitude is visible in the passage from the preface to the second edition of *Winter* in which Thomson employs this phrase: "the best, both ancient, and modern, poets have been passionately fond of retirement and solitude. The wild romantic country was their delight. And they seem never to have been more happy, than when lost in unfrequented fields, far from the little, busy world, they were at leisure, to meditate, and sing the works of nature" (303).

8. Thomson in fact directly echoes the Philips poem in *Winter*, 235–41:

> Low, the woods
> Bow their hoar Head; and, ere the languid sun
> Faint from the west emits his evening ray,
> Earth's universal face, deep-hid, and chill,
> Is one wild dazzling waste, that buries wide
> The works of man.

9. I am speaking specifically of Shaftesbury as he appears in *The Moralists*, and as his doctrine is then understood by such poets as Akenside and J. G. Cooper. This version of Shaftesburian benevolism always demands to be read, Linda Dowling reminds me, against the darker and more complex background provided by the *Philosophical Regimen*, which, however, remained unpublished during the eighteenth century.

POEMS CITED

EDITIONS CITED

For the following poets, citations are to the editions listed below:

Burns: *The Poems and Songs of Robert Burns*. Ed. James Kinsley. 3 vols. Oxford: Clarendon Press, 1968.
Chatterton: *The Complete Works of Thomas Chatterton*. Ed. Donald S. Taylor. 2 vols. Oxford: Clarendon Press, 1971.
Churchill: *The Poetical Works of Charles Churchill*. Ed. Douglas Grant. Oxford: Clarendon Press, 1956.
Collins: *The Poems of Thomas Gray, William Collins, Oliver Goldsmith*. Ed. Roger Lonsdale. London: Longmans, 1969.
Cowper: *The Poetical Works of William Cowper*. Ed. Humphrey S. Milford. Oxford: Oxford University Press, 1907.
Dryden: *The Poems of John Dryden*. Ed. James Kinsley. 4 vols. Oxford: Oxford University Press, 1958.
Etherege: *The Poems of Sir George Etherege*. Ed. James Thorpe. Princeton: Princeton University Press, 1963.
Gay: *The Poetry and Prose of John Gay*. Ed. Vinton A. Dearing and Charles E. Beckwith. 2 vols. Oxford: Clarendon Press, 1974.
Goldsmith: *The Poems of Thomas Gray, William Collins, Oliver Goldsmith*. Ed. Roger Lonsdale. London: Longmans, 1969.
Oldham: *The Poems of John Oldham*. Ed. Harold F. Brooks. Oxford: Clarendon Press, 1987.
Pope: *The Poems of Alexander Pope: A One-Volume Edition of the Twickenham Text*. Ed. John Butt. New Haven: Yale University Press, 1963.
Ramsay: *The Poetical Works of Allan Ramsay*. Ed. Charles Mackay. 2 vols. London, 1800.
Rochester: *Poems by John Wilmot, Earl of Rochester*. Ed. Vivian de Sola Pinto. Cambridge: Harvard University Press, 1953.
Swift: *Swift: Poetical Works*. Ed. Herbert Davis. Oxford: Oxford University Press, 1967.
Thomson: *The Seasons*. Ed. James Sambrook. Oxford: Clarendon Press, 1981.
Wolcot: *The Works of Peter Pindar*. 5 vols. London, 1812.

COLLECTIONS CITED

Poems cue-referenced "EP" have been quoted from David French's reprint edition of Chalmers' *English Poets: Minor English Poets, 1660–1780: A Selection from Alexander Chalmers' The English Poets*. Compiled by David P. French. 10 vols. New York: Benjamin Blom, 1967.

Poems cue-referenced "CA" have been quoted from Bell's collection of fugitive poetry: *Classical Arrangement of Fugitive Poetry*. Ed. John Bell. Vols. 1–7 (epistolary verse). London, 1790–1797.

Spelling and punctuation of eighteenth-century texts, both poetry and prose, have been modernized in all quoted passages.

Addison, Joseph. *A Letter from Italy, to the Right Hon. Charles Lord Halifax, in the Year 1701.* EP 2.488–89.

———. *An Account of the Greatest English Poets. To Mr. Henry Sacheverell, April 3, 1694.* EP 2.487–88.

———. *To Mr. Dryden.* EP 2.481.

Akenside, Mark. *An Epistle to Curio.* EP 5.509–12.

———. *Ode to Curio.* EP 5.484–86.

———. *Ode XIII. On Lyric Poetry.* EP 5.487–88.

———. *The Pleasures of Imagination.* EP 5.441–78.

Anstey, Christopher. *The New Bath Guide.* In *The Poetical Works of the Late Christopher Anstey, Esq.* Ed. John Anstey. London, 1808.

Anti-Jacobin writers [George Canning, J. H. Frere, George Ellis]. *New Morality.* In *Poetry of the Anti-Jacobin.* Ed. L. Rice-Oxley. Oxford: Basil Blackwell, 1924.

Bancks, John. *The Wish.* Qtd. in Røstvig 2.311. [See WORKS CITED.]

Barber, Mary. *The Conclusion of a Letter to the Rev. Mr. C———.* In *Poems on Several Occasions.* London, 1734.

Beattie, James. *On the Report of a Monument to be Erected in Westminster Abbey, to the Memory of a Late Author.* EP 8.269–70.

Bentley, Richard. *To Lord Melcombe.* CA 3.68–77.

Bramston, James. *The Art of Politics.* CA 5.97–117.

Browne, Isaac Hawkins. *To Himself.* CA 2.44–48.

Brown, John. *An Essay on Satire, Occasioned by the Death of Mr. Pope.* CA 5.1–21.

———. *On Honour. To the Lord Viscount Lonsdale.* CA 1.27–37.

Buckhurst. [Charles Sackville, Lord Buckhurst.] *Another Letter from Lord Buckhurst to Mr. Etherege.* [Etherege, *Poems* 35–37].

Burns, Robert. *Epistle to J. L[aprai]k, An Old Scotch Bard.* Poems and Songs 1.85–89.

———. *Epistle to Davie, a Brother Poet.* Poems and Songs 1.65–69.

———. *Epistle to J. S[mith].* Poems and Songs 1.178–83.

———. *To the Same* [J. Lapraik]. Poems and Songs 1.89–93.

Byrom, John. *An Epistle to a Gentleman of the Temple.* EP 4.421–24.

———. *Enthusiasm: A Poetical Essay, in a Letter to a Friend in Town.* EP 4.424–28.

Candour: or, an Occasional Essay on the Abuse of Wit and Eloquence. London 1739.

The Country. Qtd. in Røstvig 2.329. [See WORKS CITED.]

Cawthorn, James. *Abelard to Eloisa.* EP 4.321–24.

———. *The Vanity of Human Enjoyments: An Ethic Epistle to the Right Hon. George Lyttelton, Esq.* EP 4.342–44.

Chandler, Mary. *The Description of Bath. A Poem. In a Letter to a Friend.* London, 1734.

Chatterton, Thomas. *Epistle to the Reverend Mr. Catcott.* Works 1.412–19.

———. *The Defence.* Works 1.421–22.

Chetwood, Knightly. *To the Earl of Roscommon, on his Essay on Translated Verse.* EP 1.546–47.

POEMS CITED **195**

Churchill, Charles. *An Epistle to William Hogarth. Poetical Works* 211–30.
———. *Night. An Epistle to Robert Lloyd. Poetical Works* 49–61.
———. *The Farewell. Poetical Works* 373–88.
———. *The Ghost.* 4.268–74. *Poetical Works* 148.
Collins, William. *An Epistle: Addressed to Sir Thomas Hanmer on his Edition of Shakespear's Works. Poems* 389–400.
———. *An Ode on the Popular Superstitions of the Highlands of Scotland, Considered as the Subject of Poetry. Poems* 501–19.
Cooper, John Gilbert. *Epistles to His Friends in Town, from Aristippus in Retirement.* EP 5.359–65.
———. *The Power of Harmony.* EP 5.370–76.
Cowley, Abraham. *Ode. Upon his Majestie's Restoration and Return.* EP 1.92–96.
Cowper, William. *The Castaway. Poetical Works* 431.
———. *The Task.* 4.671–83. *Poetical Works* 197.
———. *Tirocinium: or, a Review of Schools,* 807–14. *Poetical Works* 259.
Crabbe, George. *The Village,* 2.93–100. In *Poems by George Crabbe.* Ed. Adolphus W. Ward. 3 vols. Cambridge: Cambridge University Press, 1905–1907. 1.132.
Dalacourt, James. *A Prospect of Poetry. To the Earl of Orrery.* CA 3.21–52.
———. *To James Thomson, Esq. On his Seasons.* CA 3.81–85.
Dalton, John. *To the Countess of Hertford, at Percy-Lodge, Written in the Year 1744.* CA 2.108–18.
———. *To the Lord Viscount Beauchamp. Written in the Year 1735–36.* CA 1.63–73.
Daniel, George. *The Author.* In *The Selected Poems of George Daniel of Beswick.* Ed. Thomas B. Stroup. Lexington: University of Kentucky Press, 1959.
Davies, Sneyd. *To Charles Pratt, Esq. Written in 1743.* CA 1.152–54.
———. *To the Worthy, Humane, Generous, Reverend, and Noble, Frederick Cornwallis. Written in the Year 1763.* CA 1.140–44.
Denham, Sir John. *Coopers Hill.* EP 1.333–36.
Dodsley, Robert. *An Epistle to Stephen Duck, at His First Coming to Court.* EP 4.603.
———. *The Footman. An Epistle to my Friend Mr. Wright.* EP 4.585–86.
Donne, John. *To Mr. Rowland Woodward.* In *Poetical Works,* ed. H.J.C. Grierson. 2 vols. Oxford: Clarendon Press, 1912. 1.186.
Dryden, John. *To his Friend the Author [Hoddesdon], on His Divine Epigrams. Poems* 1.4.
———. *To my Honour'd Kinsman, John Driden, of Chesterton. Poems* 4.1529–35.
———. *To my Ingenious Friend, Mr. Henry Higden, Esq; On his Translation of the Tenth Satyr of Juvenal. Poems* 1.465–66.
———. *To the Earl of Roscommon, on his Excellent Essay on Translated Verse. Poems* 1.387–89.
Duck, Stephen. *A Description of a Journey to Marlborough, Bath, Portsmouth, &c. To the Right Honourable the Lord Viscount Palmerston.* In *Poems on Several Occasions.* London, 1736.
———. *The Thresher's Labour.* In *Poems on Several Subjects.* London, 1730.

Dyer, John. *The Country Walk*. EP 4.310–11.
———. *The Fleece*. EP 4.288–309.
———. *The Ruins of Rome*. EP 4.284–88.
———. *To Mr. Wray*. Qtd. in R. M. Williams 142. [See WORKS CITED.]
An Epistle upon the Cultivation of Taste. Addressed to Miss G—— of E——. 1757. In *Instructions for a Young Lady, in Every Sphere and Period of Life*. Edinburgh, 1762.
Etherege, George. *A Letter to Lord Middleton*. Poems 46–47.
———. *A Second Letter to Lord Middleton*. Poems 48–50.
———. *Mr. Etherege's Answer* [to Charles Sackville's *A Letter . . . to Mr. George Etherege*] Poems 43–45.
Fawkes, Francis. *An Epistle to a Friend in Yorkshire*. EP 6.386–87.
———. *To His Wife. A Journey to Doncaster; Or, a Curious Journal of Five Days. Wrote with a Pencil in a Chaise*. CA 2.101–7.
Fenton, Elijah. *An Epistle to Mr. Southerne, from Kent, January 28, 1710–11*. EP 3.89–91.
———. *An Epistle to Thomas Lombard, Esq.* EP 3.89–91.
Garth, Samuel. *Claremont: Addressed to the Right Hon. the Earl of Clare, Afterwards Duke of Newcastle*. EP 2.404–6.
Gay, John. *An Epistle to the Earl of Burlington. A Journey to Exeter*. Poetry and Prose 1.203–7.
———. *Mr. Pope's Welcome from Greece*. Poetry and Prose 1.254–60.
———. *Rural Sports*, 11–16. Poetry and Prose 1.41.
Gifford, William. *An Epistle to Peter Pindar*. London, 1800.
Goldsmith, Oliver. *The Traveller, or, A Prospect of Society*. Poems 628–57.
Granville, George, Baron Lansdowne [in response to Elizabeth Higgons's *Verses Sent to the Author in his Retirement*]. *Occasioned by the Foregoing Verses. Written in the Year 1690*. EP 3.268–69.
Green, Matthew. *The Spleen. To Mr. Cuthbert Jackson*. EP 3.357–63.
Harte, Walter. *An Essay on Satire*. EP 6.258–62.
———. *To a Young Lady. With Fenton's Miscellanies*. EP 6.239–40.
———. *To Mr. Pope*. EP 6.40.
Henley, Samuel. *To a Friend, Just Leaving a Favorite Retirement, Previous to Setting Abroad. Written at the Close of Winter*. CA 4.60–65.
Hoadly, John. *To the Marchioness Grey; Sent with Phoebe, a Pastoral Opera*. CA 2.129–31.
Horace. Ode 2.15. In *The Essential Horace*, trans. Burton Raffel. San Francisco: North Point Press, 1983.
———. Ode 3.17. In *The Essential Horace*.
James, Richard. *Iter Lancastrense: A Poem*. Ed. Thomas Corser. Manchester: Chetham Society Publications, 1845.
Jenyns, Soame. *An Essay on Virtue. To the Honourable Philip Yorke, Esq.* EP 7.296.
———. *Burlesque Ode*. Qtd. in Rothstein 123. [See WORKS CITED.]
———. *Written in the Right Honourable the Earl of Oxford's Library at Wimple, An. 1729*. EP 7.293.
Jonson, Ben. *To Penshurst*. [In Herford-Simpson: see WORKS CITED.]
Langhorne, John. *Epistle to Mr. ———*. EP 6.520.

———. *Studley Park. To the Rev. Mr. Farrar.* EP 6.472–475.
———. *The Enlargement of the Mind. Epistle II. To William Langhorne, M.A. Written in 1765.* EP 6.483–84.
———. *The Enlargement of the Mind. To General Craufurd. Written at Belvidere. 1763. Epistle I.* EP 6.481–82.
Lansdowne, Baron. [See Granville, George.]
Leapor, Mary. *An Epistle to a Lady.* In *Poems by Eminent Ladies.* 2 vols. Dublin, 1757. 2.26–28
Lisle, Thomas. *To My Sisters at Crux-Easton, Written from Cairo in Egypt, August 1734.* CA 2.94–96.
Lloyd, Robert. *A Familiar Letter of Rhymes. To a Lady.* EP 4.675–77.
———. *An Epistle to C. Churchill.* EP 4.641–43.
———. *An Epistle to Mr. Colman. Written in the Year 1756.* EP 4.656–57.
———. *On Rhyme. A Familiar Epistle to a Friend.* EP 4.679–82.
———. *The Poet. An Epistle to C. Churchill.* EP 4.665–67.
———. *The Whim. An Epistle to Mr. W. Wotty.* EP 4.689–91.
———. *To **** About to Publish a Volume of Miscellanies. Written in the Year 1755.* EP 4.644–45.
———. *To George Colman, Esq. A Familiar Epistle. Written January 1, 1761, from Tissington in Derbyshire.* EP 4.645–47.
Lyttelton, George, Baron Lyttelton. *An Epistle to Mr. Pope. From Rome, 1730.* EP 6.202.
———. *To Mr. Poyntz, Ambassador at the Congress of Soissons, in 1728. Written at Paris.* EP 6.201.
———. *To the Rev. Dr. Ayscough at Oxford.* EP 6.200–201.
Marvell, Andrew. *Last Instructions to a Painter.* In *The Poems and Letters of Andrew Marvell.* 3d ed. Ed. H. M. Margoliouth. 2 vols. Oxford: Clarendon Press, 1971. 1.147–72.
Mason, William. *An Epistle to Dr. Shebbeare.* EP 8.112–14.
Masters, Mary. *To the Right Honourable the Earl of Burlington.* In *Poems on Several Occasions.* London, 1733.
Mathias, T. J. *An Heroic Epistle to the Rev. Richard Watson, D.D. F.R.S. Archdeacon of Ely, late Professor of Chemistry, now Regius Professor of Divinity in the University of Cambridge.* London, 1780.
Melmoth, William. *Of Active and Retired Life.* EP 1.9–10.
———. *To a Young Lady of Thirteen.* CA 1.131–32.
Mickle, William Julius. *Almada Hill. An Epistle from Lisbon.* EP 7.370–76.
Miller, James. *Of Politeness. An Epistle to the Right Honourable William Stanhope, Lord Harrington.* London, 1738.
———. *"Are These Things So?" and "The Great Man's Answer to 'Are These Things So?'"* Los Angeles: Clark Memorial Library, 1972.
Montagu, Lady Mary Wortley. *An Epistle from Arthur Grey, the Footman, After his Condemnation for Attempting a Rape.* In *The Poetical Works of the Right Honourable Lady M—— W—— M——e.* London, 1768.
———. *Answer to a Love Letter in Verse.* In Isobel Grundy, "Ovid and Eighteenth-Century Divorce: an Unpublished Poem by Lady Mary Wortley Montagu." *Review of English Studies* 23 (1972): 417–28.

Moore, Edward. *To the Right Hon. Henry Pelham. The Humble Petition of the Worshipful Company of Poets and News-Writers*. EP 4.258–59.

Nugent, Earl. [Robert Nugent or Craggs, Earl Nugent.] *To Clarissa*. CA 6.179–82.

———. *Of Human Enjoyments*. [Title supplied; poem untitled in Bell.] CA 1.106–19.

———. *To the Lord Viscount Cornbury*. CA 1.85–105.

Oldham, John. *Apology* [for Oldham's *Satyr Against Vertue*]. Poems 68–70.

Parnell, Thomas. *To Mr. Pope*. EP 2.318.

Philips, Ambrose. *To a Friend who Desired me to Write on the Death of King William. April 20, 1702.* EP 4.106–7.

———. *To the Earl of Dorset. Copenhagen, March 9, 1709.* EP 4.107–8.

———. *To the Honourable James Craggs, Esq., Secretary at War, at Hampton-Court, 1717.* EP 4.108–10.

———. *To the Right Hon. Charles Lord Halifax, One of the Lords Justices Appointed by His Majesty. 1714.* EP 4.108.

Philips, John. *Cyder*, 219–21. EP 2.107–18.

Pinnel, Peter. *To a Lady, on Asking My Opinion of Friendship*. CA 6.166.

Pitt, Christopher. *To Mr. Spence. Prefixed to the Essay on Pope's Odyssey*. EP 3.608.

Polwhele, Richard. *Epistle to H. Downman, M.D. of Exeter, written During a Violent Illness, August 17, 1791.* In *Poems, Chiefly by Gentlemen of Devonshire and Cornwall*. Bath, 1792.

Pope, Alexander. *An Epistle to Henry Cromwell, Esq*. Poems 271.

———. *An Essay on Man*, 4.373–82. Poems 547.

———. *Eloisa to Abelard*. Poems 252–61.

———. *Epilogue to the Satires*, Dialogue II. Poems 694–703.

———. *Epistle to Miss Blount, on Her Leaving Town, After the Coronation*. Poems 243–44.

———. *Epistle to Robert Earl of Oxford*. Poems 313–14.

———. *Imitations of Horace*, Epistle 2.1 ("To Augustus"). Poems 634–49.

———. *Part of the Ninth Ode of the Fourth Book of Horace*. Poems 674–75.

———. *Windsor Forest*. Poems 195–210.

Prior, Matthew. *An Epistle to Fleetwood Shephard, Esq. Burleigh, May 14, 1689.* In *The Literary Works of Matthew Prior*, ed. H. Bunker Wright and Monroe K. Spears. 2 vols. Oxford: Clarendon Press, 1959. 1.883–91.

Ramsay, Allan. *Epistle to the Honourable Duncan Forbes, Lord Advocate*. Poetical Works 1.95–96.

———. *To Sir William Burnet*. Poetical Works 1.76.

Roberts, William Hayward. *A Poetical Epistle to Christopher Anstey, Esq. on the English Poets, Chiefly Those, who have Written in Blank Verse*. In *Poems by Dr. Roberts of Eton College*. London, 1774.

Rochester. [John Wilmot, Earl of Rochester.] *The Latter End of the Chorus of the Second Act of Seneca's Troas, Translated*. Poems 49.

———. *Tunbridge Wells*. Poems 87–92.

Rogers, Samuel. *An Epistle to a Friend*. London, 1798.

Roscommon. [Wentworth Dillon, Earl of Roscommon.] *An Essay on Translated Verse*. EP 1.543–46.

———. *Ode upon Solitude*. EP 1.549–50.

Ryves, Eliza. *An Epistle to the Right Honourable Lord John Cavendish, Late Chancellor of the Exchequer.* London, 1784.

Savage, Richard. *The Friend. An Epistle to Aaron Hill, Esq.* In *The Poetical Works of Richard Savage,* ed. Clarence Tracy. Cambridge: Cambridge University Press, 1962.

Scott, John (of Amwell). *Winter Amusements in the Country. To a Friend in London.* EP 6.743–45.

Seward, Thomas. *On the Female Right to Literature. To a Young Lady, Written from Florence.* CA 6.17–23.

Smedley, Jonathan. *A Satyr.* [In Swift, *Poetical Works* 288–92.]

Smith, Edmund. *A Poem, to the Memory of Mr. John Philips. To a Friend.* EP 2.162–64.

Somerville, William. *Epistle to Mr. Thomson, on the First Edition of his Seasons.* EP 3.475.

———. *To the Author of the Essay on Man.* EP 3.475.

Swift, Jonathan. *On Reading Dr Young's Satires, called the Universal Passion.* Poetical Works 2.390–92.

———. *To Mr. Gay on his being Steward to the Duke of Queensbury.* Poetical Works 2.530–36.

Thompson, William. *On Mr. Pope's Works. Written Soon After His Death.* EP 5.319–21.

Thomson, James. *Summer,* 1457–66. *The Seasons* 126.

———. *Summer,* 1445–56. *The Seasons* 125–26.

———. *Spring* (1728 ed.), 55–60. *The Seasons* 5.

———. *Spring,* 461–66. *The Seasons* 24.

Tickell, Richard. *The Project. To the Rev. Dean Tucker.* CA 4.92–101.

Tickell, Thomas. *To His Excellency The Lord Privy Seal, On the Prospect of Peace.* EP 3.376–79.

Vaughn, Thomas. *The Retort.* London, 1761.

Waller, Edmund. *To the King.* EP 1.621–22.

Warton, Joseph. *Fashion: A Satire.* EP 8.139–41.

Warton, Thomas. *Newmarket: A Satire.* EP 7.534–35.

———. *Ode. Sent to a Friend, on His Leaving a Favourite Village in Hampshire.* EP 7.517.

———. *On the Marriage of King George the Third and Queen Charlotte. To the Queen.* EP 7.506–7.

Webster, Mr. *The Stage. To Joseph Addison, Esq.* CA 3.86–105.

Welsted, Leonard. *One Epistle to Mr. Pope.* Los Angeles: Clark Memorial Library, 1965.

Whaley, John. *To a Friend, Recapitulating the Particulars of a Journey to Houghton.* CA 4.21–34.

White, Gilbert. *To Thomas Pennant, Esq. The Naturalist's Summer-Evening Walk.* CA 4.66–68.

Whitehead, Paul. *Epistle to Doctor Thomson. 1755.* EP 6.339–42.

———. *The State Dunces.* EP 6.325–28.

Whitehead, William. *On Nobility. An Epistle to the Earl of Ashburnham.* EP 7.209–10.

Williams, Helen Maria. *To Dr. Moore, in answer to a Poetical Epistle written to me by him in Wales, September 1791.* In *Poems on Various Subjects.* London, 1823.

Winchilsea. [Anne Finch, Countess of Winchilsea.] *To a Friend, in Praise of the Invention of Writing Letters.* In *Anne Finch, Countess of Winchilsea: Selected Poems,* ed. Denys Thompson. Manchester, England: Carcanet Press, 1987.

Wolcot, John. [Peter Pindar.] *A Commiserating Epistle to James Lowther, Earl of Lonsdale and Lowther.* Works 3.17–25.

———. *A Poetical and Congratulatory Epistle to James Boswell, Esq. on his Journal of a Tour to the Hebrides with the Celebrated Doctor Johnson.* Works 1.325–28.

———. *Hair Powder: A Plaintive Epistle to Mr. Pitt.* Works 292–305.

———. *The Royal Tour and Weymouth Amusements; a Solemn and Reprimanding Epistle to the Laureat.* Works 3.330–40.

Woodhouse, James. *To the Right Honorable Lord Lyttelton. An Epistle.* In *Poems on Several Occasions.* London, 1766.

Wycherley, William. *For Solitude and Retirement against the Publick, Active Life.* In *The Complete Works of William Wycherley,* ed. Montague Summers. 4 vols. London: Nonesuch, 1924. 4.205–13.

Young, Edward. *An Epistle to the Right Hon. George Lord Lansdowne.* EP 5.223–27.

———. *Two Epistles to Mr. Pope, concerning the Authors of the Age.* EP 5.227–31.

WORKS CITED

Addison, Joseph. "Dissertatio de Insignioribus Romanorum Poetis." In *Poems on Several Occasions*. London, 1724.

———.[See *The Spectator*.]

Aden, John M. *Something Like Horace: Studies in the Art and Allusion of Pope's Horatian Satires*. Nashville: Vanderbilt University Press, 1969.

Althusser, Louis. "Ideology and Ideological State Apparatuses (Notes Toward an Investigation)." In *Lenin and Philosophy and Other Essays*. New York: Monthly Review Press, 1971.

Altman, Janet Gurkin. *Epistolarity: Approaches to a Form*. Columbus: Ohio State University Press, 1982.

Appleby, Joyce. *Economic Thought and Ideology in Seventeenth-Century England*. Princeton: Princeton University Press, 1978.

Armstrong, Nancy. *Desire and Domestic Fiction*. Oxford: Oxford University Press, 1987.

Ashton, John. *Social Life in the Reign of Queen Anne Taken from Original Sources*. London: Chatto and Windus, 1919.

The Athenian Oracle. 4 vols. 3d ed. London, 1728.

Attridge, Derek. "The Language of Poetry: Materiality and Meaning." *Essays in Criticism* 31 (1981): 228–45.

———, Geoff Bennington, and Robert Young, eds. *Post-structuralism and the Question of History*. Cambridge: Cambridge University Press, 1987.

Augustine, St. *Confessions*. Trans. R. S. Pine-Coffin. Harmondsworth, Middlesex, England: Penguin Books, 1982.

Balzac, Jean-Louis Guez de. *The Letters of Mounsier de Balzac Translated into English . . . by W[illiam] T[irwhyt] Esq*. London, 1634.

Beasley, Jerry C. "Portraits of a Monster: Robert Walpole and Early Prose Fiction." *Eighteenth-Century Studies* 14 (1981): 406–31

Beer, Gillian. "'Our unnatural No-voice': The Heroic Epistle, Pope, and Woman's Gothic." In *Modern Essays on Eighteenth-Century Literature*, ed. Leopold Damrosch, Jr. Oxford: Oxford University Press, 1988.

Bell, Howard J. "*The Deserted Village* and Goldsmith's Social Doctrines." *PMLA* 59 (1944): 747–72.

Bender, John. "Prison Reform and the Sentence of Narration in *The Vicar of Wakefield*." In *The New Eighteenth Century: Theory, Politics, English Literature*, ed. Felicity Nussbaum and Laura Brown. New York: Methuen, 1987.

Bennington, Geoff. "Demanding History." In *Post-Structuralism and the Question of History*, ed. Derek Attridge, Geoff Bennington, and Robert Young. Cambridge: Cambridge University Press, 1987.

Benveniste, Emile. *Problems in General Linguistics*. Trans. Mary Elizabeth Meek. Miami: University of Miami Press, 1971.

Berkeley, Joseph. *Of The Principles of Human Knowledge*. In *Works*, ed. Alexander Campell Fraser. 3 vols. Oxford: Clarendon Press, 1821.

Blair, Hugh. *Lectures on Rhetoric and Belles Lettres*. New York, 1826.

Bogel, F. V. *Literature and Insubstantiality in Later Eighteenth-Century England.* Princeton: Princeton University Press, 1984.
Bolingbroke, Lord. *Letters on the Study and Use of History.* In *The Works of Lord Bolingbroke.* 4 vols. London, 1844. Reprint. London: Frank Cass, 1967.
———. *The Idea of a Patriot King.* [*Works* 2.429.]
Breton, Nicholas. *A Poste with a Packet of Mad Letters.* In *Works*, ed. Alexander Grosart. 2 vols. London, 1879. Reprint. New York: AMS Press, 1966.
Brewer, John. *Party Ideology and Popular Politics at the Accession of George III.* Cambridge: Cambridge University Press, 1976.
———. *The Sinews of Power: War, Money, and the English State, 1688–1783.* New York: Alfred A. Knopf, 1989.
Briggs, Peter M. "'The brain, too finely wrought': Mind Unminded in Churchill's Satires." *Modern Language Studies* 14 (1984): 39–53.
Brower, Reuben A. *Alexander Pope: The Poetry of Allusion.* Oxford: Clarendon Press, 1959.
Browne, Sir Thomas. *Religio Medici.* In *Works*, ed. Charles Sayle. 3 vols. London: Grant Richards, 1904.
Browning, Reed. *Political and Constitutional Ideas of the Court Whigs.* Baton Rouge: Louisiana State University Press, 1982.
Brown, Peter. *Augustine of Hippo.* New York: Dorset Press, 1986.
Budick, Sanford. *Poetry of Civilization: Mythopoeic Displacement in the Verse of Milton, Dryden, and Pope.* New Haven: Yale University Press, 1974.
Burns, Robert. *The Letters of Robert Burns.* Ed. J. DeLancey Ferguson. 2 vols. Oxford: Clarendon Press, 1931.
Byrd, Max. *Visits to Bedlam: Madness and Literature in the Eighteenth Century.* Columbia: University of South Carolina Press, 1974.
Carretta, Vincent. *The Snarling Muse: Verbal and Visual Political Satire from Pope to Churchill.* Philadelphia: University of Pennsylvania Press, 1983.
Chalker, John. *The English Georgic.* Baltimore: Johns Hopkins University Press, 1969.
Chapin, Chester. *Personification in Eighteenth-Century English Poetry.* New York: Columbia University Press, 1955.
Cibber, Colley. *The Character and Conduct of Cicero Considered, from the History of his Life, by the Reverend Dr. Middleton.* London, 1747.
Cicero, Marcus Tullius. "On Duties." In *Cicero on the Good Life.* Trans. Michael Grant. Harmondsworth, Middlesex, England: Penguin Books, 1971.
———. "On Old Age." In *Cicero: Selected Works*, trans. Michael Grant. Harmondsworth, Middlesex, England: Penguin Books, 1960.
Clough, Cecil H. "The Cult of Antiquity: Letters and Letter Collections." In *Cultural Aspects of the Italian Renaissance: Essays in Honour of Paul Oskar Kristeller*, ed. Cecil H. Clough. Manchester: Manchester University Press, 1976.
Colie, Rosalie. "John Locke and the Publication of the Private." *Philological Quarterly* 45 (1966): 24–45.
———. *Light and Enlightenment: A Study of the Cambridge Platonists and the Dutch Arminians.* Cambridge: Cambridge University Press, 1957.
Cowley, Abraham. *The Complete Works in Verse and Prose of Abraham Cowley.* Ed. Alexander B. Grosart. 2 vols. Reprint. New York: AMS Press, 1967.

Cox, Stephen D. *"The Stranger Within Thee": Concepts of the Self in Late-Eighteenth-Century Literature*. Pittsburgh: University of Pittsburgh Press, 1980.
The Craftsman. By Caleb D'Anvers. 14 vols. London, 1731–1737.
Culler, Jonathan. "The Call to History." In *Framing the Sign: Criticism and its Institutions*. Norman: University of Oklahoma Press, 1988.
——. *The Pursuit of Signs: Semiotics, Literature, Deconstruction*. Ithaca: Cornell University Press, 1981.
Damrosch, Leopold. "Burns, Blake, and the Recovery of Lyric." *Studies in Romanticism* 21 (1982): 637–60.
——. *The Imaginative World of Alexander Pope*. Berkeley and Los Angeles: University of California Press, 1987.
Davenant, Charles. *The True Picture of a Modern Whig, Set Forth in a Dialogue Between Mr. Whiglove and Mr. Double, Two Under-Spur-Leathers to the Late Ministry*. 6th ed. London, 1701.
——. *Tom Double Returned Out of the Country: Or, the True Picture of a Modern Whig, Set Forth in a Second Dialogue Between Mr. Whiglove and Mr. Double, at the Rummer Tavern in Queen-street*. London, 1702.
Davidow, Lawrence Lee. "The English Verse Epistle from Jonson to Burns." Ph.D. diss., Princeton University, 1974.
Day, Angel. *The English Secretary, or, Methods of Writing Epistles and Letters*. London, 1599. Reprint. Gainesville, Fla.: Scholars' Facsimiles and Reprints, 1967.
Day, Martin S. "Anstey and Anapestic Satire in the Late Eighteenth Century." *ELH* 15 (1948): 122–46.
——. "The Influence of Mason's *Heroic Epistle*." *Modern Language Quarterly* 14 (1953): 235–52.
Defoe, Daniel. *A Plan of the English Commerce*. London, 1728.
——. *The Compleat Gentleman*. Ed. Karl D. Bülbring. London: Foxcroft Library Editions, 1972.
——. *The True-Born Englishman*. In *Daniel Defoe*, ed. James T. Boulton. New York: Shocken Books, 1965.
DeJean, Joan. "Fictions of Sappho." *Critical Inquiry* 13 (1987): 806–24.
de Lauretis, Teresa. *Alice Doesn't: Feminism, Semiotics, Cinema*. Bloomington: Indiana University Press, 1984.
Dennis, John. *The Grounds of Criticism in Poetry* (1704). In *The Critical Works of John Dennis*, ed. Edward Niles Hooker. 2 vols. Baltimore: Johns Hopkins University Press, 1943.
Dickinson, H. T. *Bolingbroke*. London: Constable, 1970.
——. *Liberty and Property: Political Ideology in Eighteenth-Century Britain*. New York: Holmes and Meier, 1977.
Dollimore, Jonathan, and Alan Sinfield, eds. *Political Shakespeare: New Essays in Cultural Materialism*. Ithaca: Cornell University Press, 1985.
Donne, John. *Letters to Severall Persons of Honour*. Ed. Charles E. Merrill, Jr. New York: Sturgis and Walton, 1910.
Dowling, William C. *Jameson, Althusser, Marx*. Ithaca: Cornell University Press, 1981.
Dryden, John. "A Discourse Concerning the Original and Progress of Satire." In *Dryden: A Selection*, ed. John Conaghan. London: Methuen, 1978.

———. Dedicatory epistle to *Aurenge-Zebe*. In *Dryden: The Dramatic Works*, ed. Montague Summers. 6 vols. New York: Gordian Press, 1968.

———. "Preface of the Translator, with a Parallel of Poetry and Painting Prefixed to *De Arte Graphica* (1695)." In *The Works of John Dryden*, ed. Walter Scott. Rev. George Saintsbury. 18 vols. London: William Paterson, 1892.

———. *The Works of Virgil in English*. Ed. William Frost. Vol. 6 of *The Works of John Dryden*, ed. H. T. Swedenberg et al. 20 vols. Berkeley and Los Angeles: University of California Press, 1956– .

Duckworth, Alistair M. "'Whig' Landscapes in Defoe's *Tour*." *Philological Quarterly* 61 (1982): 453–65.

Duff, William. *An Essay on Original Genius*. London, 1767.

Elkin, Peter K. *The Augustan Defence of Satire*. Oxford: Clarendon Press, 1973.

Elledge, Scott, ed. *Eighteenth-Century Critical Essays*. 2 vols. Ithaca: Cornell University Press, 1961.

Ellis, John. "Ideology and Subjectivity." In *Culture, Media, Language*, ed. Stuart Hall, Dorothy Hobson, Andrew Lowe, and Paul Willis. London: Hutchinson, for the Centre for Contemporary Cultural Studies, University of Birmingham, 1980.

Erskine-Hill, Howard. "Alexander Pope: The Political Poet in His Time." *Eighteenth-Century Studies* 15 (1981–82): 123–48.

———. *The Augustan Idea in English Literature*. London: Edward Arnold, 1983.

Ewell, Barbara C. "Unity and the Transformation of Drayton's Poetics in *England's Heroicall Epistles*: From Mirrored Ideals to 'The Chaos in the Mind'." *Modern Language Quarterly* 44 (1983): 231-50.

Fabricant, Carole. "The Aesthetics and Politics of Landscape in the Eighteenth Century." In *Studies in Eighteenth-Century British Art and Aesthetics*, ed. Ralph Cohen. Berkeley and Los Angeles: University of California Press, 1985.

Farley-Hills, David. *Rochester's Poetry*. Totowa, N.J.: Rowan and Littlefield, 1978.

Farrington, Benjamin. *The Faith of Epicurus*. New York: Basic Books, 1967.

Fielding, Henry. *An Essay on Conversation*. In *Miscellanies by Henry Fielding, Esq.*, ed. Henry Knight Miller. 2 vols. Middletown, Conn.: Wesleyan University Press, 1972.

Frost, William. *Dryden and the Art of Translation*. New Haven: Yale University Press, 1955.

Fry, Paul H. *The Poet's Calling in the English Ode*. New Haven: Yale University Press, 1980

Fussell, Paul. *The Rhetorical World of Augustan Humanism*. Oxford: Clarendon Press, 1965.

Garrison, James D. *Dryden and the Tradition of Panegyric*. Berkeley and Los Angeles: University of California Press, 1975.

Gillis, Cristina Marsden. *The Paradox of Privacy: Epistolary Form in "Clarissa."* Gainesville: University Presses of Florida, 1984.

Girard, René. *Violence and the Sacred*. Trans. Patrick Gregory. Baltimore: Johns Hopkins University Press, 1977.

Goldgar, Bertrand A. *Walpole and the Wits: The Relation of Politics to Literature, 1722–1742*. Lincoln: University of Nebraska Press, 1976.

Goldsmith, Oliver. *The Collected Works of Oliver Goldsmith*. Ed. Arthur Friedman. 5 vols. Oxford: Oxford University Press, 1966.
Gray, Thomas. *Correspondence of Thomas Gray*. Ed. Paget Toynbee and Leonard Whibley. 3 vols. Oxford: Clarendon Press, 1935.
The Guardian: A Corrected Edition. With a Preface Historical and Biographical, by Alexander Chalmers. 2 vols. London, 1806.
Guilhamet, Leon. *The Sincere Ideal: Studies on Sincerity in Eighteenth-Century English Literature*. Montreal: McGill-Queens University Press, 1974.
Guillén, Claudio. *Literature as System*. Princeton: Princeton University Press, 1971.
Hadot, Pierre. "Forms of Life and Forms of Discourse in Ancient Philosophy." *Critical Inquiry* 16 (1990): 483–504.
Haight, Elizabeth Hazelton. "Epistula Item Quaevis Non Magna Poema Est: A Fresh Approach to Horace's First Book of Epistles." *Studies in Philology* (1958): 187–200.
Hall, Stuart, Dorothy Hobson, Andrew Lowe, and Paul Willis, eds. *Culture, Media, Language*. London: Hutchinson, for the Centre for Contemporary Cultural Studies, University of Birmingham, 1980.
Hatch, Ronald B. "George Crabbe and the Tenth Muse." *Eighteenth-Century Studies* 7 (1974): 274–94.
Havens, Raymond D. "Assumed Personality, Insanity, and Poetry." *Review of English Studies* NS 4 (1953): 26–37.
Henkel, Jacqueline. "Linguistic Models and Recent Criticism: Transformational-Generative Grammar as Literary Metaphor." *PMLA* 105 (1990): 448–63.
Hibbard, George R. "The Country House Poem of the Seventeenth Century." *Journal of the Warburg and Courtauld Institutes* 19 (1956): 159–74.
Hobbes, Thomas. *Leviathan*. Ed. A. R. Waller. Cambridge: Cambridge University Press, 1904.
Hobson, Marian. "History Traces." In *Post-Structuralism and the Question of History*, ed. Derek Attridge, Geoff Bennington, and Robert Young. Cambridge: Cambridge University Press, 1987.
Holmes, G. S., and W. A. Speck, eds. *The Divided Society: Parties and Politics in England, 1694–1716*. New York: St. Martin's Press, 1967.
Houpt, Charles T. *Mark Akenside: A Biographical and Critical Study*. 1944; Folcroft, Pa.: Folcroft Press, 1970.
Huizinga, Johan. *Erasmus of Rotterdam*. London: Phaidon Publishers, 1952.
Hume, David. *A Treatise of Human Nature*. Ed. L. A. Selby-Bigge. Rev. P. H. Nidditch. Oxford: Clarendon Press, 1978.
Irving, William H. *The Providence of Wit in the English Letter Writers*. Durham, N.C.: Duke University Press, 1955.
Jameson, Fredric. *The Prison-House of Language: A Critical Account of Structuralism and Russian Formalism*. Princeton: Princeton University Press, 1972.
Johnson, James William. *The Formation of English Neo-Classical Thought*. Princeton: Princeton University Press, 1967.
Johnson, Samuel. *Lives of the English Poets*. Ed. George Birkbeck Hill. 3 vols. Oxford: Clarendon Press, 1905.

———. "Preface to Shakespeare" (1765). In *Johnson on Shakespeare*, ed. Arthur Sherbo. Vols. 7 and 8 of *The Yale Edition of the Works of Samuel Johnson*. New Haven: Yale University Press, 1958– .
———. *Rasselas*. In *Samuel Johnson: Selected Poetry and Prose*, ed. Frank Brady and W. K. Wimsatt. Berkeley and Los Angeles: University of California Press, 1977.
———. *The Idler and the Adventurer*. Ed. W. J. Bate, John M. Bullitt, and L. F. Powell. Vol. 2 of *The Yale Edition of the Works of Samuel Johnson*. New Haven: Yale University Press, 1958– .
———. *The Rambler*. Ed. W. J. Bate and Albrecht B. Strauss. Vols. 3–5 of *The Yale Edition of the Works of Samuel Johnson*. New Haven: Yale University Press, 1958–.
Jonson, Ben. *Timber*. In *Works*, ed. C. H. Herford and Percy and Evelyn Simpson. 11 vols. Oxford: Clarendon Press, 1947.
Jose, Nicholas. *Ideas of the Restoration in English Literature*. Cambridge: Harvard University Press, 1984.
Kenny, Virginia C. *The Country-House Ethos in English Literature, 1688–1750*. New York: St. Martin's Press, 1984.
Ketcham, Michael G. *Transparent Designs: Reading, Performance, and Form in the "Spectator" Papers*. Athens: University of Georgia Press, 1985.
Knox, Vicesimus. *Essays, Moral and Literary*. 2d ed. 2 vols. London, 1779.
Kramnick, Isaac. *Bolingbroke and His Circle*. Cambridge: Harvard University Press, 1968.
Lacan, Jacques. *Écrits: A Selection*. Trans. Alan Sheridan. New York: W. W. Norton, 1977.
Landry, Donna. "The Resignation of Mary Collier." In *The New Eighteenth Century: Theory, Politics, English Literature*, ed. Felicity Nussbaum and Laura Brown. New York: Methuen, 1987.
Laslett, Peter. *The World We Have Lost*. 2d ed. New York: Charles Scribner's Sons, 1971.
Law, William. *The Way to Divine Knowledge*. London, 1757.
Lemaire, Anike. *Jacques Lacan*. Trans. David Macey. London: Routledge and Kegan Paul, 1977.
Livingston, Donald W. *Hume's Philosophy of Common Life*. Chicago: University of Chicago Press, 1984.
Locke, John. *An Essay Concerning Human Understanding*. Ed. Peter H. Nidditch. Oxford: Clarendon Press, 1975.
———. *Thoughts Concerning Education*. In *Works*. 10 vols. London, 1823.
Loftis, John. *Comedy and Society*. Stanford: Stanford University Press, 1957.
Long, A. A. *Hellenistic Philosophy: Stoics, Epicureans, Sceptics*. London: Duckworth, 1974.
Lonsdale, Roger. "A Garden, and a Grave: The Poetry of Oliver Goldsmith." In *The Author in his Work: Essays on a Problem in Criticism*, ed. Louis L. Martz and Aubrey Williams. New Haven: Yale University Press, 1978.
Lukács, Georg. *History and Class Consciousness*. Cambridge: MIT Press, 1971.
Lynn, Caro. *A College Professor of the Renaissance: Lucio Marineo Siculo Among the Spanish Humanists*. Chicago: University of Chicago Press, 1937.
Mack, Maynard. *The Garden and the City: Retirement and Politics in the Later Poetry of Pope*. Toronto: University of Toronto Press, 1969.

MacPherson, C. B. *The Political Theory of Possessive Individualism*. Oxford: Oxford University Press, 1962.
Mandeville, Bernard. *The Fable of the Bees*. Ed. F. B. Kaye. 2 vols. Oxford: Clarendon Press, 1924.
Manlove, Colin N. *Literature and Reality, 1600-1800*. London: Macmillan, 1978.
Markley, Robert. "Sentimentality as Performance: Shaftesbury, Sterne, and the Theatrics of Virtue." In *The New Eighteenth Century: Theory, Politics, English Literature*, ed. Felicity Nussbaum and Laura Brown. New York: Methuen, 1987.
Marx, Karl, and Friedrich Engels, "Manifesto of the Communist Party." In *Karl Marx and Friedrich Engels: Basic Writings on Politics and Philosophy*, ed. Lewis S. Feuer. New York: Doubleday, 1959.
Masao, Miyoshi. "Thinking Aloud in Japan." *Raritan* 9 (1989): 29-44.
Mason, John. *An Essay on the Power and Harmony of Prosaic Numbers*. London, 1749.
Mauss, Marcel. "A Category of the Human Mind: the Notion of Person." In *The Category of the Person*, ed. Michael Carrithers, Steven Collins, and Steven Lukes. Cambridge: Cambridge University Press, 1985.
Mayo, Thomas Franklin. *Epicurus in England*. Ph.D. diss., Columbia University, 1933.
McGuirk, Carol. *Robert Burns and the Sentimental Era*. Athens: University of Georgia Press, 1985.
McKillop, Alan D. *The Background of Thomson's "Liberty."* Rice Institute Pamphlet 38, no. 2. Houston: Rice Institute Press, 1951.
Meehan, Michael. *Liberty and Poetics in Eighteenth-Century England*. Dover, N.H.: Croom Helm, 1986.
Melmoth, William, trans. *The Letters of Pliny the Consul*. London, 1748.
Middleton, Conyers. *The History of the Life of Marcus Tullius Cicero*. 3 vols. London, 1742.
Miles, Gary B. *Virgil's Georgics*. Berkeley and Los Angeles: University of California Press, 1980.
Mill, J. S. *A System of Logic*. 5th ed. 2 vols. London, 1862.
Miller, D. A. *Narrative and Its Discontents*. Princeton: Princeton University Press, 1981.
Milton, John. *Works*. Ed. Frank Allen Patterson et al. 18 vols. New York: Columbia University Press, 1931-1938.
Montaigne, Michel Eyquem de. *The Essays of Michael Lord of Montaigne*. Trans. John Florio. 3 vols. London: J. M. Dent, 1928.
Moore, Cecil A. *Backgrounds of English Literature, 1700-1760*. Minneapolis: University of Minnesota Press, 1953.
Morley, David. "Texts, readers, subjects." In *Culture, Media, Language,* ed. Stuart Hall, Dorothy Hobson, Andrew Lowe, and Paul Willis. London: Hutchinson, for the Centre for Contemporary Cultural Studies, University of Birmingham, 1980.
Morris, David. *Alexander Pope: The Genius of Sense*. Cambridge: Harvard University Press, 1984.
Munker, Dona F. "The Paultry Burlesque Stile: Seventeenth-Century Poetry and Augustan 'Low Seriousness.'" *Seventeenth-Century News* 33 (1975): 14-22.

Nietzsche, Friedrich Wilhelm. *Zur Genealogie der Moral.* In *Werke.* 3 vols. Munich: Carl Hansen Verlag, 1981.
Nussbaum, Felicity, and Laura Brown, eds. *The New Eighteenth Century: Theory, Politics, English Literature.* New York: Methuen, 1987.
Pater, Walter. *The Renaissance.* Ed. Donald L. Hill. Berkeley and Los Angeles: University of California Press, 1980.
Pocock, John Greville Agard. *The Machiavellian Moment: Florentine Political Thought and the Atlantic Republican Tradition.* Princeton: Princeton University Press, 1975.
Pollak, Ellen. *The Poetics of Sexual Myth: Gender and Ideology in the Verse of Swift and Pope.* Chicago: University of Chicago Press, 1985.
Pope, Alexander. "Preface" to *The Iliad* (1715). In *Selected Prose of Alexander Pope*, ed. Paul Hammon. Cambridge: England: Cambridge University Press, 1987.
——. *The Dunciad Variorum.* Vol. 5 of *The Twickenham Edition of the Works of Alexander Pope*, ed. James Sutherland. London: Methuen, 1943.
Price, Martin. "The Sublime Poem: Pictures and Powers." *Yale Review* 58 (1969): 194–213.
Prior, Matthew. *The Literary Works of Matthew Prior.* Ed. H. Bunker Wright and Monroe K. Spears. 2 vols. Oxford: Clarendon Press, 1959.
Putnam, Hilary. *The Many Faces of Realism.* LaSalle, Ill.: Open Court, 1987.
——. *Reason, Truth, and History.* Cambridge: Cambridge University Press, 1981.
Rabinowitz, Peter J. "Who Was That Lady? Pluralism and Critical Method." *Critical Inquiry* 5 (1979): 585–89.
Redford, Bruce. *"The Converse of the Pen": Acts of Intimacy in the Eighteenth-Century Familiar Letter.* Chicago: University of Chicago Press, 1986.
Reynolds, Joshua. *The Literary Works of Sir Joshua Reynolds.* Ed. Henry William Beechey. 2 vols. London, 1835.
Richetti, John. *Philosophical Writing: Locke, Berkeley, Hume.* Cambridge: Harvard University Press, 1983.
Ricks, Christopher. "Allusion: The Poet as Heir." In *Studies in the Eighteenth Century III: Papers Presented at the Third David Nichol Smith Memorial Seminar, Canberra, 1973*, ed. R. F. Brissenden and J. C. Eade. Toronto: University of Toronto Press, 1976.
Rollin, Charles. *Method of Teaching and Studying the Belles Lettres.* 4 vols. London, 1734.
Rosenmeyer, Thomas. *The Green Cabinet.* Berkeley and Los Angeles: University of California Press, 1969.
Rothstein, Eric. *Restoration and Eighteenth-Century Poetry, 1660-1780.* London: Routledge and Kegan Paul, 1981.
Røstvig, Maren-Sofie. *The Happy Man: Studies in the Metamorphoses of a Classical Ideal.* 2 vols. Vol. 1: 1600–1700. Oslo: Akademisk forlag, 1954. Vol 2: 1700–1760. Oslo: Oslo University Press, 1958.
Rymer, Thomas. *A Short View of Tragedy.* London, 1693.
Said, Edward. "Swift's Tory Anarchy." *Eighteenth-Century Studies* 3 (1969): 48–66.

Schilling, Bernard N. *Dryden and the Conservative Myth: A Reading of Absalom and Achitophel.* New Haven: Yale University Press, 1961.

Seamon, Roger. "Poetics Against Itself: On the Self-Destruction of Modern Scientific Criticism." *PMLA* 104 (1989): 294–305.

Sekora, John. *Luxury: The Concept in Western Thought from Eden to Smollett.* Baltimore: Johns Hopkins University Press, 1977.

Seneca [Lucias Annaeus Seneca, "The Younger"]. *The Stoic Philosophy of Seneca.* Trans. Moses Hadas. New York: W. W. Norton, 1958.

Shaftesbury, Anthony Ashley Cooper, Third Earl of. *Characteristics of Men, Manners, Opinions, Times, etc.* Ed. John M. Robertson. 2 vols. New York: E. P. Dutton, 1900.

Sitter, John E. *Literary Loneliness in Mid-Eighteenth-Century England.* Ithaca: Cornell University Press, 1982.

Smith, Paul. *Discerning the Subject.* Minneapolis: University of Minnesota Press, 1988.

Sorokin, Pitirim A. *Social and Cultural Dynamics.* 4 vols. New York: American Book Company, 1937.

Spacks, Patricia. *An Argument of Images: The Poetry of Alexander Pope.* Cambridge: Harvard University Press, 1971.

The Spectator. Ed. Donald F. Bond. 5 vols. Oxford: Clarendon Press, 1965.

Spence, Joseph. *Observations, Anecdotes, and Characters of Books and Men.* Ed. James M. Osborne. 2 vols. Oxford: Clarendon Press, 1966.

Sprinker, Michael. *Imaginary Relations: Aesthetics and Ideology in the Theory of Historical Materialism.* London: Verso, 1987.

Starobinski, Jean. "The Style of Autobiography." Trans. Seymour Chatman. In *Autobiography: Essays Theoretical and Critical,* ed. James Olney. Princeton: Princeton University Press, 1980.

Steele, Richard. [See *The Spectator.*]

Stone, Lawrence. *The Crisis of the Aristocracy, 1558–1641.* Oxford: Oxford University Press, 1966.

———. *The Family, Sex, and Marriage in England 1500–1800.* New York: Harper and Row, 1977.

Suleiman, Susan R., and Inge Crosman, eds. *The Reader in the Text: Essays on Audience and Interpretation.* Princeton: Princeton University Press, 1980.

Swift, Jonathan. *A Tale of a Tub.* Ed. A. C. Guthkelch and D. Nichol Smith. 2d ed. Oxford: Clarendon Press, 1958.

———. *Gulliver's Travels.* Ed. Harold Williams. Oxford: Basil Blackwell, 1965.

———. *Journal to Stella.* Ed. Harold Williams. 2 vols. Oxford: Clarendon Press, 1948.

Tave, Stuart. *The Amiable Humorist.* Chicago: University of Chicago Press, 1960.

Taylor, Donald S. *Thomas Chatterton's Art: Experiments in Imagined History.* Princeton: Princeton University Press, 1979.

Temple, Sir William. "Upon the Gardens of Epicurus." In *Miscellanea. The Second Part. In Four Essays.* 3d ed. London, 1692.

Tompkins, Jane P., ed. *Reader-Response Criticism from Formalism to Post-Structuralism.* Baltimore: Johns Hopkins University Press, 1980.

Viala, Alan. "Prismatic Effects." *Critical Inquiry* 14 (1988): 563–73.

Wallace, John M. "*Coopers Hill*: the Manifesto of Parliamentary Royalism, 1641." *ELH* 41 (1974): 494–540.
Warburton, William. *Letters from a Late Eminent Prelate to One of his Friends.* London, 1808.
Warton, Joseph. *Essay on the Genius and Writings of Pope.* 2 vols. London, 1782.
Wasserman, Earl. *The Subtler Language: Critical Readings of Neoclassic and Romantic Poems.* Baltimore: Johns Hopkins University Press, 1959.
Weston, John C. "Robert Burns's Use of the Scots Verse-Epistle Form." *Philological Quarterly* 49 (1970): 188–210.
Wilkinson, Andrew M. "The Decline of English Verse Satire in the Middle Years of the Eighteenth Century." *Review of English Studies* NS 3 (1952): 222–33.
Willeman, Paul. "Notes on Subjectivity." *Screen* 19 (1978): 41–69.
Williams, Ralph M. *Poet, Painter, and Parson: The Life of John Dyer.* New York: Bookman Associates, 1956.
Williams, Raymond. *The Country and the City.* London: Chatto and Windus, 1973.
Wimsatt, W. K. *The Verbal Icon.* Lexington: University of Kentucky Press, 1954.
Wordsworth, William. "Preface" to *Lyrical Ballads* (1850). *The Prose Works of William Wordsworth.* Ed. W.J.B. Owen and Jane Worthington Smyser. 3 vols. Oxford: Clarendon Press, 1974.

INDEX

Addison, Joseph, 6–7, 81, 125, 129, 131, 159; *An Account of the Greatest English Poets. To Mr. Henry Sacheverell*, 71; comparison of Horatian and Juvenalian satire, 113; *A Letter from Italy*, 59; *To Mr. Dryden*, 78
Addisonian politeness, 129, 131, 134, 136; attacked as false ideal, 160. *See also* polite citizens
Adorno, Theodor, 108
aestheticism: as antibourgeois ideology, 158–59, 161
aesthetic response: as imaginary ownership of property, 159, 161, 190n.4
Akenside, Mark, 146, 152, 172; *An Epistle to Curio*, 121–24; *Ode to Curio*, 122–24; *To Liberty*, 121; *The Pleasures of Imagination*, 107, 109, 159, 164
Althusser, Louis, 13–15, 178n.5
Altman, Janet, 21
Anstey, Christopher: *The New Bath Guide*, 52, 139–41, 143
The Anti-Jacobin, 97, 153, 155, 157, 185n.2
anti-Petrarchan poetry, 8
Appleby, Joyce, 16
aristocracy: exiled to legendary past in midcentury poetry, 124; as survivors of a lost world, 63, 66, 72, 121; as symbolic presence in epistolary poetry, 63, 66, 72, 80–81, 96
aristocratic nihilism in poetry, 67, 69
aristocratic speech as poetic norm, 70–72, 120, 123, 141
Aristotelian theory of friendship, 46, 168, 171; transformed into ideology of companionate marriage, 134–35, 188n.20
Aristotle, 4, 80
Armstrong, Nancy, 188n.17
ars dictaminis 37
Ashton, John, 140
The Athenian Oracle, 33, 134, 188n.18
Attridge, Derek, 33
Auden, W. H., 112
Augustan audience: defined, 54; as excluded presence in Augustan poetry, 96–98, 109, 131, 143, 158; given claim to patrician sensibility by Shaftesburian ethical theory, 105, 128
Augustan collapse, 95, 98, 112–15, 151, 172
Augustan middle state, 58, 64, 76, 114; redefined as bourgeois "middle order of mankind," 124–25, 137, 141. *See also* polite citizens
Augustan poetry as Republic in exile, 58, 79, 83, 85–86, 90
Augustan universal, 43–44, 90; as identical principle in Dryden and Johnson, 78
Augustine, Saint. *See* Saint Augustine
Augustinian introspection, 39, 41, 43; as source of literary truth, 44
Augustinian middle state, 76, 114, 175
Augustus (Caesar Augustus), 57; as symbolic figure in Roman poetry, 58–59
Austen, Jane, 135

Bacon, Francis, 40
Balzac, Jean-Louis Guez de, 31
Bancks, John: *The Wish*, 133
Barber, Mary: *The Conclusion of a Letter to the Rev. Mr. C———*, 133
Barthes, Roland, 5, 7, 14, 145
Bath: as symbolic locale, 139
Bathurst, Alan Baron, 66, 122
Beasley, Jerry, 182n.2
Beattie, James: *On the Report of a Monument to be Erected in Westminster Abbey, to the Memory of a Late Author*, 156
Beckett, Samuel, 67
Beer, Gillian, 27–29
Bell, Howard, 186n.8
Bender, John, 186n.8
Benjamin, Walter, 108
Bennington, Geoff, 179n.6
Bentley, Richard: *To Lord Melcombe*, 169
Benveniste, Emile, 31, 61
Berkeley, George, 41
Blackmore, Sir Richard, 66–67, 69; *The Nature of Man*, 181n.3
Blair, Hugh, 35
blank verse: as poetic expression of radical republicanism, 122–23, 146
Bleich, David, 5

Bloch, Ernst, 74
Blount, Thomas, 180n.5
Boehme, Jacob, 175
Bogel, F. V., 183n.3
Bolingbroke, Henry St. John, Viscount, 21, 35, 39, 66, 71, 73, 95–96, 98, 119, 121–22, 126–27, 135–37, 141, 145, 150–51, 154, 160, 178n.4
bourgeoisie: as emergent class in Augustan writing, 95, 105, 116–17, 124, 126–29, 131–32, 138–42, 159. *See also* polite citizens
Boyle, John, fifth earl of Orrery, 65
Boyse, Samuel, 116, 129; *To the Author of the Polite Philosopher*, 185n.2
Bradley, F. H., 22
Bramston, James: *The Art of Politics*, 79–81
Brecht, Bertholt, 72
Breton, Nicholas, 30
Briggs, Peter, 186n.6
Brower, Reuben, 54
Browne, Sir Isaac Hawkins: *To Himself*, 113
Browne, Sir Thomas, 29
Browning, Reed, 181n.2
Brown, John: *An Essay on Satire*, 51, 64, 70, 84–85, 97, 100, 114; *On Honour. To the Lord Viscount Lonsdale*, 186n.8
Brown, Peter, 39
Budick, Stanford, 85
Burke, Edmund, 21, 155, 157
Burney, Francis, 135
Burns, Robert, 129; *An Epistle to David Sillar [Epistle to Davie, a Brother Poet]*, 138–39; *An Epistle to J. L[aprai]k, An Old Scotch Bard*, 136; *Epistle to J. S[mith]*, 138
Butler, Joseph, 101
Butler, Samuel: *Hudibras*, 145–46
Byrd, Max, 190n.6
Byrom, John, 32; *Enthusiasm. A Poetical Essay, in a Letter to a Friend in Town*, 100–101; *An Epistle to a Gentleman of the Temple*, 76–77, 99–100, 175
Byron, George Gordon, Baron, 162; *Don Juan*, 29

Caligula, 113
Cambridge Platonism, 103, 183n.5
Candour, 51, 110
capitalism. *See* market society
Carew, Thomas, 53
Caroline, Queen, 131
Carretta, Vincent, 95
cash nexus. *See* market society
Cato, Marcus Porcius, 56
Cawthorn, James, *Abelard to Eloisa*, 28; *The Vanity of Human Enjoyments: An Ethic Epistle to the Right Hon. George Lyttelton, Esq.*, 108, 129
Chalker, John, 127
Chandler, Mary: *The Description of Bath. A Poem. In a Letter to a Friend*, 139–40
Chapin, Chester, 147
Charles II, 53
Chatterton, Thomas, 186n.5; *The Defense*, 163; *Epistle to the Reverend Mr. Catcott*, 162–63; Rowley poems, 124, 162
Chesterfield, Philip Dormer Stanhope, earl of, 21
Chetwood, Knightly: *To the Earl of Roscommon, on his Essay on Translated Verse*, 70
Churchill, Charles, 115, 119, 120–23, 125, 138, 144, 147, 152, 160, 162; *An Epistle to William Hogarth*, 32, 115, 118, 121; *The Farewell*, 118; *The Ghost*, 117; *Gotham*, 148, 186n.6; *Night. An Epistle to Robert Lloyd*, 51, 115–18, 139, 148; inverts Augustan morality as expressed in Thomson's *Winter*, 185n.4
Cibber, Colley, 56, 149
Cicero, Marcus Tullius, 37, 55–56, 61, 64, 90–92; as martyr of Republic, 56
Cincinnatus, 61, 63
civic humanism, 125. *See also* classical republicanism
classical republicanism, 82, 125. *See also* civic humanism
Clough, Cecil H., 180n.7
Cobbett, William, 62
Coleridge, Samuel Taylor, 171, 175
Colie, Rosalie, 26, 180n.7
Collier, Jeremy, 66, 69
Collier, Mary, 129, 133, 136
Collins, William, 124, 157, 162, 171; *An Epistle to Sir Thomas Hanmer*, 165, 169; *Ode on the Popular Superstitions of the Highlands*, 169–70
Colman, George (the elder), 115
commerce, 94, 107, 126; as benign force in history, 108, 184n.11. *See also* Tory mercantilism

companionate marriage, 134; as domestic version of otium ideal, 135; as ricorso of classical republicanism transposed to private sphere, 135. *See also* Aristotelian theory of friendship
concordia discors, 126
Condillac, Étienne Bonnot, Abbé de, 41
Condorcet, Antoine-Nicolas de, 167
Congreve, William, 13, 67, 71
Cooper, John Gilbert, 172; *Epistles to His Friends in Town, from Aristippus in Retirement*, 90, 157–58, 160–61; *The Power of Harmony*, 103, 106, 109, 157
correctness. *See* decorum
country-house poem, 53, 86
Country ideology, 16, 60–61, 63, 96, 119, 121, 125–26, 136, 152, 154–55
The Country, 168
Cowley, Abraham, 88; *Ode. Upon his Majestie's Restoration and Return*, 53–54
Cowper, William, 138, 147, 162, 172; *The Castaway*, 23, 162; *An Epistle to Robert Lloyd, Esq.*, 190n.1; *The Task*, 95, 97, 114–15, 157, 162, 173, 182n.4; *Tirocinium: or, a Review of Schools*, 124–25; *To Lady Austen*, 190n.1; *To the Rev. William Bull*, 190n.1
Cox, Stephen, 23, 106, 184n.8, 186n.5
Crabbe, George, 138; *The Village*, 114–15
credit: as force of social transformation, 17, 55, 73, 79, 94, 108, 125; Shaftesburian benevolism as ideology of, 108
Crosman, Inge, 177n.1
Cudworth, Ralph, 108
Culler, Jonathan, 6, 179n.6
Curll, Edmund, 81
cyclical theory of history, 75–76, 94, 113, 125, 164, 167
Cyrenaic hedonism, 115, 117

Dacier, André, 29
Dalacourt, James: *A Prospect of Poetry. To the Earl of Orrery*, 71; *To James Thomson, Esq. On his Seasons*, 174
Dalton, John: *To the Countess of Hereford, at Percy-Lodge, Written in the Year 1744*, 93
Damrosch, Leopold, 67
Daniel, George of Beswick: *The Author*, 88
Davenant, Charles, 73, 94, 119, 137, 140, 160, 184n.11

Davidow, Lawrence, 60
Davies, Sneyd, 175; *To Charles Pratt, Esq. Written in 1743*, 176; *To the Worthy, Humane, Generous, Reverend, and Noble, Frederick Cornwallis*, 161
Day, Angel, 35, 45
Day, Martin S., 190n.28
decorum, 34
Defoe, Daniel, 17, 81, 98–99, 107–8, 125, 158, 189n.21; *The True-Born Englishman*, 118
DeJean, Joan, 180n.3
de Lauretis, Teresa, 13, 178n.5
Delphic oracle, 39
demystification, 85, 130
Denham, Sir John, 34, 111; *Coopers Hill*, 93, 126, 172, 187n.11
Dennis, John, 77, 98
Derrida, Jacques, 178n.6
Descartes, René, 29, 40–41
Dickens, Charles, 102
Dickinson, H. T., 16
Dodsley, Robert: *An Epistle to Stephen Duck*, 132; *The Footman. An Epistle to my Friend Mr. Wright*, 70–71; *Modern Reasoning*, 181n.10
Dollimore, Jonathan, 179n.7
Domitian, 113
Donne, John, 21, 26, 48; *To Mr. Rowland Woodward*, 29
double audience in epistolary discourse, 32
Dowling, Linda, 191n.9
Drayton, Michael: *Englands Heroicall Epistles*, 26–27
Dryden, John, 13, 29, 60, 67, 71, 78, 101, 113, 123, 129–31, 144, 155, 163, 173; *Absalom and Achitophel*, 53, 80; *To Dr. Charleton*, 84; *To John Hoddesdon*, 31; *Macflecknoe*, 146; *To My Honoured Kinsman, John Driden*, 61, 87–88, 121, 142; *To My Ingenious Friend, Mr. Henry Higden*, 112; *To Mr. Congreve*, 60–61; translation of *The Aeneid*, 53, 81
Duck, Stephen, 129, 133, 136, 188n; *A Description of a Journey to Marlborough, Bath, Portsmouth, &c. To the Right Honourable the Lord Viscount Palmerston*, 130–31; *The Thresher's Labour*, 130–31
Duckworth, Alistair, 86, 98

Duff, William, 171
Dyer, John: *A Country Walk*, 124; *The Fleece*, 75, 107; *The Ruins of Rome*, 54–55, 182n.1; *To Mr. Wray*, 158

elegiac Augustanism, 97, 114, 120, 157, 162, 172
Eliot, T. S., 23; *The Love Song of J. Alfred Prufrock*, 9; *The Wasteland*, 22
Elkin, Peter, 112
Ellis, John, 17, 179n.8
Engels, Friedrich, 151
Ennius, Quintus, 55
Epicurus, 37–39, 46–47, 90, 161
An Epistle upon the Cultivation of Taste. Addressed to Miss G—— of E——. 1757, 133–34, 137
epistolary audience: as autonomous presence, 13, 48, 60–61, 68, 81; as internal to poetic discourse, 12, 45, 48, 51; as figment of Augustan discourse, 97, 161. *See also* interpellation
epistolary dialectic, 29–31, 176
epistoler: defined, 12
Epistulae Obscurorum Virorum, 37
Erasmus, Desiderius, 36, 46
Erskine-Hill, Howard, 18, 58, 119
Etherege, George, 70; *A Letter to Lord Middleton*, 67; *Mr. Etherege's Answer*, 67; *A Second Letter to Lord Middleton*, 24
Evelyn, John, 93
Ewell, Barbara, 26
Excise Crisis of 1733, 55

Fabricant, Carole, 86
Farley-Hills, David, 68, 189n.24
Farrington, Benjamin, 37–38, 46
Fawkes, Francis: *To His Wife. A Journey to Doncaster*, 92–93; *An Epistle to a Friend in Yorkshire*, 45, 134–35
Felton, Henry, 70
feminism: as ideological feature of bourgeois ascendancy, 134; radical strain originating in Augustan critique of modernity, 135–36, 189n.22
Fenton, Elijah: *An Epistle to Mr. Southerne*, 59; *An Epistle to Thomas Lombard*, 30
Fielding, Henry, 69, 120
Fish, Stanley, 5
French Revolution, 138, 152–55, 176
Frost, William, 53–54

Fry, Paul, 30
Fussell, Paul, 39, 72

Garrison, James, 150
Garth, Samuel: *Claremont: Addressed to the Right Hon. the Earl of Clare*, 63–64, 82, 87, 122
Gay, John, 72, 83, 120, 135, 146, 173; *An Epistle to the Earl of Burlington. A Journey to Exeter*, 87; *Mr. Pope's Welcome from Greece*, 85; *Rural Sports*, 93; *Trivia*, 94
George I, 85
George III: as "Farmer George," 149–51
georgic mythology, 62, 74
Gibson, Walker, 3
Gifford, William: *The Baeviad*, 149; *An Epistle to Peter Pindar*, 51, 153–56, 176; *The Maeviad*, 149
Gillis, Christina, 21, 31
Girard, René, 25
Glorious Revolution of 1688, 99
Glover, Richard, 155; *Leonidas*, 164; *London: or, the Progress of Commerce*, 107
Godwin, William, 102
Golden Age, 63
Goldgar, Bertrand, 18, 154, 184n.12
Goldsmith, Oliver, 21, 118, 120, 122, 124, 138, 141, 147, 156, 162, 172; *The Deserted Village*, 98, 114–15, 152; *The Traveller*, 98, 121, 146, 162
Granville, George, Baron Lansdowne: response to Elizabeth Higgons's *Verses Sent to the Author in his Retirement*, 47, 119, 142
Gray, Thomas, 23, 49, 124, 146, 157–58, 166, 168, 171; *Elegy Written in a Country Churchyard*, 164
Greenblatt, Stephen, 19
Green, Matthew: *The Spleen. To Mr. Cuthbert Jackson*, 142
Guilhamet, Leon, 26
Guillén, Claudio, 27

Hadot, Pierre, 181n.8
Haight, Elizabeth, 35
Hamilton, William (of Gilbertfield), 137
Harte, Walter: *To a Young Lady. With Fenton's Miscellanies*, 31; *To Mr. Pope*, 50–51
Hatch, Ronald, 114

Havens, R. D., 18, 163
Heath, Stephen, 14
Hegel, Georg Wilhelm Friedrich, 50, 102
Henkel, Jacqueline, 178n.3
Henley, Samuel: *To a Friend, Just Leaving a Favorite Retirement*, 174–76
Herodotus, 94
Hesiod, 94
Hesiodic miracle, 61–63
Hibbard, G. S., 87
Hill, Aaron, 46, 127
Hobbes, Thomas, 40–41, 43, 67, 82, 100–103, 114
Hobson, Marian, 178n.6
Holland, Norman, 5, 177n.3
Home, John, 169
Homer, 11
Horace (Quintus Horatius Flaccus), 13, 30, 35, 38–39, 50, 53–54, 57–59, 64–65, 80, 91–93, 113, 143; Ode 2.15, 56; Ode 4.5, 59
Horatian verse epistle, 27–30, 37
Houpt, Charles T., 187n.10
Huizinga, Johan, 36
Hume, David, 3, 22, 40, 42–44
Hurd, Richard, 21, 106, 124
Hutcheson, Francis, 101

ideological state apparatuses, 14
ideology of form, 123
interior landscape of Augustan poetry, 10, 86, 91–93, 96–98, 170; left vacant at death of Pope, 109–10
internal audience, theory of, 3–5, 7–9
interpellation, 13–15; and epistolary audience, 90
Irving, William H., 70, 180n.5

Jameson, Fredric, 6
James, Richard: *Iter Lancastrense*, 92
Jauss, Hans Robert, 5
Jenyns, Soame: *An Essay on Virtue. To the Honourable Philip Yorke, Esq.*, 105; burlesque ode, 146, 157; *Written in the Earl of Oxford's Library*, 89
Johnson, J. W., 74, 76, 129
Johnson, Samuel, 7, 26, 33, 43, 70, 77–78, 84, 90, 122–23, 129, 189n.20
Jonson, Ben, 21, 36, 53, 60; *To Penshurst*, 87, 122
Jose, Nicholas, 181n.1

Juvenal (Decimus Junius Juvenalis), 51–52, 92–93, 112, 114–15, 123, 155
Juvenalian revival of 1790s, 155, 185n.2

Kant, Immanuel, 161
Kenny, Virginia, 74
Ketcham, Michael, 189n.25
Knight, Richard Payne: *The Progress of Civil Society*, 107
Knox, Vicesimus, 35, 65, 129
Kramnick, Isaac, 15–17, 75, 94, 99, 151
Kristeva, Julia, 179n.8

Lacan, Jacques, 23
Laclau, Ernesto, 14, 45, 83
Landry, Donna, 187n.13, 188n.16
Langhorne, John. *The Enlargement of the Mind. Epistle II. To William Langhorne, M. A.*, 47–48, 161; *Epistle to Mr.———*, 47; *Studley Park. To the Rev. Mr. Farrar*, 109, 168, 172
Laslett, Peter, 122, 180n.6
Latitudinarian theology, 101
Law, William, 42–43, 76, 99, 102
Leapor, Mary, 129; *An Epistle to a Lady*, 132–33
lector: defined, 12
Leicester House opposition, 127
Lemaire, Anike, 23
library as symbolic center of otium world, 89–90
Lisle, Thomas: *To My Sisters at Crux-Easton, Written from Cairo in Egypt, August 1734*, 142
literature as moral explanation, 44
Livingston, Donald, 181n.9
Livy (Titus Livius), 53, 83
Lloyd, Robert, 145, 157, 162; *An Epistle to C. Churchill*, 115; *An Epistle to Mr. Colman*, 147; *A Familiar Epistle to ******, 148; *A Familiar Letter of Rhymes*, 25, 34–35; *The Poet. An Epistle to Charles Churchill*, 115–16; *On Rhyme. A Familiar Epistle to a Friend*, 51–52; *The Whim. An Epistle to Mr. W. Wotty*, 144
Lloyd, Robert, and Colman, George: *Two Odes*, 146
Locke, John, 3, 21, 25, 29, 40–44, 137
Loftis, John, 18, 66
logos, 49
Long, A. A., 49

Longinus, 123, 164–65
Lonsdale, Roger, 114
Lucretius: *De Rerum Naturae*, 46–47
Lukacs, Georg, 17
luxury, 17, 75–76, 94, 128
Lynn, Caro, 180n.7
Lyttelton, George, Lord: *An Epistle to Mr. Pope. From Rome*, 58–59; *To Mr. Poyntz*, 49; *To the Rev. Dr. Ayscough at Oxford*, 50

Macaulay, Thomas Babington, first baron Macaulay, 123
Machiavelli, Niccolò, 13, 75
Mack, Maynard, 40, 83
Macpherson, C. B., 16, 81
Macpherson, James: Ossianic poems, 124, 162
Mandeville, Bernard, 82, 99–101, 103–6
Manlove, Colin, 182n.3
Marineo, Lucio, 180n.7
market society, 73, 82–84, 86–87, 91–95, 99–100, 107, 116, 119–20, 135–37
Markley, Robert, 105
Marvell, Andrew: *To His Coy Mistress*, 4–5, 7–9, 12, 24; *Last Instructions to a Painter*, 55
Marx, Karl, 16, 18, 102, 108, 151, 178n.4; *The Communist Manifesto*, 15
Masao, Miyoshi, 10–11
Mason, John, 65
Mason, William, 52, 146; *An Epistle to Dr. Shebbeare*, 143; *An Heroic Epistle to Sir William Chambers*, 30, 143
Masters, Mary: *To the Right Honourable the Earl of Burlington*, 132
materialism: as unsupported theoretical position, 15
Mathias, T. J., 52, 145; *An Heroic Epistle to the Rev. Richard Watson*, 30; *The Pursuits of Literature*, 149
Mauss, Marcel, 65
Mayo, Thomas, 181n.8
McKillop, Alan, 18, 127, 187n.12
Meehan, Michael, 181n.3
Melmoth, William, 64–65, 71, 91; *Of Active and Retired Life*, 108–9; *To a Young Lady of Thirteen*, 134
Mickle, William Julius, 35; *Almada Hill. An Epistle from Lisbon*, 26, 128; translation of *The Lusiad*, 107, 128
midcentury poetic revival, 28, 52, 98, 121, 123–24, 144, 146–47, 157–58, 163–65, 167, 169–74

Middleton, Conyers, 56, 64
Miles, Gary, 55
Miller, David, 153
Miller, James: *Are These Things So?*, 110; *The Great Man's Answer*, 110; *Of Politeness. An Epistle to the right Honourable William Stanhope, Lord Harrington*, 128
Mill, John Stuart, 3, 41
Milton, John, 53, 76–77, 122, 146; *Il Penseroso*, 52
mob: as moral category in Augustan poetry, 80–81, 105, 110
Montagu, Lady Mary Wortley: *Answer to a Love Letter in Verse*, 135; *An Epistle from Arthur Grey*, 24
Montaigne, Michel Eyquem de, 29–30, 39, 89, 184n.11
Montesquieu, Charles Louis de Secondat, Baron, 21
Moore, Cecil, 107, 125
Moore, Edward: *To the Right Hon. Henry Pelham*, 154, 190n.3
Moore, John, 137
More, Hannah, 105
More, Saint Thomas, 46
Morley, David, 14, 178n.5
Morris, David, 18, 167
mos maiorum, 55
Mountague, Walter, 40
Moyle, Walter, 75–76
Munker, Dona, 145
Muses' Empire conceit, 60

Nash, Beau, 139, 141
natural sociability, 102–3
neo-Harrington mystique of land ownership, 60–61, 63, 119
Nero, 113
New Criticism, 3–5
New Historicism, 17, 19
Newton, Sir Isaac, 108–9
Nietzsche, Friedrich Wilhelm, 82, 97
Nosce teipsum, 29, 39, 41
Nugent, Earl: *To Clarissa*, 24–25; *Of Human Enjoyments*, 46; *To the Lord Viscount Cornbury*, 76

Oldham, John: *Apology* [for Oldham's *Satyr Against Virtue*], 68–70

On the Abuse of Wit and Eloquence, 113
Ong, W. J., 3
Orrery, Lord. *See* Boyle
otium, 45–47, 50, 74, 86–88, 98, 11, 157, 159, 171, 190n.2; as bourgeois wish-fantasy, 142. *See also* Pomfret, John: *The Choice*
Otway, Thomas, 70
Ovidian verse epistle, 27–29

parliamentary royalism, 126; defined, 187n.11
Parnell, Thomas: *To Mr. Pope*, 166
Pater, Walter, 22, 40, 157
Paul, Saint. *See* Saint Paul
Pelagianism, 101–3, 106, 175
Peter Pindar (John Wolcot), 30, 52, 121, 123, 145, 148–49, 151–53, 155–56; *A Commiserating Epistle to James Lowther, Earl of Lonsdale and Lowther*, 120–21, 152–53; *Hair Powder: A Plaintive Epistle to Mr. Pitt*, 151–52; *A Poetical and Congratulatory Epistle to James Boswell* 149; *The Royal Tour and Weymouth Amusements*; *A Solemn and Reprimanding Epistle to the Laureate*, 150–51
Petrarch (Francesco Petrarca), 37, 89; *Epistulae Metricae*, 36
Petrarchan love poetry, 8–9, 23, 27
Pêcheux, Michel, 14
Philips, Ambrose: *To the Earl of Dorset. Copenhagen, March 9, 1709*, 173; echoed in Thomson, *Winter*, 191n.8; *To the Honourable James Craggs, Esq.*, 125, 150; *To a Friend*, 25; *To the Right Hon. Charles Lord Halifax*, 85
Philips, John: *Cyder*, 168
Pinnel, Peter: *To a Lady, on Asking my Opinion of Friendship*, 134
Pitt, Christopher: *To Mr. Spence*, 164–65
placket-rhyme poetry, 66–68, 70
Plato, 43, 83, 100
Pliny the Younger (Gaius Plinius Caecilius Secundus), 38, 64, 71, 91–92, 129; *Epistulae*, 37
Plotinus, 39, 43, 100
plutocracy. *See* titled upstarts
Pocock, J.G.A., 16–17, 54, 73, 75, 94, 99, 125, 184n.10
poetic discourse as public utterance, 11, 32–34
poetic imitation, 78

poetry as ideological intervention, 12, 15–17, 19
polite citizens, 98–99, 132, 137, 139, 141, 151, 157–58; described in *Universal Journal*, 188n.15. *See also* Addisonian politeness, bourgeoisie
Pollak, Ellen, 180n.3, 188n.19
Polwhele, Richard: *Epistle Written During a Violent Illness*, 84
Polybius, 126
Pomfret, John: *The Choice*, 98, 142, 188n.20
ponos, 63
Pope, Alexander, 7, 13, 17, 30, 34, 39, 47–48, 50, 72, 83, 95, 106, 109, 113, 116–17, 120, 123, 129–31, 135–37, 141–42, 144, 155, 162–64, 170, 173; *To Augustus*, 150; *The Dunciad*, 55, 62, 64, 80, 93, 144, 146, 148; *Eloisa to Abelard*, 9, 24, 27–28, 52, 167–68; *Epilogue to the Satires*, 69, 97, 110; *Epistle to Arbuthnot*, 10, 12–13, 35, 81, 83, 156, 171; *Epistle to Bathurst*, 18; *Epistle to Henry Cromwell, Esq.*, 146; *Epistle to Miss Blount*, 166–67; *Epistle to Mr. Jervas*, 10; *Epistle to Robert Earl of Oxford*, 74; *Essay on Criticism*, 70, 165; *Essay on Man*, 35, 71–72, 121; *Imitations of Horace*, Epistle 2.1, 70; paraphrase of Horace, Ode 4.9, 60; translation of Homer, 63, 81, 164–65; *Windsor Forest*, 62, 108, 126
possessive individualism, 16. *See also* market society, solipsism
pre-Romanticism, 171, 173
Price, Martin, 165, 171
Prince, Gerald, 177n.2
Prior, Matthew, 41, 146; *An Epistle to Fleetwood Shephard, Esq.*, 145–46
Probationary Odes, 149
progressive linearism. *See* progressive theory of history
progressive theory of history, 101, 107–8, 118, 164, 169
proletarian poetry, 130, 132, 136
Pulteney, William, 121
Puritanism, 53, 67, 146
Putnam, Hilary, 179n.6

Rabinowitz, Peter J.: weakness of audience theory, 177n.3
Ramsay, Allen: *An Epistle to the Honourable*

Ramsay, Allen (cont.)
  Duncan Forbes, 137; *To Sir William Burnet*, 105
reader-response criticism, 5
Redford, Bruce, 179n.1
Reform Bill of 1832, 153
Renaissance neoplatonism, 60
ressentiment, 153
Restoration, 53, 126
Restoration poetry, 66
retrospective radicalism, 15, 72, 79
Reynolds, Sir Joshua, 33
Rezeptionsästhetik, 5
Richardson, Jonathan, 26
Richardson, Samuel, 21, 26
Richetti, John, 22, 26
Ricks, Christopher, 60
ricorso, 13, 18, 82, 96, 122, 126, 135
Riffaterre, Michael, 19, 179n.9
Rivers, Isabel, 18
Roberts, William Hayward: *A Poetical Epistle to Christopher Anstey, Esq. on the English Poets*, 122, 174, 189n.26
Robespierre, 154
Rochester. *See* Wilmot, John
Rogers, Samuel: *An Epistle to a Friend*, 89
Rolliad, 145, 149
Rollin, Charles, 59, 77–78
Roman ancestor-worship, 65
Roman roads, 91–92
Romanticism, 172, 175–76
Ronsard, Pierre de, 36
Roscommon, Dillon Wentworth, earl of: *An Essay on Translated Verse*, 59, 69–70; *Ode Upon Solitude*, 46
Rosenmeyer, Thomas, 63
Røstvig, Maren-Sofie, 40, 88
Rothstein, Eric, 117, 138, 142, 146, 180n.4
Royal Society, 40
Rymer, Thomas, 58
Ryves, Eliza: *An Epistle to the Right Honourable Lord John Cavendish*, 133

Sackville, Charles, sixth earl of Dorset, 67
Said, Edward, 145
Saint Augustine, 31–32, 39–40, 43, 46–49, 89, 100–102
Saint-Évremond, Charles de Saint-Denis, 59
Saint Paul, 37–38, 43, 62, 89, 101
Saintsbury, George, 123
Saint-Simon, Claude-Henri de Rouvroy, Comte de, 167
Sarbiewski, Casimire, 36
Sartre, Jean Paul, 6–7
satire, 44, 51, 64, 73, 83–85, 88, 94–95, 97, 101, 107, 110–13, 115
satirist as moral physician, 85, 111
Savage, Richard: *The Friend. An Epistle to Aaron Hill, Esq.*, 46, 105
Scarron, Paul: *La Légende de Bourbon*, 140
Schilling, Bernard, 80
Scipio Aemilianus, Publius Cornelius (Scipio Africanus Minor), 88
Scott, John (of Amwell): *Winter Amusements in the Country. To a Friend in London*, 172–76
Screen theory, 14
Scriblerus, Martinus, 148
Seamon, Roger, 178n.3
Sekora, John, 76, 94, 184n.9
semiotic horizon, 6
Seneca, Lucius Annaeus, 38, 49, 63, 89–90; *Epistulae*, 37
Seward, Thomas: *On the Female Right to Literature*, 136
Shaftesbury, Anthony Ashley Cooper, third earl of, 58, 98, 101–3, 105–8, 110, 128, 136, 157–60, 175, 183n.4; equation of moral and aesthetic sense, 104
Shakespeare, William, 24, 137, 165; Sonnet 130, 8
Shomberg, Alexander: *Bagley*, 147
Sidney, Sir Philip, 4
Sitter, John, 43, 100, 157
Smart, Christopher, 162
Smedley, Jonathan: *A Satyr*, 154
Smith, Adam, 101, 184n.8
Smith, Edmund: *A Poem, to the Memory of Mr. John Philips. To a Friend*, 122
Smith, Paul, 178n.5
Smollett, Tobias, 21
sociopoetics, 3, 19
Socrates, 39, 83, 90, 100
solipsism, 3, 11, 16, 22–23, 25, 27, 40, 51, 77, 100, 106, 118, 144–45, 147, 158, 161–63, 166–68, 170, 172, 175; as egoism or pride, 100, 102, 106; as source of poetic inspiration, 124
Somerville, William: *The Chase*, 127; *To the Author of the Essay on Man*, 50, 72

Sorokin, P. A., 167
Southerne, Thomas: *To Mr. Congreve*, 60
Southern, R. W., 37
Spacks, Patricia, 23
The Spectator, 98, 107, 125, 128; and autonomy of bourgeois consciousness, 159–60, 164–65; as vade mecum of bourgeois aspiration, 81, 129, 133–34, 137, 147, 157, 188n.14
Spence, Joseph, 150, 164–65, 180n.5
Spenser, Edmund, 60, 146
Sprinker, Michael, 178n.5
Starobinski, Jean, 31–32
Steele, Sir Richard, 35, 81, 128, 159
Sterne, Laurence, 148
Stillingfleet, Benjamin, 100
Stoicism, 48–50
Stone, Lawrence, 16, 134
style: as embodiment of republican virtue, 64–65
Suleiman, Susan R., 177n.1
Swift, Jonathan, 13, 62, 72, 83, 95, 106, 112, 120, 136, 141, 144, 154–55, 170–71; *To Mr. Gay on his being Steward to the Duke of Queensbury*, 95; *Poetry: A Rapsody*, 145

Tave, Stuart, 112
Taylor, Donald, 190n.5
Temple, Sir William, 74
Thompson, William: *On Mr. Pope's Works*, 110
Thomson, James, 155; *The Castle of Indolence*, 161; *Liberty*, 122, 127, 182n.1; *The Seasons*, 61–62, 89, 108–9, 127, 154–55, 164, 168, 173–75,
Thornton, Bonnell, 145, 148–49
Tickell, Richard, 145; *The Project. To the Rev. Dean Tucker*, 149
Tickell, Thomas, 7, 131; on classical learning as source of Addisonian politeness, 129; *To His Excellency the Lord Privy Seal, On the Prospect of Peace*, 49
titled upstarts (parvenu aristocracy), 98, 118–19, 121, 137, 152, 160, 186n.7, 187n.7; identified by post-Augustan poets as successors to Robinocracy, 120
Tompkins, Jane, 177n.1
Tory demise of 1714, 145
Tory mercantilism, 125–27
Tunbridge Walks, 140

Ungleichzeitigkeit, 74
Upon the Cultivation of Taste. See *An Epistle upon the Cultivation of Taste*
Upton, John, 182n.3

Valéry, Paul, 25
Vaughn, Thomas: *The Retort*, 118
Viala, Alain, 3, 19
vir bonus, 84
Virgil (Publius Vergilius Maro), 6–7, 11, 38, 53–54, 56, 58, 62, 64–65, 83, 93–94; *The Aeneid*, 6, 59; *Georgics*, 55, 57, 59, 61; imagined as tutulary spirit of English Augustanism, 58
vita activa, 48–49

Wallace, John M., 187n.11
Waller, Edmund, 34; *To the King*, 126
Walpole, Sir Robert, 10, 12, 18–19, 48, 51, 56, 72–77, 79, 81–84, 86, 88, 90–91, 95, 97, 110, 113, 119–21, 125–26, 128, 136, 145, 149–50, 154, 160; as monster, 95–96
Warburton, William, 31, 106
Warton, Joseph, 27–28, 49, 52, 67, 98, 113, 121, 124, 128, 158, 164, 166–68, 171; *Fashion: A Satire*, 51–52
Warton, Thomas, 28, 52, 98, 121, 124, 158, 166, 168, 170–71; *Newmarket: A Satire*, 170; *Ode. Sent to a Friend*, 168–71
Wasserman, Earl, 126
Webster, Mr.: *The Stage*, 81
Welsted, Leonard: *One Epistle to Mr. Pope*, 109
Weston, John C., 189n.23
Whaley, John: *To a Friend, Recapitulating the Particulars of a Journey to Houghton*, 93
Whig panegyric, 107–8, 125, 127, 150, 154
White, Gilbert: *To Thomas Pennant, Esq. The Naturalist's Evening Walk*, 176
Whitehead, Paul, 110, 129; *Epistle to Doctor Thomson*, 11; *The State Dunces*, 109
Whitehead, William: *On Nobility*, 69
Wilde, Oscar, 4
Wilkes, John, 152
Wilkinson, Andrew M., 183n.6
Willeman, Paul, 14, 178n.5

William of Orange, 55, 99, 119, 126
Williams, Charles Hanbury: *The Country Girl*, 186n.9
Williams, Helen Maria: *To Dr. Moore, in answer to a Poetical Epistle written to me by him in Wales, September 1791*, 118–19, 176
Williams, Raymond, 15–16, 53–54, 72, 79, 87–88, 94, 130–31
Wilmot, John, Earl of Rochester, 67–68; *An Epistle from Artemisia to Chloe*, 68; *To the Postboy*, 67; translation of Seneca's *Troades*, 67–68; *Tunbridge Wells*, 140
Wimsatt, W. K., 3–4, 6, 43
Winchelsea, Anne Finch, countess of, 36
Wittgenstein, Ludwig, 11
Wolcot, John. *See* Peter Pindar
Wollstonecraft, Mary, 136

women's poetry: as expression of bourgeois aspiration, 132–33
Woodhouse, James, 129, 136; *To the Right Honourable Lord Lyttelton. An Epistle*, 132
Wordsworth, William, 33, 130, 163, 171, 176; *Lyrical Ballads*, 175
Wyatt, Sir Thomas, 21; *They Flee from Me*, 8
Wycherley, William: *For Solitude and Retirement against the Publick, Active Life*, 45

Yeats, William Butler: *The Rose of the World*, 9
Young, Edward, 6–7; *An Epistle to the Right Hon. George Lord Lansdowne*, 89; *Letter to Mr. Tickell*, 6; *Night Thoughts*, 164; *Two Epistles to Mr. Pope*, 10, 77, 118; *The Universal Passion*, 112

GPSR Authorized Representative: Easy Access System Europe - Mustamäe tee
50, 10621 Tallinn, Estonia, gpsr.requests@easproject.com

www.ingramcontent.com/pod-product-compliance
Lightning Source LLC
Chambersburg PA
CBHW050632300426
44112CB00012B/1765